MFA HIGHLIGHTS european painting and sculpture after 1800

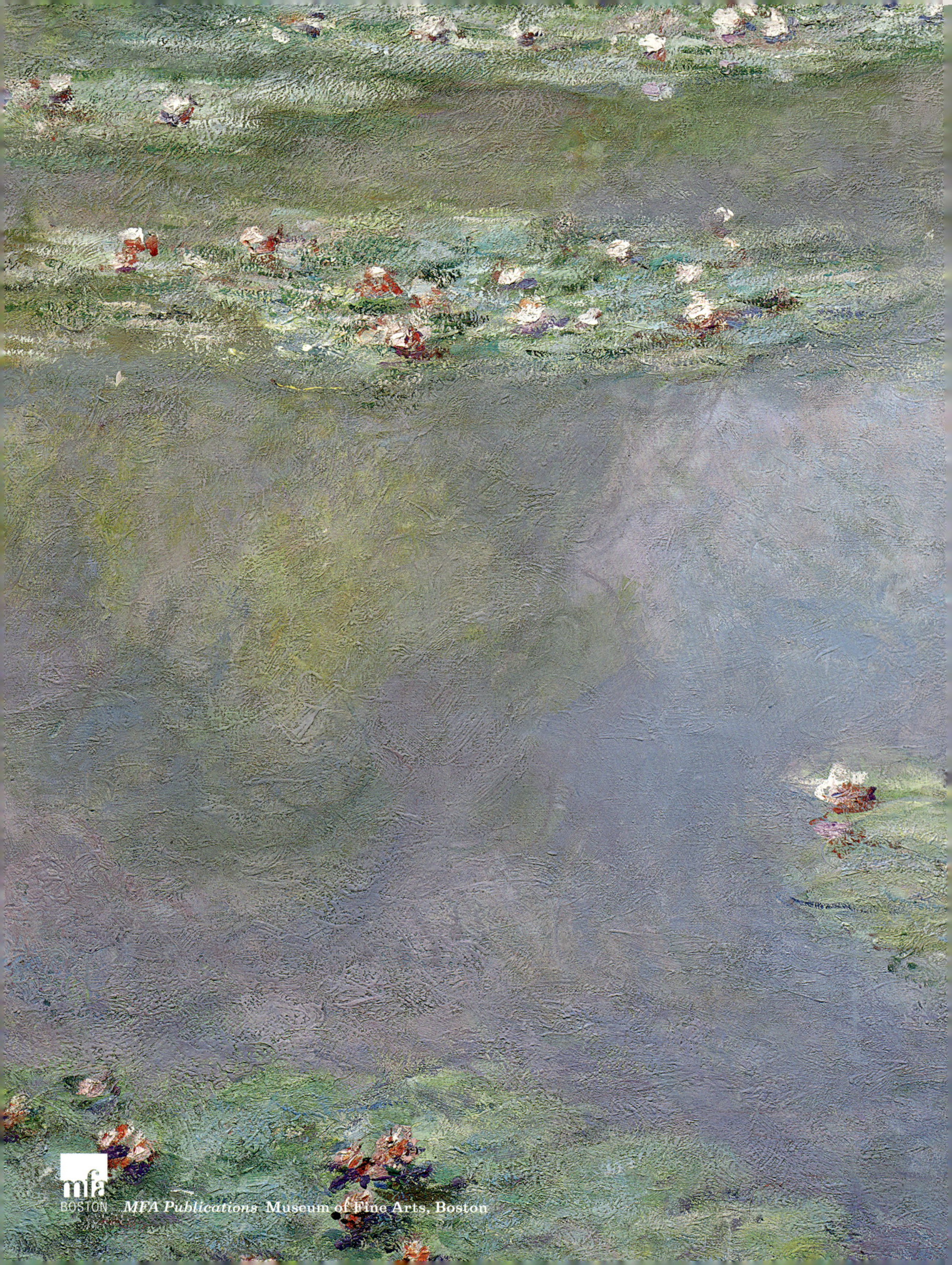
mfa
BOSTON
MFA Publications Museum of Fine Arts, Boston

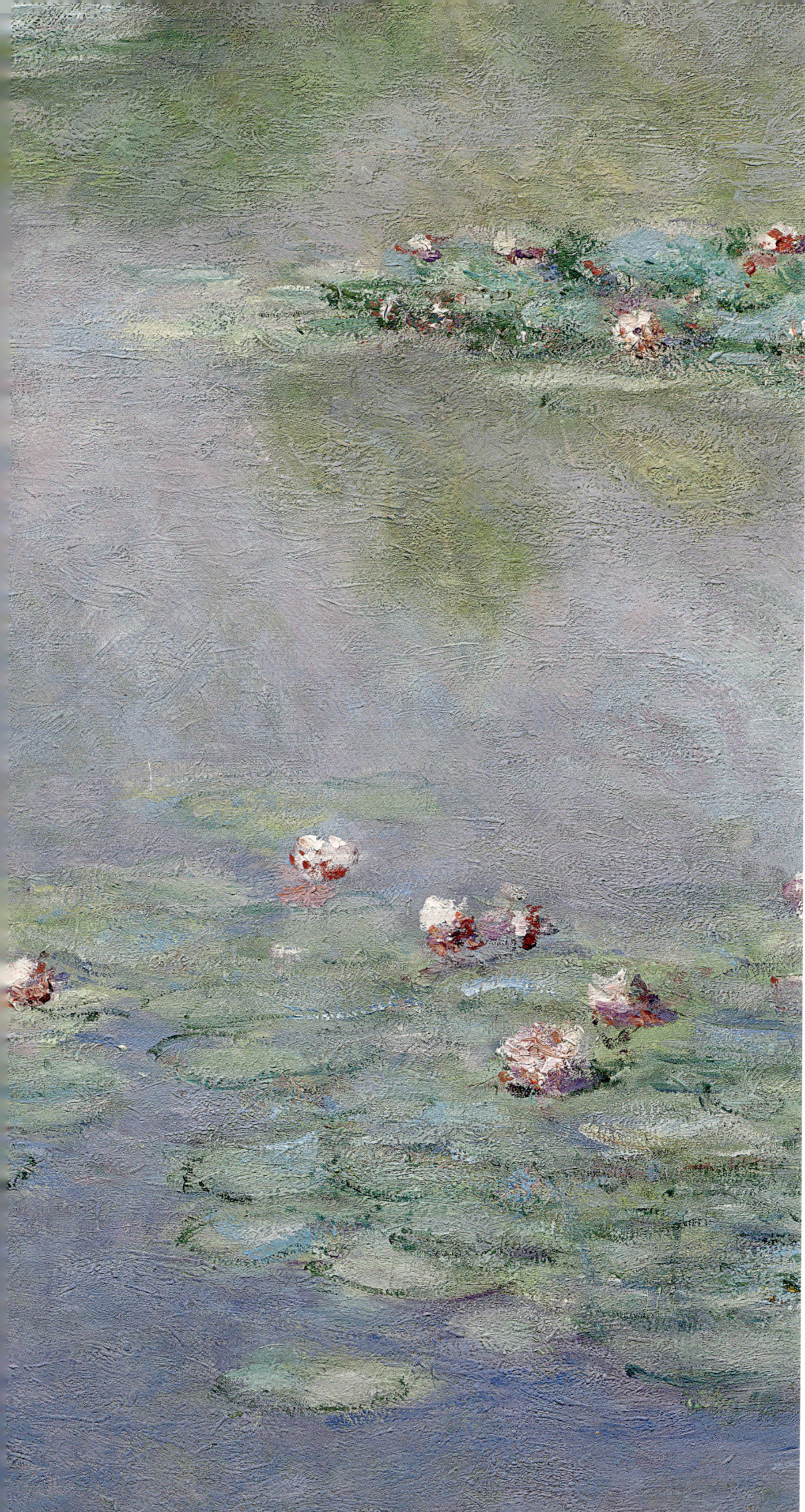

MFA HIGHLIGHTS european painting and sculpture after 1800

Emily A. Beeny
Marietta Cambareri

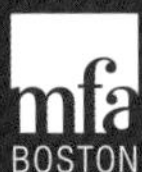

MFA Publications
Museum of Fine Arts, Boston
465 Huntington Avenue
Boston, Massachusetts 02115
www.mfa.org/publications

Support for this publication was provided by the Ann and William Elfers Publications Fund and the Anne Poulet European Decorative Arts and Sculpture Publication Fund.

© 2016 by Museum of Fine Arts, Boston

ISBN 978-0-87846-840-9
Library of Congress Control Number: 2015955028

All rights reserved. No part of this book may be reproduced in any form or by any electronic or mechanical means, including information storage and retrieval systems, without written permission from the publisher, except in the case of brief quotations embodied in critical articles and reviews.

The Museum of Fine Arts, Boston, is a nonprofit institution devoted to the promotion and appreciation of the creative arts. The Museum endeavors to respect the copyrights of all authors and creators in a manner consistent with its nonprofit educational mission. If you feel any material has been included in this publication improperly, please contact the Department of Rights and Licensing at 617 267 9300, or by mail at the above address.

While the objects in this publication necessarily represent only a small portion of the MFA's holdings, the Museum is proud to be a leader within the American museum community in sharing the objects in its collection via its website. Currently, information about more than 330,000 objects is available to the public worldwide. To learn more about the MFA's collections, including provenance, publication, and exhibition history, kindly visit *www.mfa.org/collections*.

For a complete listing of MFA publications, please contact the publisher at the above address, or call 617 369 3438.

All illustrations in this book were photographed by the Imaging Studios, Museum of Fine Arts, Boston, except where otherwise noted.

Grateful acknowledgment is made to the copyright holders for permission to reproduce the works listed on p. 204.

Edited by Fronia W. Simpson and Jennifer Snodgrass
Proofread by Kathryn Blatt
Typeset by Fran Presti-Fazio
Design and production by Christopher DiPietro and Terry McAweeney
Series design by Lucinda Hitchcock
Printed and bound at Verona Libri, Verona, Italy

Distributed in the United States of America and Canada by
ARTBOOK | D.A.P.
155 Sixth Avenue
New York, New York 10013
www.artbook.com

Distributed outside the United States of America and Canada by
Thames & Hudson, Ltd.
181A High Holborn
London WC1V 7QX
www.thamesandhudson.com

FIRST EDITION
Printed and bound in Italy
This book was printed on acid-free paper.

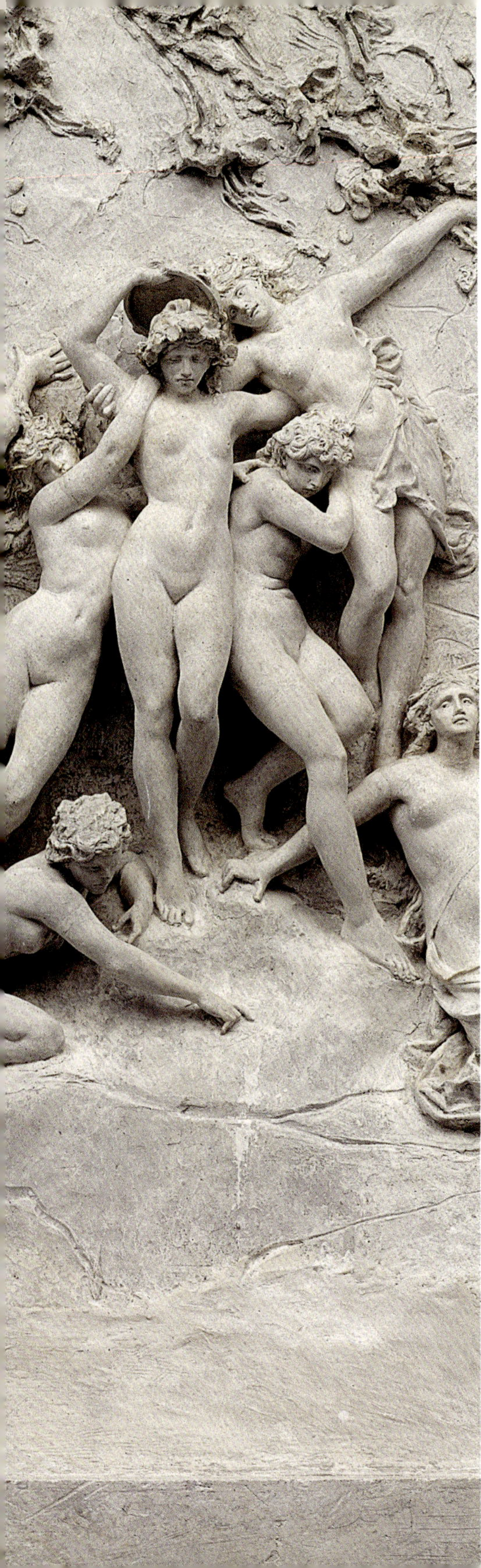

Contents

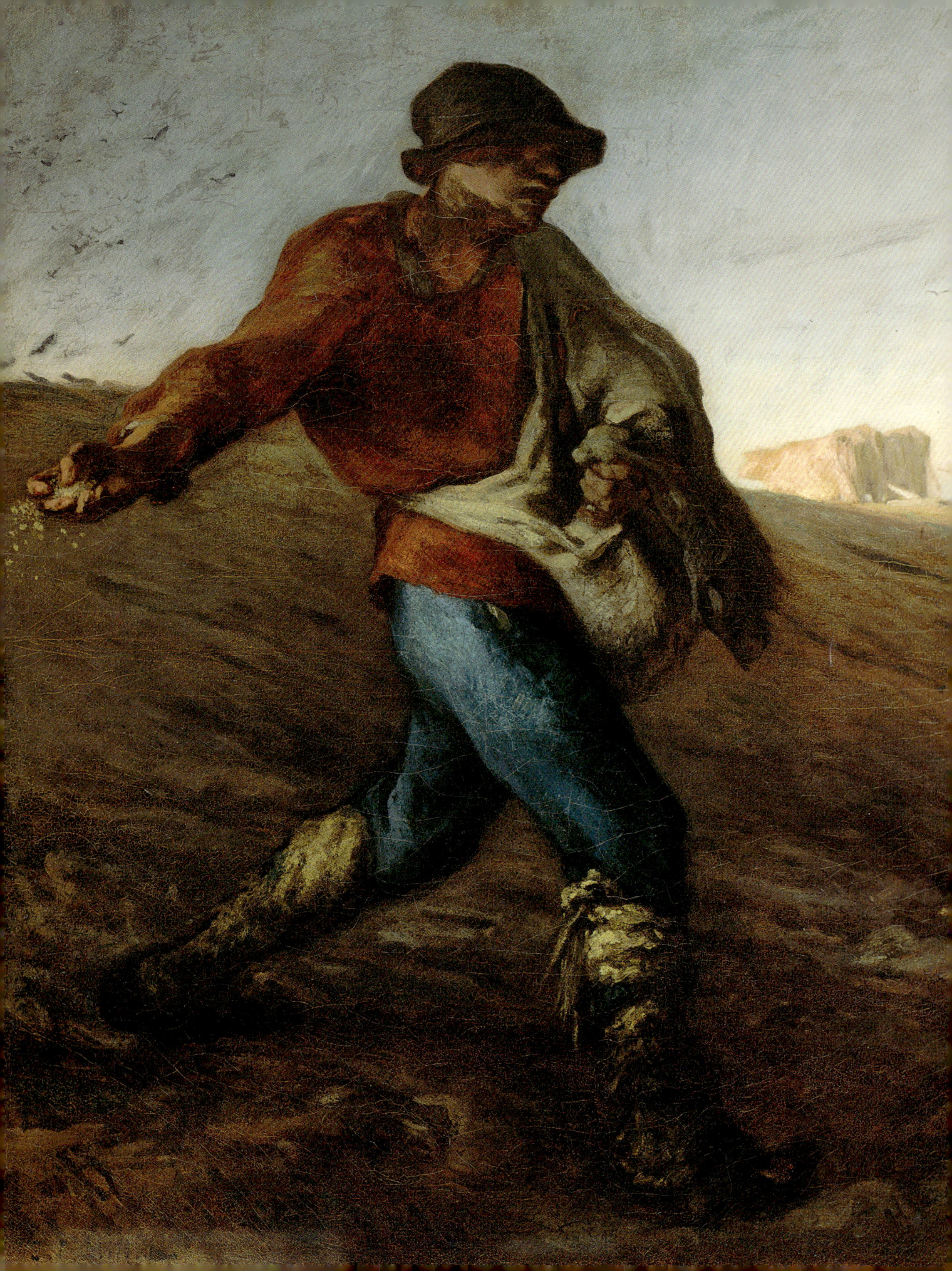

Director's Foreword

The Museum of Fine Arts collections of nineteenth- and twentieth-century painting and sculpture are familiar and beloved by many. In some cases the broad sweep of an artist's achievement is represented, in others core groupings of an artist's work or work from a specific period create extraordinary impact, and in still other cases singular works of beauty and importance encourage us to pause and reflect. For generations the collections have been treasured, linking the sensibility of a new country and growing metropolis with the deep artistic traditions of older cultures an ocean away. Early in the history of the MFA, some works that are now regarded as great historical masterpieces were acquired as contemporary paintings and sculpture, linking us to other places through the sensibility of artists. Nineteenth- and early twentieth-century Europe experienced a continuous series of political, economic, and social upheavals, paralleled in successive revolutions in art—both how it was made and how it was experienced. Our collection animates these moments, allowing us to think actively about the past and to celebrate the sensibility of artists whose work lives on forever.

Matthew Teitelbaum
Ann and Graham Gund Director
Museum of Fine Arts, Boston

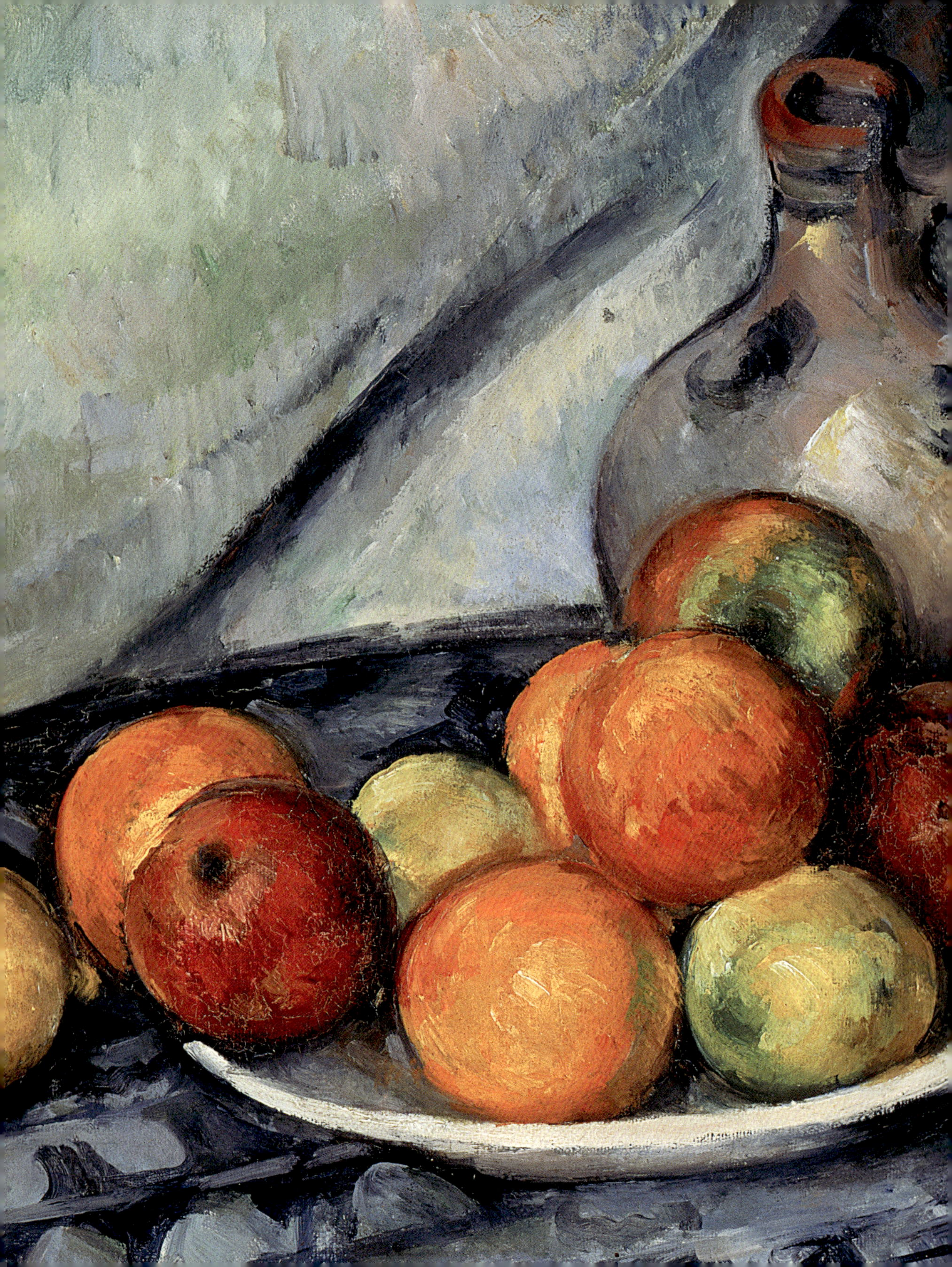

Acknowledgments

This book has benefited from the guidance and support of many colleagues at the MFA. I am particularly grateful to Marietta Cambareri, Curator of Decorative Arts and Sculpture and Jetskalina H. Phillips Curator of Judaica, Art of Europe, for her devotion to the project and for her illuminating entries on sculpture. I also wish to thank Ronni Baer, William and Ann Elfers Senior Curator of Paintings, Art of Europe, for her steadfast advocacy, her sound advice, and her help winnowing down a collection of more than five hundred pictures to these highlights. I am most grateful to Jennifer Snodgrass, Senior Editor, for shepherding the book through every phase of its development and execution, and to Julia Welch, Curatorial Fellow, for her expert research support and early editing. Additional thanks go to generous colleagues, past and present, in the Art of Europe department: Frederick Ilchman, Chair and Mrs. Russell W. Baker Curator of Paintings; Thomas Michie, Russell B. and Andrée Beauchamp Stearns Senior Curator of Decorative Arts and Sculpture; George T. M. Shackelford, former Chair and currently Deputy Director of the Kimbell Art Museum; Deanna Griffin, former Director of Administration; Katie Hanson, Assistant Curator of Paintings; John Hawley, Curatorial Fellow; former curatorial fellows Martha Clawson, Claire Whitner, and Rebecca Tilles; Betsy Griffin, former Department Administrator; and a wonderful team of graduate interns, including Hope Stockton, Caroline Shields, Omer Ziyal, Elizabeth Saari Browne, Jamee Bender, and Noelani Kirschner. Special thanks for insight and inspiration are also due to Erica E. Hirshler, Croll Senior Curator of American Paintings, and to the MFA's paintings conservation team, especially Irene Konefal and Jean Woodward, as well as Rhona MacBeth, Eijk and Rose-Marie van Otterloo Conservator of Paintings; Lydia Vagts, Cunningham Associate Conservator of Paintings; and Charlotte Ameringer and Louise Orsini. I am grateful to Fronia W. Simpson for her thoughtful, elegant edits, and to Christopher DiPietro and Terry McAweeney for creating a lovely book based on Lucinda Hitchcock's series design. Emiko K. Usui, Director of MFA Publications, made sure this book happened, and Malcolm Rogers, Ann and Graham Gund Director Emeritus, fostered the series to which it belongs. I thank them both. Support for this publication was provided by the Ann and William Elfers Publications Fund and the Anne Poulet European Decorative Arts and Sculpture Publication Fund. Finally, I wish to thank Carol Togneri, Chief Curator of the Norton Simon Museum, for her generosity and patience as I finished writing from afar, and Abraham Frank, for a sunlit life in Los Angeles.

Emily A. Beeny
Associate Curator
Norton Simon Museum

I, in turn, would like to thank Emily Beeny for her beautiful introductory texts and entries, dedication to this project, and commitment to the collection even after her departure for sunnier shores. I reiterate her thanks to our colleagues at the MFA, especially in Art of Europe and MFA Publications.

My particular thanks go to Malcolm Rogers, Ann and Graham Gund Director Emeritus, and Katherine Getchell, Chief Brand Officer and Deputy Director, for their support of this series, and especially of the Art of Europe department's participation in it. My greatest debt is to my former colleague George Shackelford, for his wisdom, support, and incomparable knowledge of the Museum's collection of European paintings and sculpture. I recall with gratitude the late Tracey Albainy, an early and staunch supporter of my work on this project. I thank Courtney Harris, Curatorial Research Fellow, Decorative Arts and Sculpture, Art of Europe, for wide-ranging help, and my Art of Europe curatorial colleagues Frederick Ilchman, Chair and Mrs. Russell W. Baker Curator of Paintings; Thomas Michie, Russell B. and Andrée Beauchamp Stearns Senior Curator of Decorative Arts and Sculpture; Ronni Baer, William and Ann Elfers Senior Curator of Paintings; and Katie Hanson, Assistant Curator of Paintings. I also wish to acknowledge my former AoE colleagues Chris Newth, now Director of Curatorial Administration; Meghan Melvin, now Jean S. and Frederic A. Sharf Curator of Design; and Bet McLeod, Rebecca Tilles, Claire Whitner, Natasha Khandekar, and Nicole Myers. Victoria Reed, Monica S. Sadler Curator for Provenance, and a series of interns working with her on the history of the sculpture collection, provided significant new research. Many current and former colleagues in Objects Conservation and Research Science contributed to the care and presentation of the sculptures in this book, in particular Jessica Arista; Arthur Beale; Michele Derrick, Schorr Family Associate Research Scientist; Susanne Gänsicke; Pamela Hatchfield, Robert P. and Carol T. Henderson Head of Objects Conservation; Abigail Hykin; Richard Newman; and Gerri Strickler, as well as Irene Konefal and Meredith Montague. For helping to facilitate new photography, I thank our Collections Care and Facilities staff, Anna Barnet, Maggie Loh, Jennifer O'Reilly, Gillian Fruh, and our colleagues in the Imaging Studios: Greg Heins, John Woolf, and especially Michael Gould, who photographed many of the sculptures, adding to the book his sensitive point of view on the works.

I am honored to acknowledge the curators who preceded me in shaping and studying the collection of European sculpture at the MFA, and the donors who enriched it from the earliest days. Finally, I thank Matthew Teitelbaum, Ann and Graham Gund Director, for inspiring new perspectives as we look forward to the future of the collection.

Marietta Cambareri
Curator of Decorative Arts and Sculpture and Jetskalina H. Phillips Curator of Judaica, Art of Europe
Museum of Fine Arts, Boston

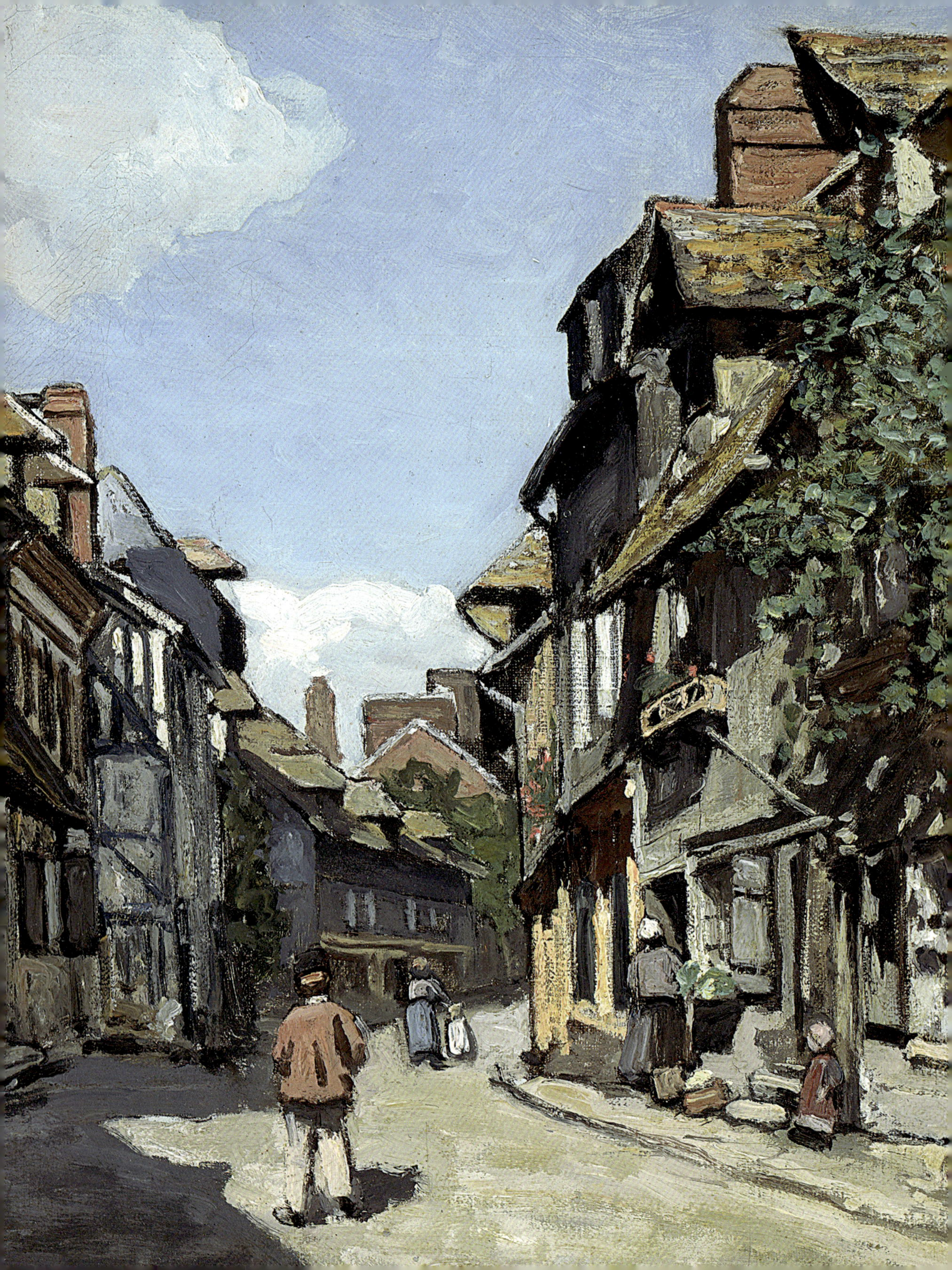

Introduction: Between Market and Museum

Emily A. Beeny

Europe in the nineteenth and early twentieth centuries witnessed drastic, often violent, change in every aspect of life, from politics to religion, from industry to art. Revolutions and rising nation-states redrew the map of the Continent; colonial expansion fed its growing urban and industrial centers with goods and raw materials from every corner of the globe. Technological advances—from railways to vaccines, from photography to atomic warfare—transformed human experience in profound, irreversible ways. Our current understanding of what "art" might mean—an exploration of form, a response to perceptual experience, an expression of the self—owes much to this turbulent period.

Defined for the purposes of this book as the geographic area between Russia and the Atlantic Ocean, Scandinavia and the Mediterranean Sea, Europe in the nineteenth and twentieth centuries had many cultural centers, including London, Rome, Berlin, Madrid, Stockholm, Brussels, and Vienna. Paris emerged as a particularly dynamic hub for artistic innovation, the incubator for a succession of avant-garde movements. The story of painting and sculpture in modern Europe is generally told through these movements, the so-called "isms": Neoclassicism, Romanticism, Realism, Impressionism, Post-Impressionism, Symbolism, Expressionism, Cubism, Surrealism . . . the list goes on. It is a story of rupture—a series of radical breaks with tradition and institutions—propelled by its own relentless momentum and starring a sequence of heroic insurgencies. It is a tale of endlessly renewed novelty and perpetual obsolescence in which innovation is measured against the art of the past. For the modern obsession with progress is also an obsession with history. This entanglement of future and past means that the story of painting and sculpture in the age of "isms" is not so straightforward as it might at first appear. The objects in this book testify to the richness and complexity of European art in the modern era, its diverse agendas and conflicting narratives.

Two phenomena helped chart the course of art in the period: the modern market and the modern museum. The market, a loose conglomeration of dealers, galleries, critics, and collectors, fed on novelty and underwrote the ultimate success of avant-garde artists from the Barbizon landscape painters of the mid-nineteenth century to the Cubists of the early twentieth. The museum, a new kind of institution, made the whole history of Western art suddenly available, offering artists a place to confront the masters of centuries past and carve out a place beside them. If, as the poet Charles Baudelaire insisted in "The Painter of Modern Life" (1859), modern art was composed of two halves—on the one hand "the transitory, the ephemeral, the contingent," and on the other "the eternal and unchanging"—the market and the museum corresponded to those halves, tugging artists in opposing directions.

The significant art movements of the nineteenth and twentieth centuries began with a cosmopolitan cohort of artists living in Rome at the end of the eighteenth. This generation, which included the Italian and Danish sculptors Antonio Canova and Bertel Thorvaldsen and the French painter Jacques-Louis David, helped launch a severe style, inspired by ancient Greek and Roman statuary and known as Neoclassicism. Its ascendancy coincided with a period of political unrest: the outbreak of the French Revolution in 1789 and Napoleon's campaigns of the early nineteenth century, which unseated monarchs, routed clerics, and fomented nationalist and democratic movements across the Continent. David's monumental history paintings of the 1780s typify the style, emphasizing contour, modeling, and the body beautiful in heroic action. David himself joined cause with the French revolutionaries and later with Napoleon, associating Neoclassicism explicitly with the political paroxysms of its era.

A period of religious revival and political retrenchment followed Napoleon's defeat in 1815. The 1810s and 1820s witnessed an outpouring of religious art, sprung again from Rome, where a circle of German-speaking expatriates sought to return painting to the service of faith, drawing inspiration from Raphael and the early Italian masters. These artists, called the Nazarenes, were among the first Romantics. Less visually defined than Neoclassicism, Romanticism was more an intellectual development than a stylistic one. Living in uncertain times, Romantic artists—like their Neoclassical predecessors—looked to the past for inspiration and consolation. The Romantics, however, were interested in a past at once more chronologically proximate and more psychologically remote. Whether the Middle Ages, the Renaissance, or the seventeenth century, the Romantics longed for a time before the revolutions and civil wars of recent memory, a moment when the world had seemed whole. Introspection, pessimism, and nostalgia were hallmarks of the Romantic age, though its artistic products were wildly diverse. Just as emblematic of Romanticism as the Nazarenes' careful Renaissance pastiches are the light-drenched seascapes of J. M. W. Turner and the sensuous, painterly histories of Eugène Delacroix, both inspired by seventeenth-century precedents.

At the same moment when so many artists were looking inward, exploring their personal beliefs through the literature and art of the past, others were striking out to work directly from nature. In England, John Constable painted clouds; in Italy, Camille Corot studied light. In France the so-called Generation of 1830 set out for the village of Barbizon, on the edge of the Forest of Fontainebleau, to portray nature in all its untrammeled beauty. In this group was Jean-François Millet, who focused less on the landscape than on its human inhabitants. The MFA collection is particularly rich in Millet's portrayals of peasants, pictures that helped make Realism the scandal of the Parisian art world in the 1840s and 1850s. Realists held that ordinary people and everyday life were as worthy of representation as classical heroes or biblical stories. This assertion had political, as well as aesthetic, implications. As Gustave Courbet, the movement's great spokesman, insisted, "Realism is essentially democratic art." The advent of Realism accompanied a wave of revolutions that swept Europe in 1848, the year Karl Marx and Friedrich Engels published their *Communist Manifesto*.

Millet and Courbet pioneered a phenomenon known as the *succès de scandale*, achieving notoriety by shocking their public. As the century wore on, such scandals became a common tactic for radical artists. Édouard Manet capitalized on his own notoriety in the 1860s, painting brazen nudes, irreverent history pictures, and stark portrayals of modern subjects. These works secured his position as the leader of a generation whose younger members joined together in the 1870s under the banner of Impressionism. To get around the Salon jury, the Impressionists exhibited their work independently in a series of eight shows from 1874 to 1886. The brightly colored, freely brushed canvases of Claude Monet and Auguste Renoir looked unfinished to contemporary viewers, appearing as insubstantial, unaccomplished sketches with no subject matter to speak of. Indeed, "Impressionism" began as a disparaging term, coined by a hostile critic. A small circle of collectors and admirers, however, recognized in Impressionism an attempt to keep pace with modern experience and perception, capturing fleeting impressions, changing fashions, shifting light. A more sympathetic critic, Edmond Duranty, christened this style "la nouvelle peinture": the new painting.

In the 1880s and 1890s the "new painting" and its avant-garde exponents fragmented into the myriad factions today called Post-Impressionism: the Neo-Impressionists Georges Seurat and Paul Signac knitted tiny dots of contrasting color into bright, continuous images; the Cloisonists Paul Gauguin and Émile Bernard applied pigment in bold, outlined fields; the independents Paul Cézanne and Vincent van Gogh struggled to give shape to highly personal visions and experiences. Post-Impressionism coincided and overlapped with Symbolism, which took a more inward path. Rejecting observed reality as an illusion, Symbolists of the fin de siècle sought new visual strategies to convey thought, emotion, and unconscious drives. This was the era, after all, of Sigmund Freud's research in Vienna and the birth of modern psychology. In the torquing bodies of Auguste Rodin's late sculpture or the pastel dreamscapes of Odilon Redon, form and color take on new meaning, no longer transcribing outward appearances but conjuring inner states.

In the early twentieth century two groups took the expressive use of form and color to new extremes: the French Fauves and the German Expressionists. In October 1905 Henri Matisse, Maurice de Vlaminck, and their radical comrades shocked the Parisian public with their first exhibition of canvases covered in dazzling, nonmimetic color. The critic Louis Vauxcelles nicknamed them "fauves" (wild beasts), calling their display an "orgy." At the same moment, two groups of German artists were banding together with a kindred interest in aggressive, unreal color and crudely expressive form: in Dresden, Ernst Ludwig Kirchner, Erich Heckel, and the group known as Die Brücke (The Bridge); in Munich, Vasily Kandinsky, Franz Marc, and the artists of Der Blaue Reiter (The Blue Rider). Together, these groups made up German Expressionism. Like the Fauves, the Expressionists drew inspiration from Gauguin and Van Gogh. They also looked to non-Western—particularly African—art, newly available in Europe thanks to colonial expansion and the proliferation of anthropological museums. For the Expressionists, art produced outside Europe provided a more sincere, "primitive" alternative to the Western canon, an opportunity to purify art by returning to its imagined origins.

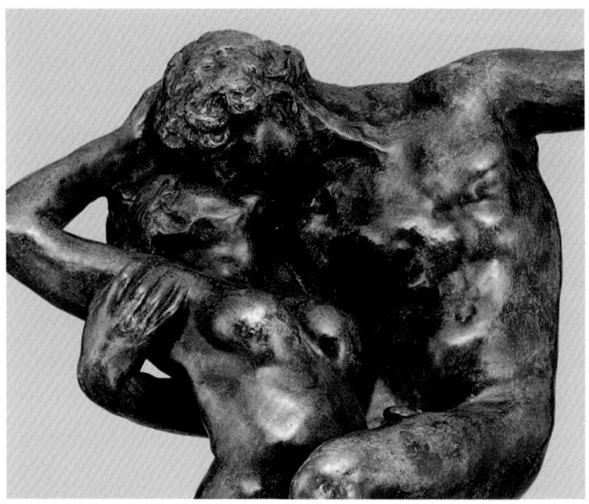

Auguste Rodin, *Eternal Springtime* (detail)

The most famous use of African art to enrich and estrange modern European practice, however, arrived in the work of Pablo Picasso, the Spanish painter and sculptor who settled in Paris at the turn of the century. In 1907, two years after the Fauves' scandalous exhibition, Picasso made waves with a new approach that dissected the bodies of his nude models into spiky, geometric shapes. Picasso's careful study of African sculpture had suggested to him the distance between representation and imitation, allowing him to explore the abstract properties of visual signs—curves and lines for eyes and mouths, squares and wedges for noses and breasts. We understand the meaning of each individual shape only in context, for each form on its own bears little relation to the feature it represents. The same critic who had coined the term *Fauves* invented *Cubism* as an insult to Picasso and his colleagues. Embracing the term, they made Cubism a crucial episode in the story of abstraction.

For abstraction—the severing of form from meaning—became a central concern in European art of the 1910s and 1920s. Could painting and sculpture exist without subject matter? If so, should they? The Dutch artist Piet Mondrian experimented with what he called "pure painting": pictures that pictured nothing, compositions of line, shape, and color alone. Nonetheless, some artists refused to abandon signification. In the 1920s and 1930s the Surrealists explored how form could be used to generate absurd or contradictory meanings and uncanny, dreamlike effects. A growing interest in the absurd and irrational among European avant-gardes took root in the traumas of the First World War and accelerated with the rise of totalitarian states across the Continent in the 1930s, from Germany to Italy to Spain. Movements and schools are inadequate to enumerate the range of artistic responses—from open mourning to gnomic abstraction—provoked by the cataclysm of the Second World War; with few exceptions, the postwar period lies beyond the scope of this volume.

For all its variety, the rapid sequence of "isms" accounts for only one dimension of European art in the modern era. It does little, for example, to illuminate the work of sculptors and painters working within the conservative art establishment—the villains of the avant-garde narrative—all those members of all those Academies, who juried official exhibitions and received government commissions. Though their work still decorates churches, theaters, and civic buildings across Europe, their names today are largely forgotten. The shifting critical fortunes of such artists and their avant-garde adversaries can be explained in part by modern Europe's appetite for novelty, embodied in the sequence of "isms" and driven by the burgeoning art market.

During the first half of the nineteenth century, royal, aristocratic, and clerical art patronage evaporated across the Continent. Artists were left to fend for themselves, working increasingly "on spec" in hopes of selling their pictures and sculptures on the open market. Formed in the eighteenth century and fed by the political chaos of the early nineteenth, the modern art market came into its own in the 1840s and 1850s. Artists' new clientele belonged to the middle classes: factory owners and financiers enriched by the industrial revolution and empowered by more democratic forms of government. Whereas an early eighteenth-century aristocrat might have commissioned a suite of permanent decorations for his residence from a team of artists, an industrialist of the mid-nineteenth century would more likely furnish his walls with modest easel pictures and his tabletops with small bronzes, created by various unaffiliated artists and purchased from a dealer. Such objects were no longer monuments to collaboration but commodities for exchange and, indeed, speculation: "portable property," as the Victorian novelist Charles Dickens put it.

This change had profound implications for artists' working methods. Few could still afford to maintain a teaching studio, the traditional locus of technical instruction, where generations past had learned to grind colors, stretch canvases, and so on. Commercially prepared grounds and colors prepackaged in tubes now meant that easel painting required only one set of hands. Sculptors increasingly sent out their clay or plaster models to industrial foundries or specialized stone carvers for realization in durable materials. The artist's new solo status had its advantages. Freed from the constraints of personal patronage and the responsibilities of a large studio, painters and sculptors used their art to explore virtually uncharted territory: the wilderness, the modern city, the inmost reaches of the mind. The notion of art as an emotional response to nature or an expression of subjective experience was a direct result of the artist's uneasy new financial status. Independence from patrons and pupils helped feed a cult of the artist as a hero, a seer, a revolutionary. This interest in the artist himself (or, more occasionally, herself) encouraged sculptors and painters to produce more personal work, even objects that evidenced their own making: sculptures coarsely carved or covered in fingerprints; pictures licked and stroked by the brush or flat as the canvas on which they were painted.

Such works were generally unwelcome in official art exhibitions, which tended to reflect conservative taste, that is, paintings and sculptures seamlessly made and emphatically idealized. Artists who did not conform to these standards sought alternative venues for display, clubbing together to show their work independently. The Impressionists' eight group exhibitions are the most famous example, but there were many more. In London, the Grosvenor Gallery provided an alternative to the Royal Academy of Arts for members of the Pre-Raphaelite and Aesthetic movements. In Munich, Vienna, and Berlin, the Secession exhibitions of the 1890s allowed Bavarian, Austrian, and Prussian Impressionists, Post-Impressionists, and Symbolists to share their work with the public. The Salon d'Automne, launched in Paris in October 1903, offered a radical rejoinder to the official spring Salon, showcasing artists from Cézanne and Gauguin to the Fauves. The story of the first exhibition by the Expressionist group Die Brücke is emblematic of the whole trend; these artists commandeered the showrooms of a Dresden lamp factory to show their work in 1906.

Independent exhibitions were also a commercial enterprise. A handful of dealers in the mid-nineteenth century recognized the potentially enormous financial upside to investing in artists scorned by the establishment. Avant-garde art was cheap—at least initially. A dealer who knew how to pick artists, develop their reputations, and place their work with collectors stood to make a fortune. The case of the Parisian dealers Durand-Ruel is emblematic. Launched as an artist's supply shop in the 1820s, the business achieved success in the 1830s and 1840s by marketing Barbizon landscapes to middle-class collectors. But Paul Durand-Ruel, director of the firm in the later nineteenth century, is best remembered for his role in the triumph of Impressionism. He hosted the Impressionists' second group exhibition and organized public auctions to drive up their prices; he signed Monet and Renoir to contracts and mounted monographic exhibitions of their work; he opened a lucrative operation in the United States, borrowing vast sums to float his investments. It is in part to Durand-Ruel that we owe Monet's late series paintings, including the *Grainstacks*, *Water Lilies*, and *Rouen Cathedrals*. The artist showed fifteen *Grainstacks* and nothing else at Durand-Ruel's Paris gallery in 1891—the first exhibition of its kind.

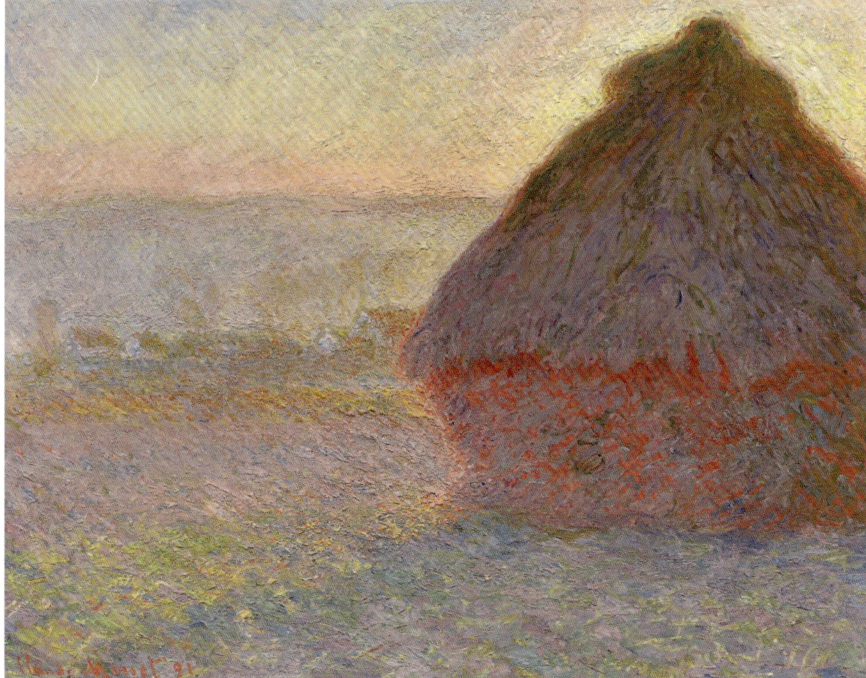

Claude Monet, *Grainstack (Sunset)*

Of course the market was not just for avant-gardes. The nineteenth-century Parisian dealer Adolphe Goupil, for example, made a specialty of academically credentialed artists like Jean-Léon Gérôme, whose canvases fetched enormous sums from the 1860s through the 1880s. Though Goupil marketed these to wealthy collectors in Europe and America, he made his real money by selling thousands of inexpensive reproductions—principally lithographs and photographs (both technologies developed in the nineteenth century)—to an enormous, international public. Those who flocked to Goupil's outposts in Havana, Warsaw, and Johannesburg might not have had the funds for an original Salon painting, but their purchase of penny prints helped transform art into a quite literal industry. Among Goupil's employees in Paris was a young Dutchman named Theo van Gogh, whose correspondence with his more famous brother testifies to the profound effect that such readily accessible reproductions had on artists of the period. Van Gogh taught himself to draw using an inexpensive primer published by Goupil and regularly compared his own mature paintings with works—by a range of artists from Millet to Gérôme—that he knew through Goupil's prints.

Inexpensive reproductions, of course, were not the only source for artists who wished to learn from their predecessors. If lithographs and photographs helped disseminate artworks, the modern museum gathered them together, sorted them by period and school, and established a theoretically permanent canon of masters. Though they had precedents in sixteenth- and seventeenth-century picture galleries, sculpture gardens, and cabinets of curiosity, public art museums emerged at

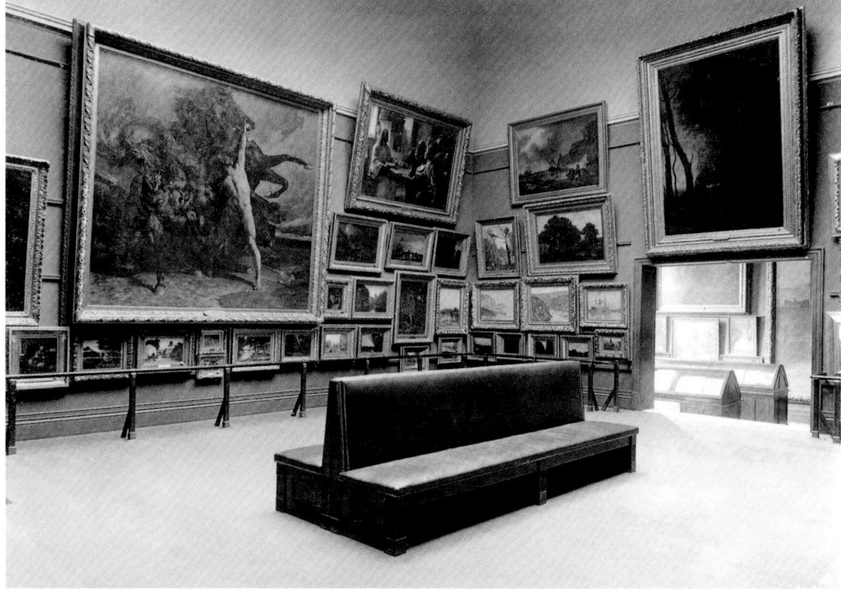

fig. 1. **The MFA's modern European paintings gallery at the turn of the twentieth century. Regnault's *Automedon*, Corot's *Dante and Virgil*, and the three first Monets acquired by the Museum are all visible.**

about the same moment as the modern art market, in the mid-eighteenth century. Rome's Capitoline Museum was the first, in 1734; granting art students access to a superb collection of antique statuary, it helped launch the Neoclassical movement. The young Neoclassicists regarded ancient sculptors as their teachers and interlocutors, even their competitors, as in the case of Canova, whose *Perseus with the Head of Medusa*, modeled on the ancient Apollo Belvedere, literally took the place of its prototype in 1801, when Napoleon's troops carried off the original along with countless other sculptures from Roman collections.

Napoleon plundered Europe in the early nineteenth century to fill a museum created by the French Revolution, the first of its scope and scale anywhere in the world. In August 1793 the former residence of the French kings—the Palais du Louvre—opened its doors as a public museum. Gathering objects from ancient Egypt, Greece, and Rome, from Renaissance Italy and Baroque Spain to the heart of Paris, the Louvre played a vital role in the development of both painting and sculpture in the modern era. Almost every French artist of the period copied there, from the Romantic Delacroix to the Impressionist Degas, from the sculptor David d'Angers to the painter Cézanne. Rodin's rough-hewn marbles would be unthinkable without the example of Michelangelo's unfinished Slave sculptures at the Louvre. As the century wore on, more modern masters found their way into the great museum: Matisse's lounging odalisques betray his study of Delacroix and Ingres in its halls. For students dissatisfied with the instruction they received at the state-sponsored École des Beaux-Arts or elsewhere, the Louvre provided an independent alternative. Hundreds of young artists registered for permission to copy in its galleries, communing with the masters of the past and dreaming of a place among them. The Louvre furnished a model for museums across the Continent. London's National Gallery was founded in 1824; Munich's Glyptothek and Berlin's Altes Museum—the world's first purpose-built art museums—opened in 1830.

If most modern artists learned to work for the market, producing easel pictures and modest sculptures for the bourgeois home, a few worked instead for the museum. These persisted in painting huge, ambitious canvases or creating monumental sculptural groups: objects willfully unsuited for domestic display. The possibility that one's work could be purchased not by a private individual, or even a king, but by one's country or city—for public display and admiration into perpetuity—was entirely new. Its closest correlate before the nineteenth century had been church patronage (artworks exhibited in houses of worship had always been more readily accessible than those displayed in princely galleries or private homes), but the museum promised a novel, secular form of devotion, one in which the work of art served not as an intermediary between the beholder and the divine but as an object of adoration in its own right. The mid-nineteenth-century writer Théophile Gautier's famous formulation—"art for art's sake"—expresses a sentiment born of the museum age.

The modern art museum arrived in America in the early nineteenth century. The Brooklyn Museum was established in 1823, and the Wadsworth Atheneum, in Hartford, Connecticut, in 1842. But most of the nation's great art museums date to the 1870s, when an economic boom following the Civil War fueled cultural projects throughout the industrial North. The MFA in Boston and the Metropolitan Museum of Art in New York were both founded in 1870. The Philadelphia Museum of Art followed in 1876, and the Art Institute of Chicago, three years later. These institutions began acquiring contemporary European art, both academic and avant-garde. Boston was particularly fortunate in this respect. A community of forward-thinking collectors amassed major holdings of Barbizon and Impressionist art during the second half of the nineteenth century, helping to make the MFA's collection of this material one of the finest in the world. Though it does not represent every episode in the story of modern art, every avant-garde and "ism," the collection shines with outstanding works from this age, torn between future and past, ephemerality and permanence, the market and the museum.

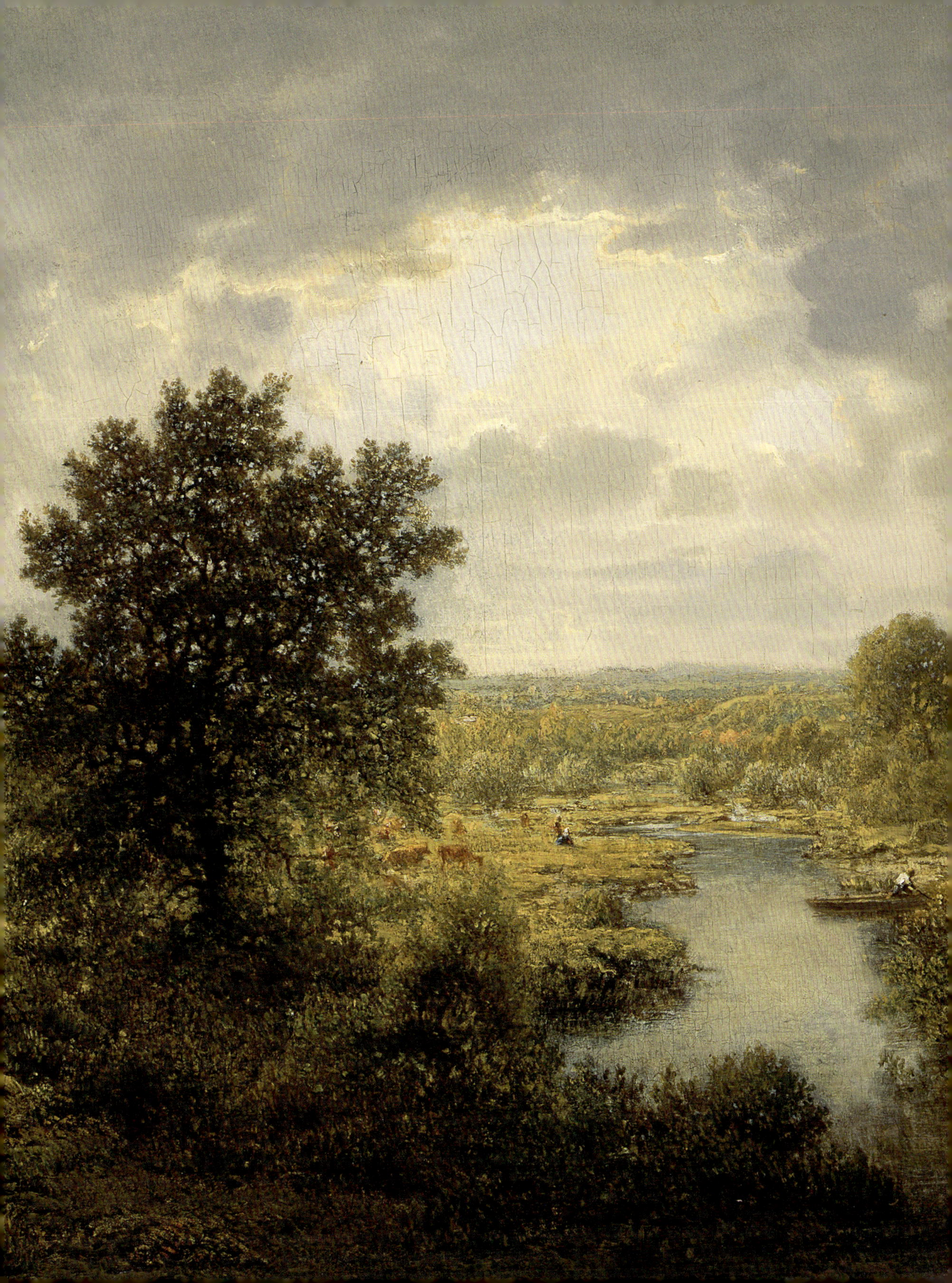

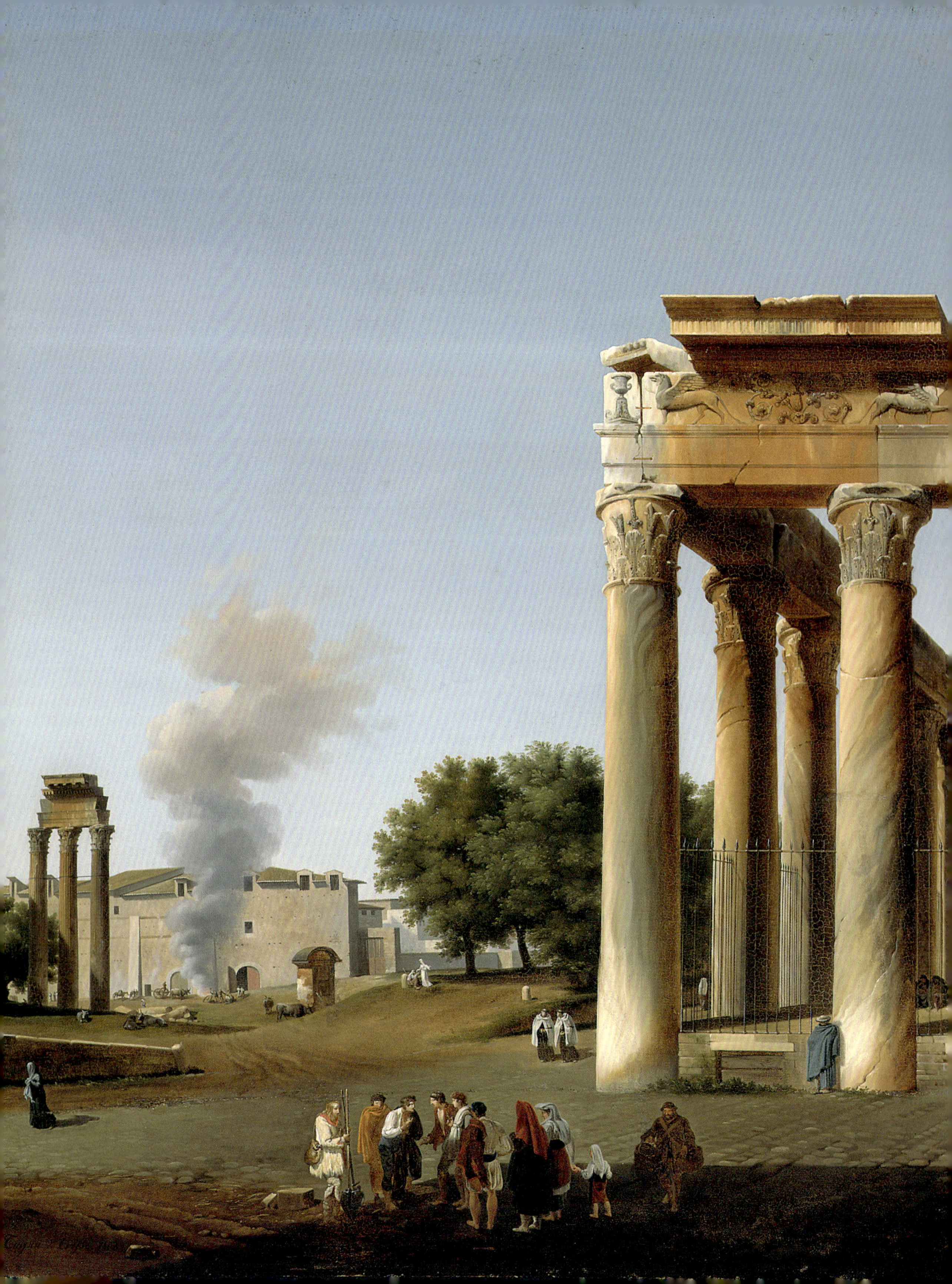

1

THE LURE OF THE PAST: neoclassicism and romanticism

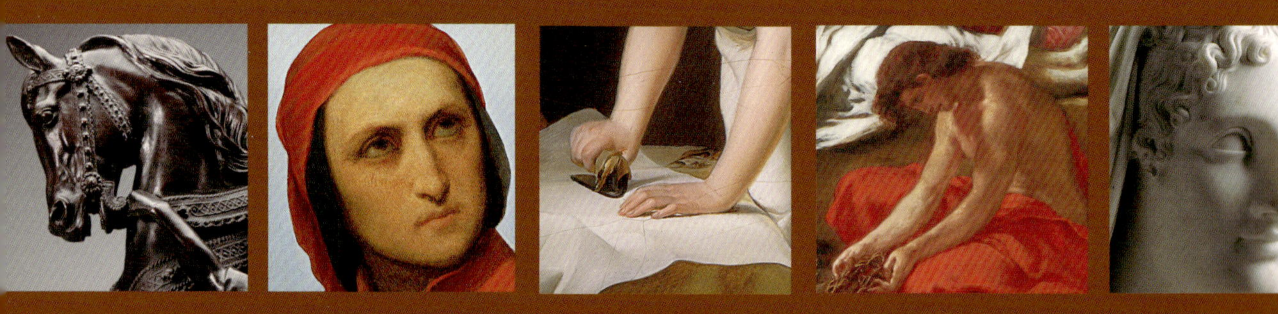

The Lure of the Past: Neoclassicism and Romanticism

Eighteenth-century Europeans set out to observe, catalogue, and understand their world with unprecedented fervor and precision. A belief that reason could comprehend every aspect of human experience animated intellectual endeavors as varied as Johann Wolfgang von Goethe's light and color experiments in Weimar, Adam Smith's theorization of capitalism in London and Edinburgh, and the compilation by Denis Diderot and Jean le Rond d'Alembert of the first great encyclopedia in Paris. From this atmosphere of inquiry and rationality emerged the modern discipline of art history, the modern art museum, and the associated artistic style known as Neoclassicism.

Excavations at Herculaneum and Pompeii in the 1730s and 1740s helped renew curiosity about the ancient world, and northern Europeans flocked to Rome throughout the century to bear witness to its classical remains. Among these travelers was a German philologist, Johann Joachim Winckelmann, who abandoned the Dresden court for the Eternal City in 1755 after publishing his *Reflections on the Imitation of Greek Works in Painting and Sculpture*. A seminal text for the Neoclassical movement, this essay exhorted painters and sculptors to turn to classical examples in order to renew modern art, which Winckelmann, like a growing number of his contemporaries, had come to regard as decadent. An international circle of young artists working in Rome embraced this credo: make it old to make it new. The Italian sculptor Antonio Canova, the French painter Jacques-Louis David, and others in their cohort spent countless hours copying antiquities in the city's public collections and, from these studies, devised their own compositions, characterized by smooth surfaces, clean lines, and idealized nude forms.

For many young artists in eighteenth-century Rome, this new style was linked to the imagined political ideals of the classical world: the Roman Republic, the Athenian democracy. Hence, at the end of the eighteenth century, when the intellectual revolutions of the Enlightenment ushered in actual political revolutions—first in North America, then in France, and, ultimately, throughout western Europe—Neoclassicism became their signature style, the sleek, valiant look of the future. Napoleon's ascendancy in the first decade of the nineteenth century, however, helped transform Neoclassicism from a revolutionary style to an official one, cultivated—and, indeed, enforced—at state art academies across the Continent. Under the leadership of the painter Jean-Auguste-Dominique Ingres and his appointed artistic heirs, Neoclassicism hardened into academic dogma.

Romanticism in the visual arts arose as a reaction to this hardening and in response to the larger disappointed hopes of the revolutionary era. Whereas Neoclassicists drew clear, rational lines between theory and practice, producing a visually coherent—even rather homogeneous—style, Romantics pursued more personal—and varied—aesthetic agendas. As the great Romantic painter Eugène Delacroix avowed, "If one understands by Romanticism the free manifestations of my personal impressions, my aversion for the stereotypes of the schools and my repugnance for academic formulae, I must admit not only that I am a Romantic but that I was so at the age of fifteen." As these words suggest, a new interest in individual, subjective experience and expression distinguished all the products of the Romantic movement, from German idealist philosophy to English Romantic poetry, from the symphonies of Ludwig van Beethoven to the paintings of Delacroix. It is to the Romantic generation that we owe our understanding of the artist as an oppositional figure, a lone, brooding genius.

Struggling to give outward, sensuous form to inward emotional states, Romantic artists found different solutions: brilliant, high-keyed color and luscious brushwork on the one hand, self-conscious archaism and pastiche, on the other. The emotional dimension of religious experience was of particular interest to the Romantics, whose era witnessed a revival of religious sentiment across the Continent. Romantic artists' study of medieval, Renaissance, and Baroque devotional art fed into their broader fascination with the art of the past. Like their Neoclassical predecessors, Romantic painters and sculptors took a lively interest in the history of art, though here again Romanticism proved its highly personal and hence endlessly varied nature: some artists turned to the Middle Ages, drawing inspiration from Dante's poetry or Gothic cathedral architecture; others looked to the Renaissance, to the paintings of Sandro Botticelli or the plays of Shakespeare; still others admired the seventeenth century, aspiring to the emotional drama of Peter Paul Rubens. Romantics rifled through the art of the past to renew their own practice, searching out models of grace and sincerity. A sense of belatedness and loss underwrote all these efforts, an overwhelming nostalgia for an imaginary past. Like the image of the brooding artistic genius, this sense of nostalgia and loss is a legacy of Romanticism, a defining feature of cultural life in modern Europe.

—E.A.B.

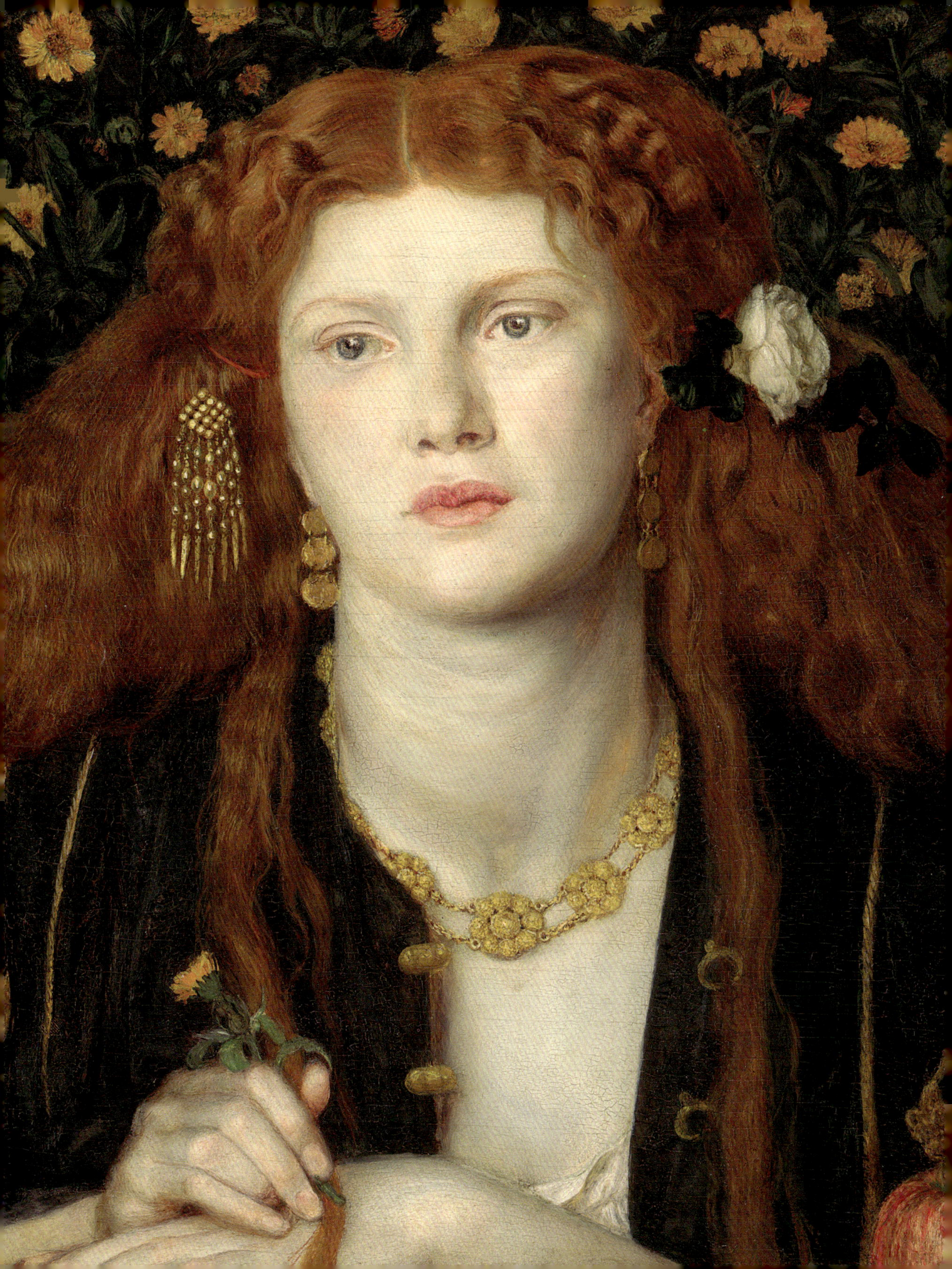

Joseph Chinard
French, 1756–1813
Profile Portrait of Anne-Louis Girodet de Roucy-Trioson, 1792

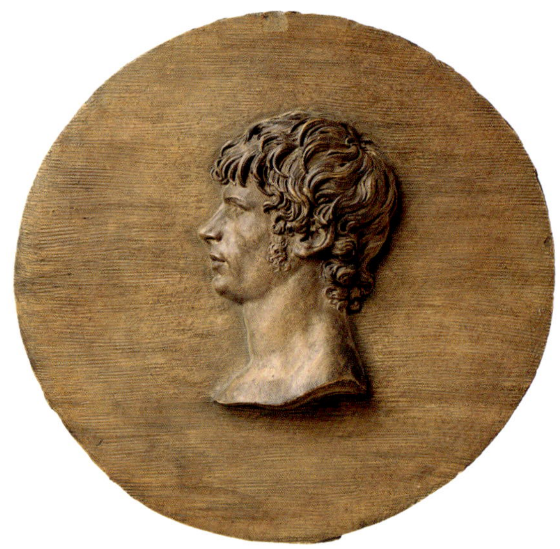

Ancient coins and Renaissance medals inspired Chinard's portrait of his fellow artist and compatriot, the painter Girodet. As in those forms, the sitter is presented in profile, set in a circular field. The isolation of the head focuses attention on the mind and the intellect of the sitter, and the severe cut of the body just below the neck also calls to mind a carved bust in the round. Chinard, however, interprets this traditional form in new ways. Comparisons with other portraits of Girodet make clear that this is a faithful likeness, not an idealized image. The terracotta medium, often used for preparatory models, mitigates the permanence and reflective surface of metal coins and medals. The fired clay retains a soft quality in the detailed curls of the hair set against the more smoothly finished flesh, as well as in the raked lines that mark the background field. The relatively small scale of the head in relation to the circular field, and its placement right at the center, instead of anchored to the lower edge, further isolate it, conveying the strong will and independent spirit of Girodet.

Signed and dated "Chinard Rome 1792," the portrait is the only evidence that the artists knew each other. It was created while they both were in Rome during the years of the French Revolution, when tensions between Italy and France were high. Girodet, who had won the Rome Prize in 1789, would flee the city in 1793 because of the political turmoil. Chinard, who had traveled to Rome in 1791, was imprisoned in 1792, the year this portrait was made, for creating sculptures that were deemed sacrilegious and for political tendencies that Italians considered dangerous. His allegorical sculpture *Truth in the Guise of Apollo Trampling Superstition* of 1791 represents Superstition as a female figure holding a cross and a chalice, emblems of the Catholic faith, and so a direct affront to Rome and to the Church itself. Although French artists might have considered their nation as rational and enlightened in contrast to old-fashioned and superstitious Italy, they also universally recognized Italy as heir to the greatest traditions of art, from antiquity through the present day. This portrait is emblematic of both lines of thought.

Terracotta
Diam. 22.5 cm (8⅞ in.)
Gift of Randolph Fuller, 1994.90

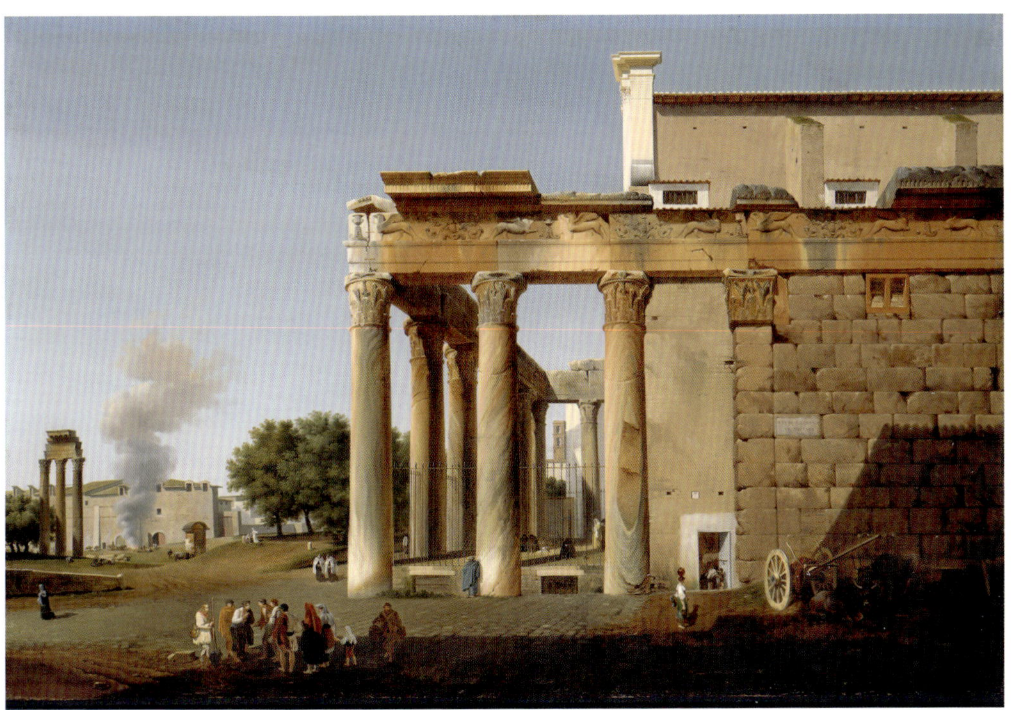

Lancelot Turpin de Crissé
French, 1782–1859
Temple of Antoninus and Faustina, 1808

Turpin de Crissé shared in his generation's fascination with the classical world and its ruined remains. In this view of the Roman Forum, he portrayed the Temple of Antoninus and Faustina—built in 141 BC and converted into a church in the sixth century AD—taking pains to exclude the later Baroque church facade barely discernible above the ancient temple's entablature. With the three columns of the Temple of Castor and Pollux and the large-scale Basilica Julia visible in the left background, the focus here is on ancient ruins, as they were inhabited and reused by the early nineteenth-century Roman population. Priests, peasants, beggars, and pilgrims populate the Forum, lending picturesque life—and occasional squalor—to the decayed splendor of their surroundings.

Turpin traveled to Rome in 1807 in search of archaeological motifs like this one. Born into a noble family, he took an early interest in classical antiquities, amassing an important collection of his own. He first learned to paint from his father, an amateur artist and an officer in the royal army, who fled France during the Revolution. Left to his own devices, the young painter turned his art from a hobby into a profession, quickly attracting patronage from members of the antiquarian circles he frequented in Paris. His most important early patron was the diplomat and archaeologist Marie-Gabriel-Auguste-Florent de Choiseul Gouffier, who underwrote Turpin's studies in Rome, and for whom he painted this picture.

Oil on canvas
114.6 x 163.2 cm (45⅛ x 64¼ in.)
Bequest of Emma B. Culbertson, 20.852

Bertel Thorvaldsen
Danish, 1768–1844
Bust of Lord Byron, 1821

This marble portrait bust of the great Romantic poet Byron was commissioned by the young Bostonian Joseph Coolidge when he visited the Roman studio of Bertel Thorvaldsen. Coolidge would have had some choices when ordering his version of the bust. He probably requested that the head be set on the severe, blocklike termination known as a herm, which was considered to be closer to ancient Greek forms. Other versions of the portrait, more like surviving Roman busts, are finished at the bottom with a smooth curving edge or draped as if the figure were wearing a toga. Soon afterward, in Venice, Coolidge met Byron, who later wrote in his journal that he was more moved by this young man's wanting the bust of a poet he loved than if a monument had been set up to him in the Paris Pantheon. In this same entry, Byron revealed ambivalence about sitting for a marble portrait bust. Sitting for a painting was one thing, but sitting for a bust was like "putting up pretensions to permanency—and smacks something of a hankering for public fame rather than private remembrance." He only did it, he said, because a friend had asked him to. Byron sat for Thorvaldsen in Rome in 1817. The sculptor found the poet a difficult sitter, who he said put on a dramatic melancholy face and moved about too much. The poet in turn was not pleased with the bust, saying that he was a sadder person than it presented him to be. Thus we find in a stony white image of Byron—with his tightly curled hair, intense gaze, soft cheeks, dimpled chin, and elegant ears—stories of human experience, pride and humility, friendship and artistic inspiration.

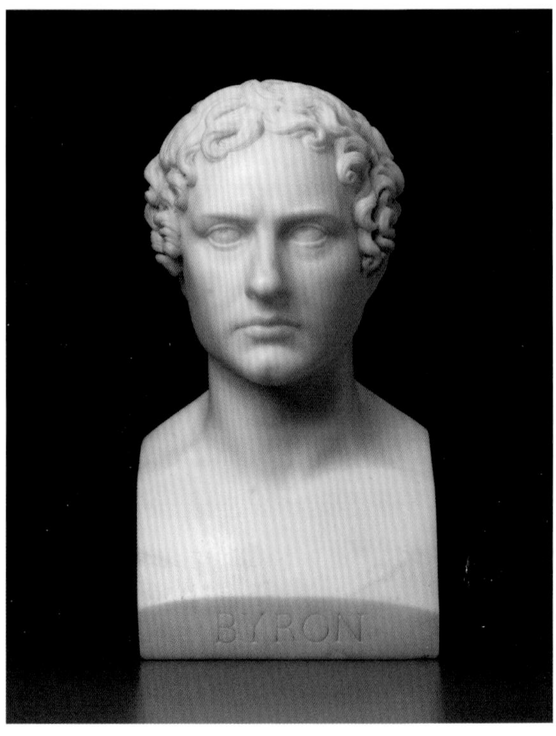

Marble
45.1 x 23 x 17.5 cm (17¾ x 9 x 6⅞ in.)
Gift of T. Jefferson Coolidge, 20.1628

Claude Michel, called **Clodion**
French, 1738–1814
The Flood, 1800

This terracotta sculpture shows a muscular man carrying the limp body of his son as he attempts to rescue him from the rising waters of a cataclysmic flood. He climbs, seeking higher ground, while behind him is the half-submerged body of a dead woman, and a young child still grasping at his mother's body. The work is a small-scale model for a life-size plaster made in 1800 by Clodion, in the hope of obtaining a commission to execute it in marble. The sculpture marks a turning point for the sculptor, who previously had produced mainly smaller-scale terracottas on more frivolous classicizing themes, such as nymphs and satyrs cavorting in landscape settings. Here he chose a dramatic subject, the powerful forces of nature overcoming struggling humanity, a theme associated with the Romantic movement.

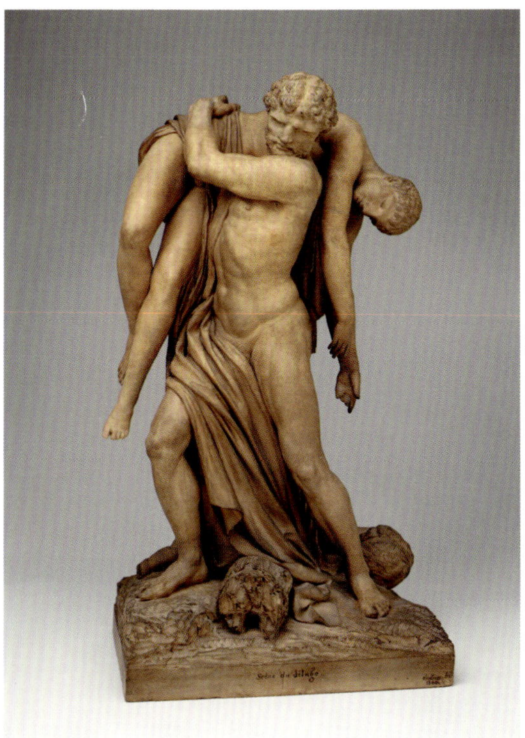

Rarely represented in sculpture, the flood was a recurring subject in paintings of the late eighteenth century, marking an interest in the forces of nature as well as a move away from classical subject matter. Clodion looked to ancient, Renaissance, and Baroque models for his figures and composition, transforming his sources into an ambitious narrative conveyed through four different figure types. His most startling invention, the half-length figure of the woman whose body seems to sink below the surface of the water and the base of the sculpture, perplexed some critics. Although the sculptor won recognition for the life-size model, a commission for the marble did not materialize.

Terracotta
54.5 x 27.9 x 22.9 cm (21½ x 11 x 9 in.)
John H. and Ernestine A. Payne Fund, 1981.398

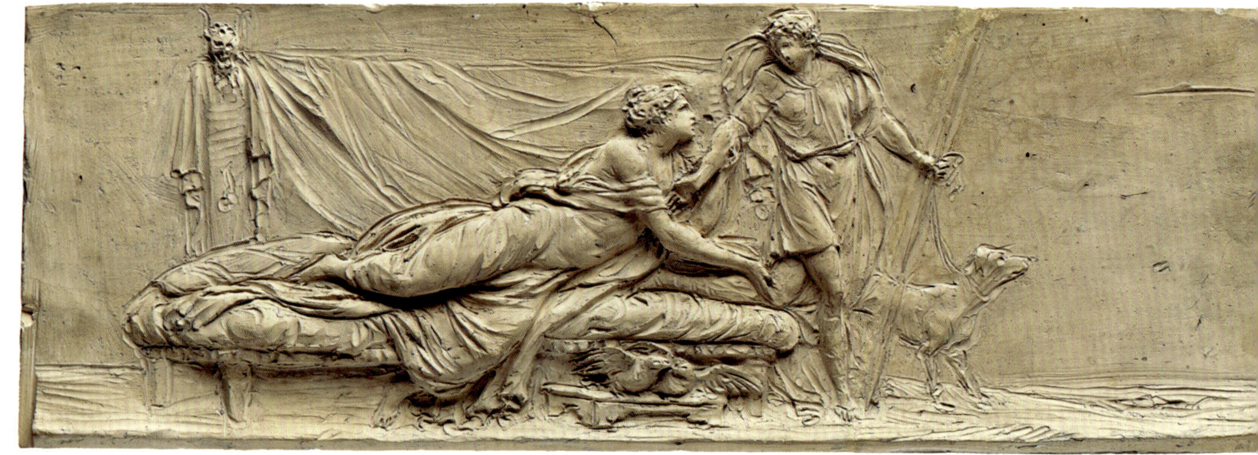

Antonio Trentanove
Italian, 1742–1812
Venus and Adonis, about 1794

Venus reclines on a cushioned bed, rousing herself to implore Adonis not to leave on his ill-fated hunt. Nonetheless, her young lover is already on his way, turning back to address her as he moves forward, his hunting dog with nose already on the scent. The scene is the prelude to the horrible death of Adonis, killed by a wild boar—a story told by Ovid in *Metamorphoses*, which ends in the transformation of the fallen hunter's blood into the anemone. This terracotta sketch was the model for a stucco relief, part of a series of the *Loves of the Gods* that decorates a room in the Laderchi Palace in Faenza, Italy. The scene is animated with exuberant, erotic details like the two turtledoves still embracing below the bed, as Venus and Adonis had been just moments before. The bed curtain wraps around the horned, phallic herm, a form that in antiquity served as a road marker thought to protect travelers; here it marks the safe precinct of Venus's bed.

The painter Felice Giani was responsible for the program of the whole room. He likely sketched the scenes that Trentanove worked out in clay for final enlargement and production in stucco. Like a drawing in clay, this small relief displays the sureness of the sculptor's touch, evident in the marks of Trentanove's pointed modeling stick, used to sketch out the forms and press in details of hair and eyes. That direct evidence of the artist's hand in the work explains why such models survive; like drawings, they were collected for that very reason. This is a particularly Italian strain of Neoclassicism, elegant and intimate, based on recent discoveries at Herculaneum and Pompeii, where more private, sometimes erotic scenes decorated homes, as opposed to the more severe style associated with marble statuary and public monuments.

Terracotta
17.1 x 48.2 x 4.1 cm (6¾ x 19 x 1⅝ in.)
Gift of Randolph Fuller, 1977.817

Louis-Léopold Boilly
French, 1761–1845
Young Woman Ironing, about 1800

The Neoclassical style is often associated with epic narrative—grand stories from Greek and Roman history—but the genre painter Boilly practiced Neoclassicism of a more intimate kind, adopting the elegant, idealizing style to subjects drawn from everyday life. He showed less interest in the often grim realities of working-class existence than in fashioning picturesque scenes that would appeal to his upper-middle-class clientele.

Boilly's laundress—at once prim and inviting in her pressed apron and plunging décolleté—irons a length of muslin in a well-appointed kitchen. At left, a spare iron warms on a stove; tongs and a bellows for stoking the fire lie on the floor. Contemporary critics complained that the girl was too elegantly dressed for her station, and the great swaths of drapery that decorate the furniture would have been an anomalous luxury in a room used only by servants. The vessels that sit on the chair, presumably meant to contain sprinkling water or starch, are made of porcelain and fine, transparent glass—materials too costly for workaday use.

In his treatment of the girl's costume, the implausible luxury items, and the crisp, translucent cloth, Boilly showcased his ability to render the specific sheens and textures of beautiful objects. His extraordinary gifts in this direction led contemporaries to compare him with such seventeenth-century Dutch fine-manner painters as Gerrit Dou and Gerard ter Borch, whose work was highly prized in late eighteenth-century France. An avid art collector, Boilly owned works by both Dou and Ter Borch and drew inspiration from their scenes of genteel domestic labor.

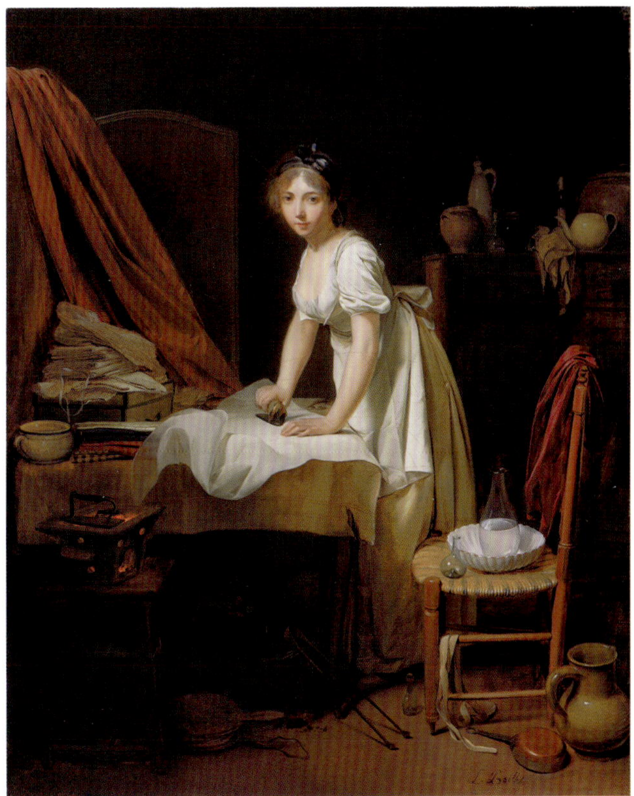

Oil on canvas
40.7 x 32.4 cm (16 x 12¾ in.)
Charles H. Bayley Picture and Painting Fund, 1983.10

Pierre-Jean David d'Angers

French, 1788-1856

Bust of Dominique François Arago, 1839

David d'Angers was one of the most prolific and creative portraitists of the Romantic period in France. This marble bust displays the most important characteristics of his style and approach to portraiture. The abstract blocklike lower termination of the bust refers to the herm in ancient Greek art: apparently developed from piles of stones set as markers on roads and dedicated to the god of travel, Hermes, the herm became a pedestal, decorated with an erect phallus, supporting the head of Hermes. Ultimately, this form was simplified as a base for portrait heads and representations of other gods and heroes. In the Neoclassical period, the herm signaled a purity associated with ancient Greece and so here inflects David d'Angers's bust with "Greek" idealism. Above this artificial cropping of the body and limbs, the naturalism of the neck, Adam's apple, and clavicles, the fleshy chin and cheeks, the deep brooding eyes, and high forehead provide a sense of the physical appearance and character of the sitter. David's subtle working of the pupils creates a suggestion of color and focus in the eyes. The exaggerated heavy eyebrows and wild and unruly curls of the hair impart a dramatic intensity to the portrait. The bust is a synthesis of all that portraiture could be for David: stark Neoclassicism tempering the naturalism of representation, and imbued with Romantic spirit and energy.

Arago was a scientist who made significant contributions to the study of astronomy and magnetism, and he was also an ardent Republican, whose political ideals were shared by his friend David d'Angers. The terracotta model for this bust, now in the museum in Angers, was surely made from life.

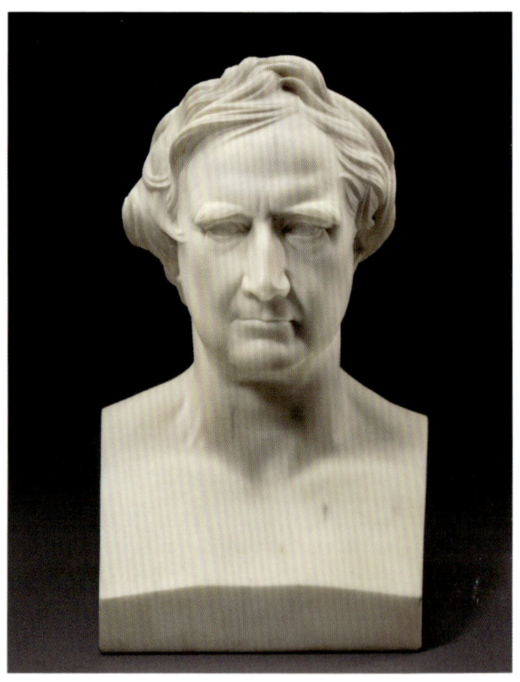

Marble

49.5 x 31.1 x 24.1 cm (19½ x 12¼ x 9½ in.)

Gift of Randolph J. Fuller, 1980.406

Antonio Canova
Italian, 1757–1822
Bust of Beatrice, 1819–22

The greatest sculptor of his day, Canova carved pure white marble statues and monuments that in their perfect finish and direct evocation of ancient statuary are the highest expression of Italian Neoclassicism. This *Bust of Beatrice*, however, is a more personal type of object, one that Canova invented late in his life. Referred to by the sculptor as "ideal heads," these busts were often made as gifts for friends for private delectation. They stood for his principal ideals as an artist, the beliefs that art could perfect nature and that ideal beauty could have moral and spiritual effects. He described making these heads with "amore caldissimo" (warmest love), and he sometimes inscribed the busts with a dedication. Canova's ideal heads often represented poets, such as Sappho, or Vestal Virgins, among other themes. The primary version of this bust was made for his friend Leopoldo Cicognara, an art critic and eventual biographer of the sculptor.

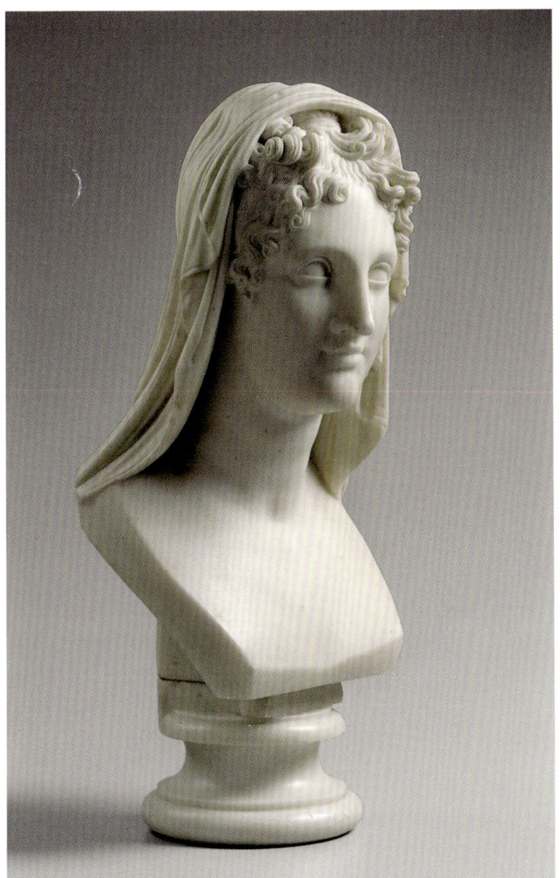

Canova's virtuosity can be seen in the deeply excavated and exuberant carving of the splendid curls of hair, the translucency of the veil, the soft finish of the skin, and the rolling flesh of the neck. The bust was conceived not as an image of Dante's muse, but as a portrait of Madame Juliette Récamier, a great Parisian beauty and the object of Canova's intense affection. Récamier rejected the plaster version of the portrait, however, displeased with the image Canova presented of her. The sculptor responded by transforming the final marble version from a likeness of his sitter into an idealized vision of Dante's beloved Beatrice. He minimized her characteristic features, including fleshier cheeks and a small bow-like smiling mouth, and smoothed out the surface of her eyes.

Marble
58.4 x 27.9 x 25.4 cm (23 x 11 x 10 in.)
William Francis Warden Fund, Edward J. and Mary S. Holmes Fund, John Lowell Gardner Fund, Russell B. and Andrée Beauchamp Stearns Fund, Helen B. Sweeney Fund, Frank B. Bemis Fund, Seth K. Sweetser Fund, H. E. Bolles Fund, Arthur Mason Knapp Fund, and Benjamin Pierce Cheney Donation, 2002.318

Ary Scheffer
Dutch (active in France), 1795–1858
Dante and Beatrice, 1851

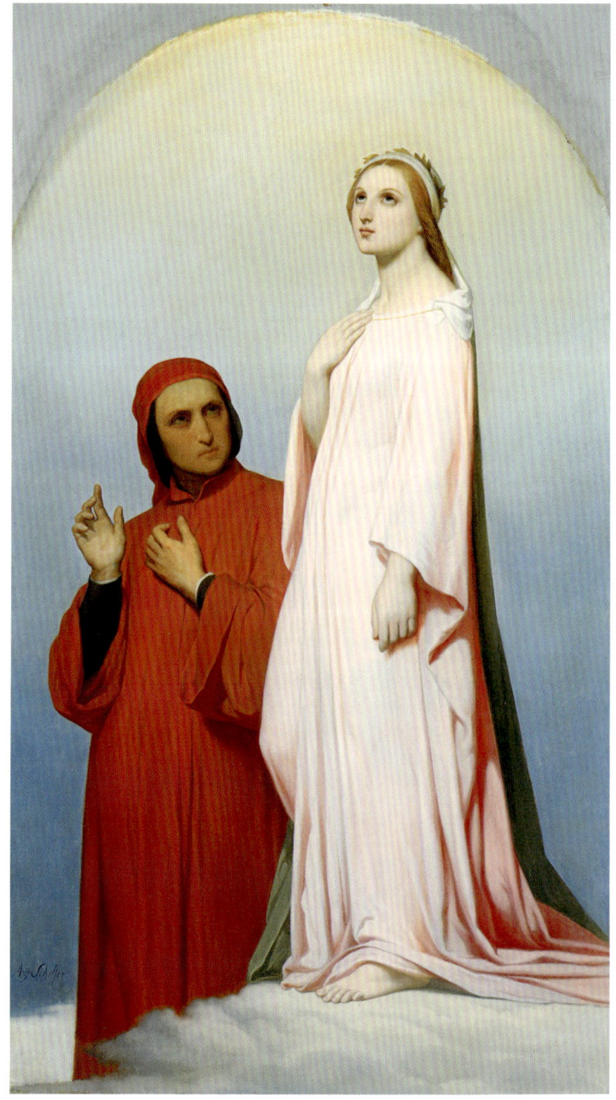

Scheffer's mature style applies the serene, sculptural forms of Neoclassicism to a Romantic repertoire of subject matter drawn from Dante, Shakespeare, and Goethe. The results strike what is sometimes called a *juste milieu*—a balance or compromise—between the two dominant aesthetic currents of the early nineteenth century. Many of Scheffer's paintings, like this one, carry the emotional resonance of religious scenes, although the stories they tell are often secular. Here the poet Dante beholds his beloved Beatrice in Paradise, standing on a cloud, her eyes turned toward a higher realm. The encounter is described in Dante's fourteenth-century *Divine Comedy* (in a translation from 1899):

> And, of a sudden, meseemed that day was added unto day, as though he who hath the power, had adorned heaven with a second sun. Beatrice was standing with her eyes all fixed upon the eternal wheels, and I fixed my sight removed from there above, on her.
>
> (Paradiso, canto 1)

These very lines are inscribed in Italian on the frame, which may have been commissioned with the painting.

This is the second version of a composition Scheffer had first painted in 1846. Like many established artists in the nineteenth century, Scheffer often produced multiple versions of his paintings to satisfy various commissions and supply prototypes for reproductive prints (engravings, lithographs, and ultimately photographs). Scheffer's work was widely reproduced, making him one of the most famous artists of his day, a leading light of Parisian cultural life, who counted the composer Franz Liszt and the poet Alphonse de Lamartine among his friends.

Oil on canvas
180 x 99 cm (70⅞ x 39 in.)
Seth K. Sweetser Fund, 21.1283

Baron Henri de Triqueti
French, 1804–1874
Dante and Virgil, modeled 1861, cast 1862

The fourteenth-century Italian poet Dante holds a scroll with an inscription from the second part (*Purgatory*) of his *Divine Comedy*: "Liberta va cercando ch'e si cara" (He goes seeking freedom, which is so dear). He is accompanied by the ancient Roman poet Virgil, one of Dante's great role models, who embraces Dante and directs him with his gestures and forward glance. In the *Divine Comedy*, Virgil guides Dante through Inferno and Purgatory but cannot, as a pagan, accompany him to Paradise. Both poets are crowned with celebratory laurel wreaths marking their fame, and Virgil, though the elder and the guide, is smooth-faced and considerably younger than Dante. Many nineteenth-century Romantic artists were inspired by Dante's work, and they were also moved to depict Dante and Virgil. The large-scale, two-figured group recalls ancient Roman tomb monuments, and its medium, bronze, also looks back to both the Renaissance and the Classical era. The group was a gift from the daughter of the artist to the Museum of Fine Arts, an appropriate home in a city that was to see the founding, in 1881, of the Dante Society of America by Henry Wadsworth Longfellow, James Russell Lowell, and Charles Eliot Norton.

Bronze
90 x 86 x 64 cm ($35\frac{3}{8}$ x $33\frac{7}{8}$ x $25\frac{1}{8}$ in.)
Gift of Mrs. Edward Lee Childe, 76.5

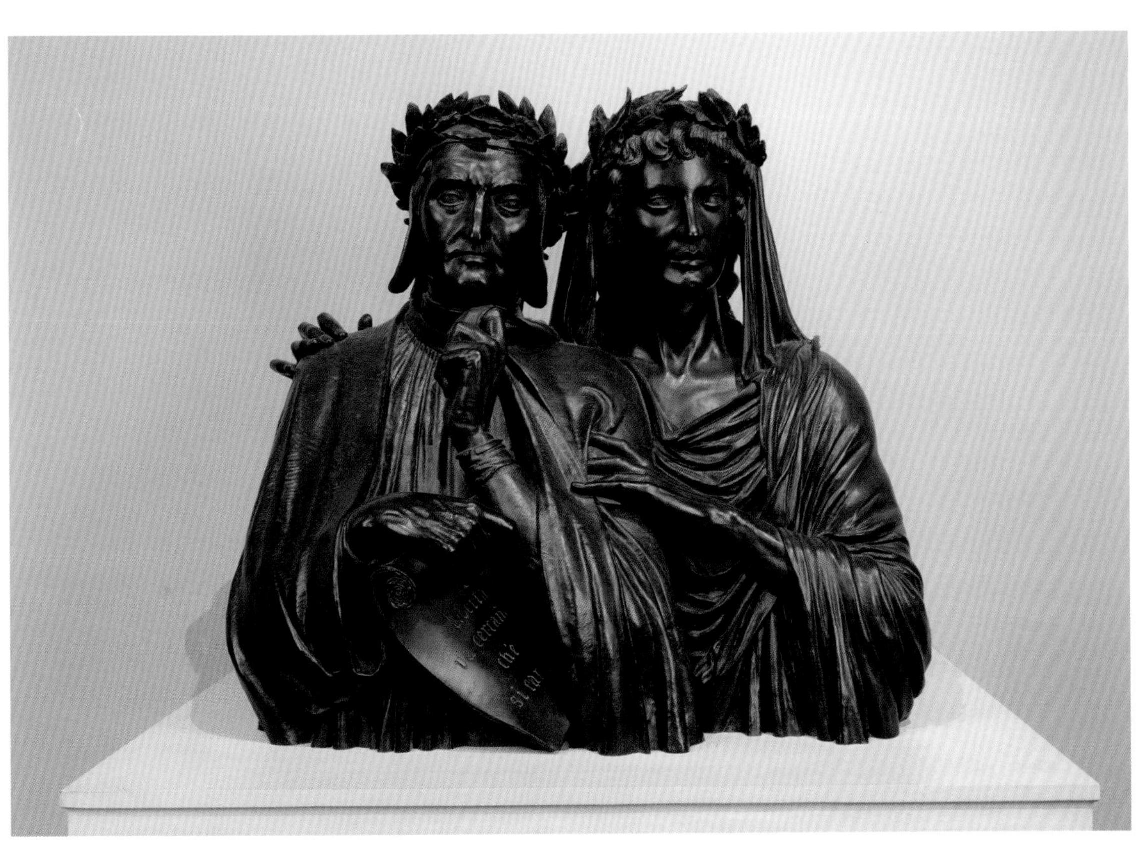

John Gibson
British, 1790–1866
Cupid Disguised as a Shepherd, about 1836

Gibson was born in Wales and trained as a carpenter. His ambitions to become a sculptor took him first to London to attend art school and then to Rome, where he studied with the two most important sculptors there, Antonio Canova and Bertel Thorvaldsen. Gibson in turn would train younger sculptors, in particular the American Harriet Hosmer, in the Neoclassical style. *Cupid Disguised as a Shepherd* is known in at least nine versions. The subject was directly inspired by the Italian Renaissance poet Torquato Tasso's pastoral play *Aminta*. The character of Cupid, the god of love, dresses up as a shepherd as he works his magic, or mischief, on local shepherds and nymphs. In his prologue, Tasso marvels that such a powerful god could be so well hidden. Gibson follows Tasso's lead by concealing beneath the shepherd's cloak Cupid's bow and his wings, which peek out below the edges of the garment at his back. The love god's open-handed gesture is one of welcome, part of the charming guile of this powerful deity. This version displays a softly polished finish that mimics the warmth of flesh and presents a delicate, sweet-faced young boy, with spiraling curls and a dreamy expression. Though brilliant white marble is the characteristic material of Neoclassical sculpture, Gibson felt it should be tempered by the application of color, which would make it even more like ancient sculpture. He applied color to other sculptures, but no traces remain on this work.

Marble
132.1 x 35.6 cm (52 x 14 in.)
Bequest of Thomas Gold Appleton, 84.271

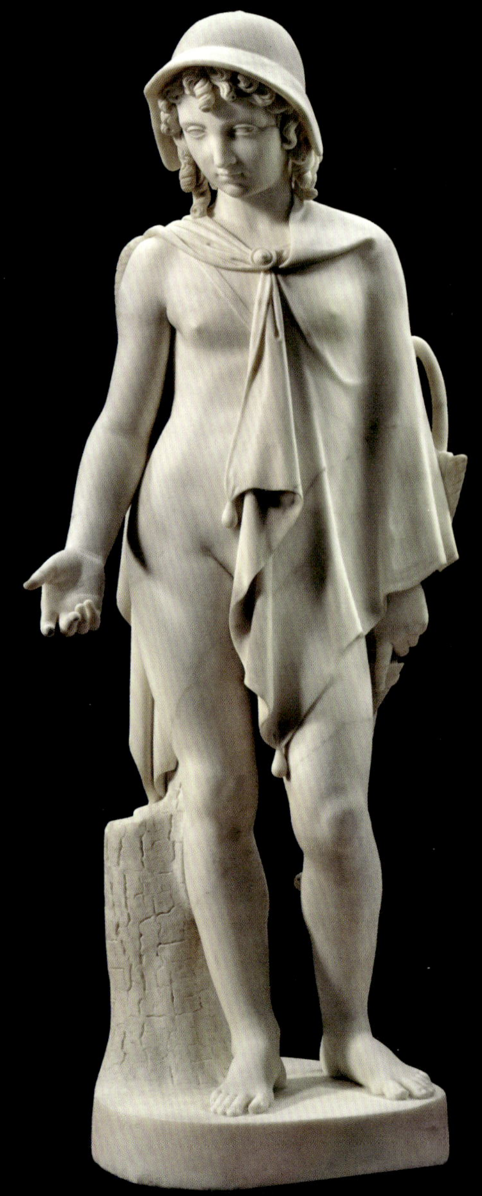

Giulio Monteverde
Italian, 1837–1917
Young Columbus, 1871

Waves lapping at his feet, the young Christopher Columbus sits on a mooring post, looking dreamily across the seas, as if into his future. Monteverde's marble sculpture displays the nineteenth century's Romantic fascination with the youth of famous men, presented with a charming naturalism and attention to detail. From the cap on his head to the buttons on his jacket and the texture of his breeches, Columbus is a picture of a Renaissance youth seen through nineteenth-century eyes. The youngster's complex, cross-legged posture shows him as he pauses in his reading, holding his place in his book. Monteverde's virtuoso carving techniques are displayed in the spiraling curls and the frothy waves.

This sculpture was ordered as a gift for the newly founded Museum of Fine Arts when the donor visited the artist's studio in Rome. The commission marks an important new purpose for the marble statue, bought not as decoration for a private home but specifically to be displayed in a museum setting.

Marble
H. 145 cm (57⅛ in.)
Gift of Augustus Porter Chamberlain, 71.8

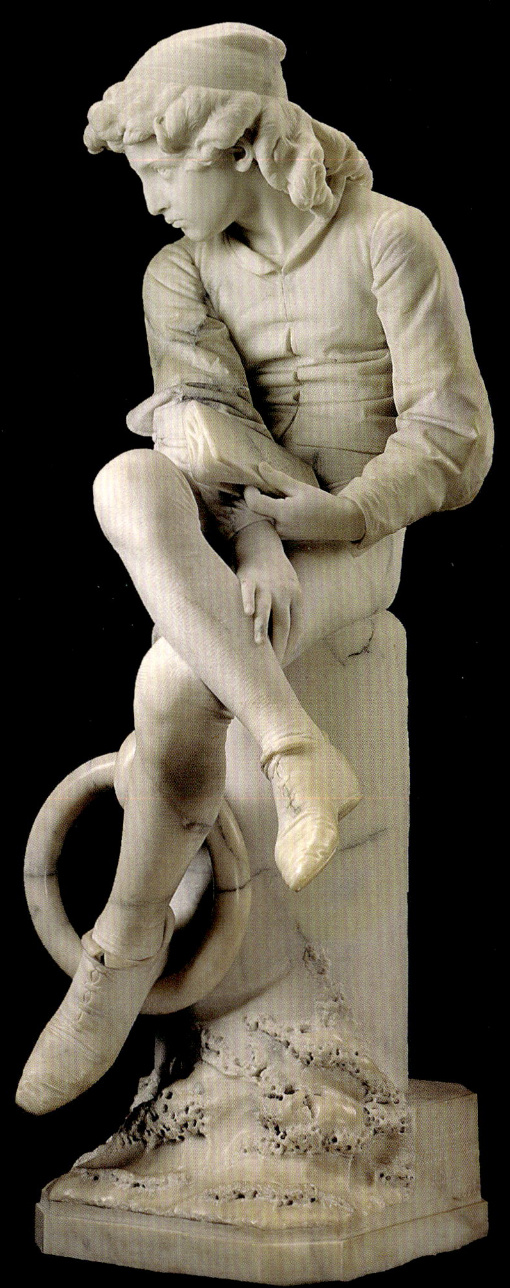

Jean-Auguste Barre
French, 1811–1896
Mary of Burgundy, about 1837–42

A rare example in sculpture of the Romantic revival movement known as the Troubadour Style, this bronze statuette presents a poignant scene from the life of a Renaissance monarch. She is the fifteenth-century Valois princess and archduchess of Austria, Mary of Burgundy, whose marriage to Holy Roman Emperor Maximilian I of Austria established a powerful dynastic union. Mary and her husband were avid hunters, a sport reserved for royalty, and she was killed in an accident while out hawking. This statuette shows her as if lost in a reverie, unaware of imminent tragedy signaled by the rearing horse and the running page struggling to control the animal.

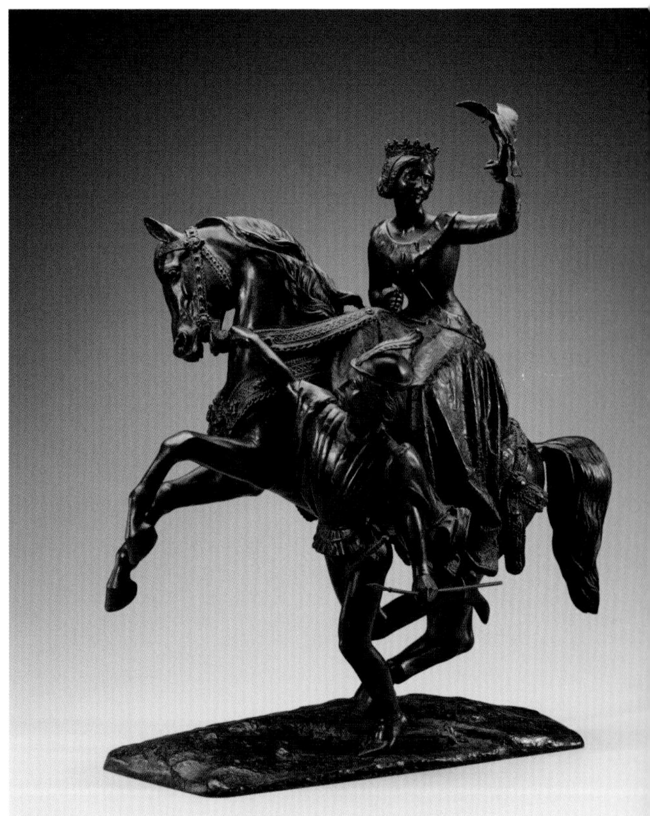

Barre was trained as a medalist, making him particularly adept at creating precise details in the bronze medium, evident here in the ornament of the bridle and reins. The rearing horse was a favored motif for Renaissance artists and a technical challenge for bronze casters. Barre met the challenge of his predecessors, modeling the sculpture with all the weight balanced on the two rear legs of the horse and the toes of one foot of the running page. This sculpture also marks the revival of the use of bronze for small-scale statues, a medium that had fallen out of favor in the eighteenth century, when porcelain was preferred.

Bronze
49.8 x 33 x 14.9 cm (19⅝ x 13 x 5⅞ in.)
Museum purchase with funds donated by
The Swan Society, 2002.26

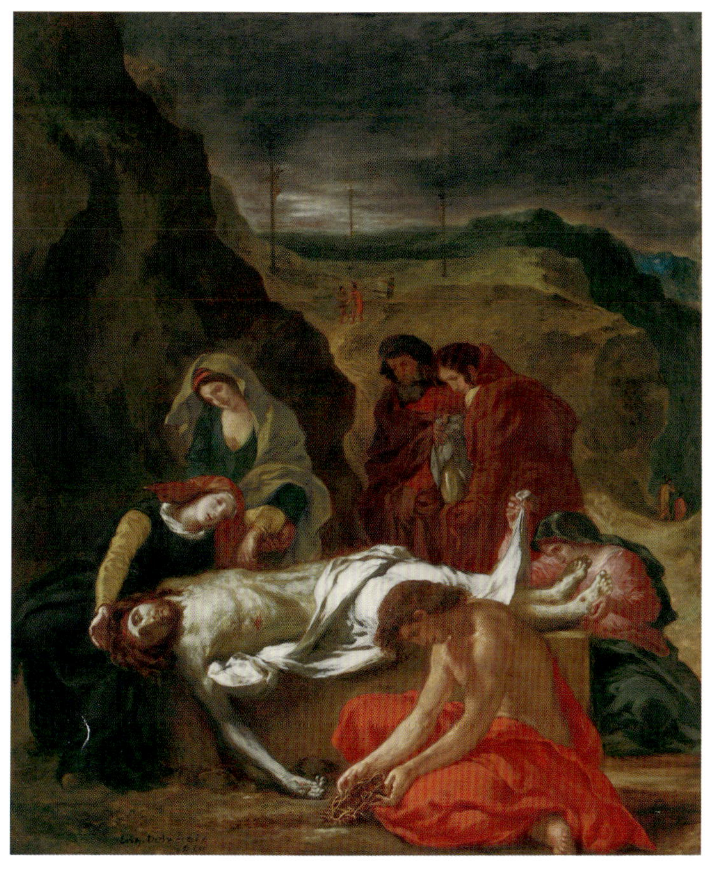

Eugène Delacroix
French, 1798–1863
The Lamentation (Christ at the Tomb), 1848

Oil on canvas
162.6 x 132.1 cm (64 x 52 in.)
Gift by contribution in memory of Martin Brimmer, 96.21

Delacroix was the greatest painter of the French Romantic movement. He pioneered a bold, free manner, using fluidly brushed expanses of color to convey heightened emotional states. Though he is best remembered for his Orientalist subjects, Delacroix was also among the most compelling religious painters of the early nineteenth century, which witnessed a revival of Christian sentiment across Europe.

Drawing inspiration from the Renaissance and Baroque masters Titian and Rubens, Delacroix here treated a time-honored subject—the Lamentation over Christ's dead body—with an unmistakably Romantic intensity. The Virgin Mary, seated at left, weeps over her son's livid corpse. A white shroud drawn over Christ heightens the pallor of his skin and creates a vivid contrast to the flame-red tunic of the young disciple, John, contemplating the crown of thorns at right. In the dim, glowering distance looms Golgotha hill with its three crosses, a reminder of the Crucifixion.

Widely hailed in Delacroix's lifetime as his greatest religious picture, the scene stirred a powerful response even in its own maker. "The general effect," he wrote on seeing this work some years after he had painted it, "inspires an emotion that astonishes even myself. You cannot tear yourself from it."

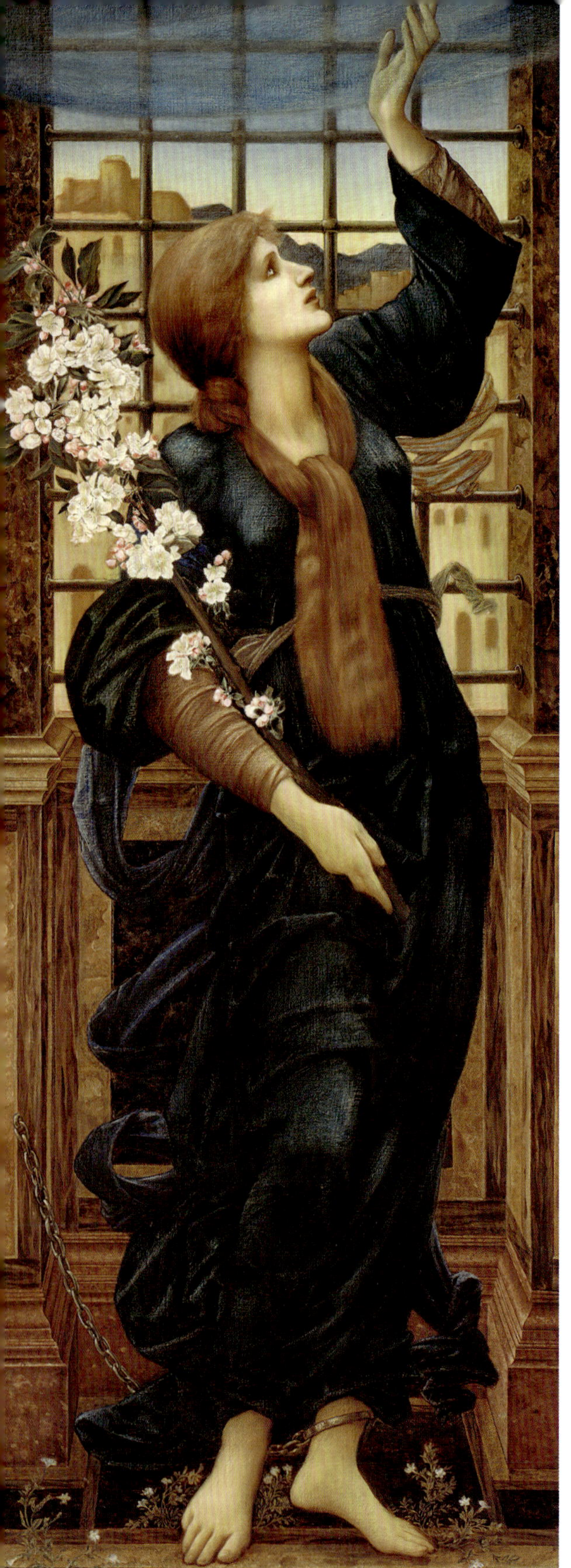

Sir Edward Coley Burne-Jones
English, 1833–1898
Hope, 1896

Hope—along with Faith and Charity—is one of the three theological virtues in the Christian tradition. Most often represented by a figure holding an anchor, Hope appears instead in Burne-Jones's painting as a prisoner in a cell. Though she wears a shackle around one ankle, her eyes turn to the open sky, which seems to waft in through her prison bars even as flowers spring up at her feet. A branch of apple blossom completes the allegory, suggesting the promise of spring, an annually renewed miracle, a reason to hope in the face of despair.

Burne-Jones studied theology at Oxford as a young man but abandoned his academic education at age twenty-two after seeing a drawing by the Pre-Raphaelite Dante Gabriel Rossetti. The older artist's work so fired Burne-Jones's imagination that he immediately began producing his own art and soon moved to London to become Rossetti's pupil. Like the Pre-Raphaelites, Burne-Jones drew inspiration from medieval and early Renaissance art, particularly that of the fifteenth-century Florentine painter Sandro Botticelli, whose graceful, elongated figure style he plainly emulated in pictures like this one. The effect of elongation is here exaggerated by the vertical format of the canvas, which revisits an earlier composition used as the basis for a stained-glass window at Christ Church, Oxford, one of three Burne-Jones designed representing Faith, Hope, and Charity.

Oil on canvas
179 x 63.5 cm (70½ x 25 in.)
Given in memory of Mrs. George Marston Whitin by her four daughters, Mrs. Laurence Murray Keeler, Mrs. Sydney Russell Mason, Mrs. Elijah Kent Swift, and Mrs. William Carey Crane, 40.778

Dante Gabriel Rossetti
English, 1828–1882
Bocca Baciata (Lips That Have Been Kissed), 1859

The title of this painting, *Bocca Baciata* (literally, "kissed mouth"), matches Rossetti's frankly sensuous treatment of its model, whose lips appear almost bruised. Those words—inscribed on the back of the panel—come from a story in Giovanni Boccaccio's fourteenth-century collection *Decameron*, in which the Babylonian princess Alatiel takes eight lovers before marrying a king. The story concludes with a proverb: "A kissed mouth loses no savor, but rather renews itself like the moon." The moral of both proverb and painting—that a woman's desirability does not rely on her virginity—shocked Victorian audiences, including Rossetti's close friend William Holman Hunt, who decried the picture's "gross" and "revolting" sensuality.

Hunt and Rossetti were two of the three founding members of the Pre-Raphaelite Brotherhood, a radical artists' collective formed in London in 1848. The Brotherhood (or PRB, as it was called) rejected contemporary academic standards, expressing a Romantic urge to renew artistic practice by emulating masters of the past. As the group's name suggests, the particular period that most interested the PRB was that of the late Middle Ages and early Renaissance: art before Raphael, which they considered purer in its forms and more sincere in its expression than work produced during the High Renaissance or any subsequent period.

Thus Rossetti's fellow Pre-Raphaelites were doubly astonished by this picture, in which his style took a sudden and definitive turn toward Titian and High Renaissance Venice. The shift may have been inspired by his model (and mistress) Fanny Cornforth, born Sarah Cox, whose pale skin and russet cloud of hair recalled Titian's favorite models. The first owner of the painting, George Price Boyce, was also a member of the Pre-Raphaelite circle, and he, too, may have been Cornforth's lover. Boyce never referred to the picture by its Italian title, calling it instead his "portrait of Fanny."

Oil on panel
32.1 x 27 cm (12⅝ x 10⅝ in.)
Gift of James Lawrence, 1980.261

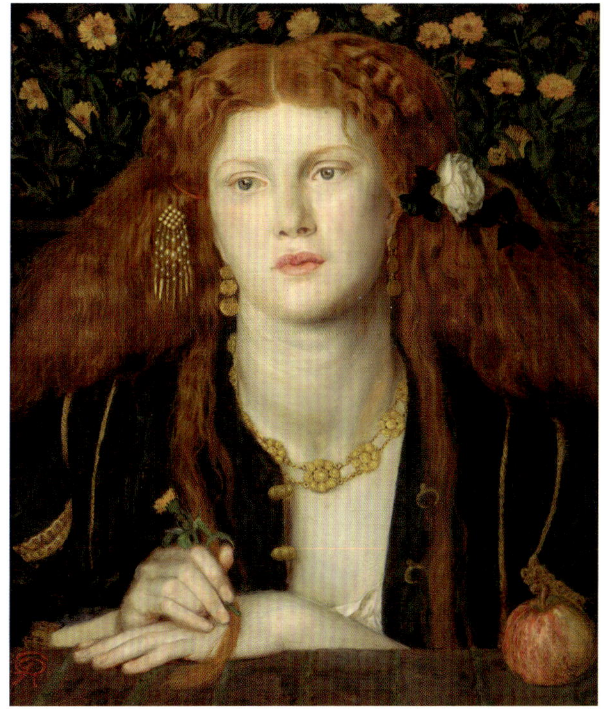

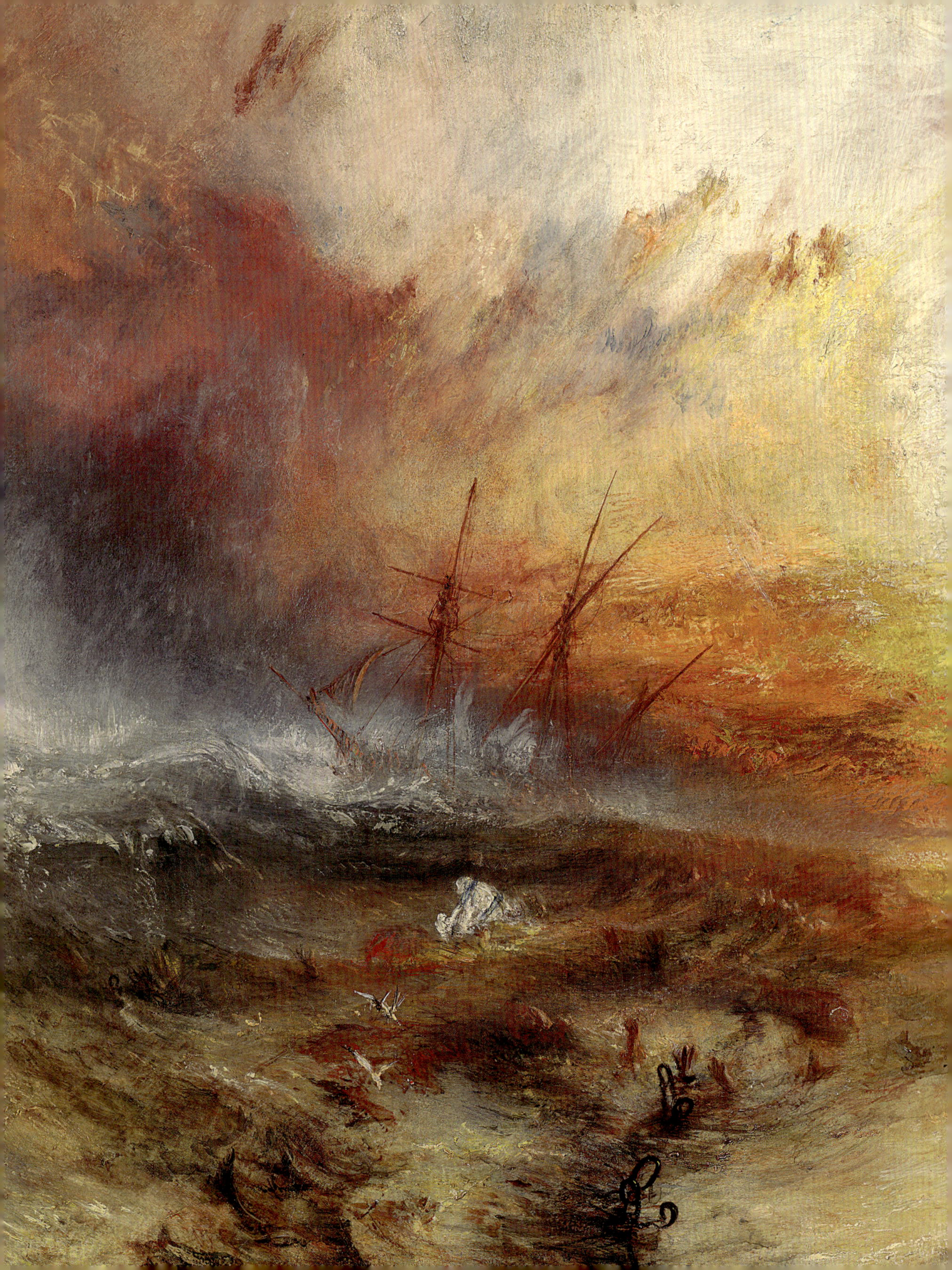

2

REPRESENTING NATURE: romantic landscape and the realist revolution

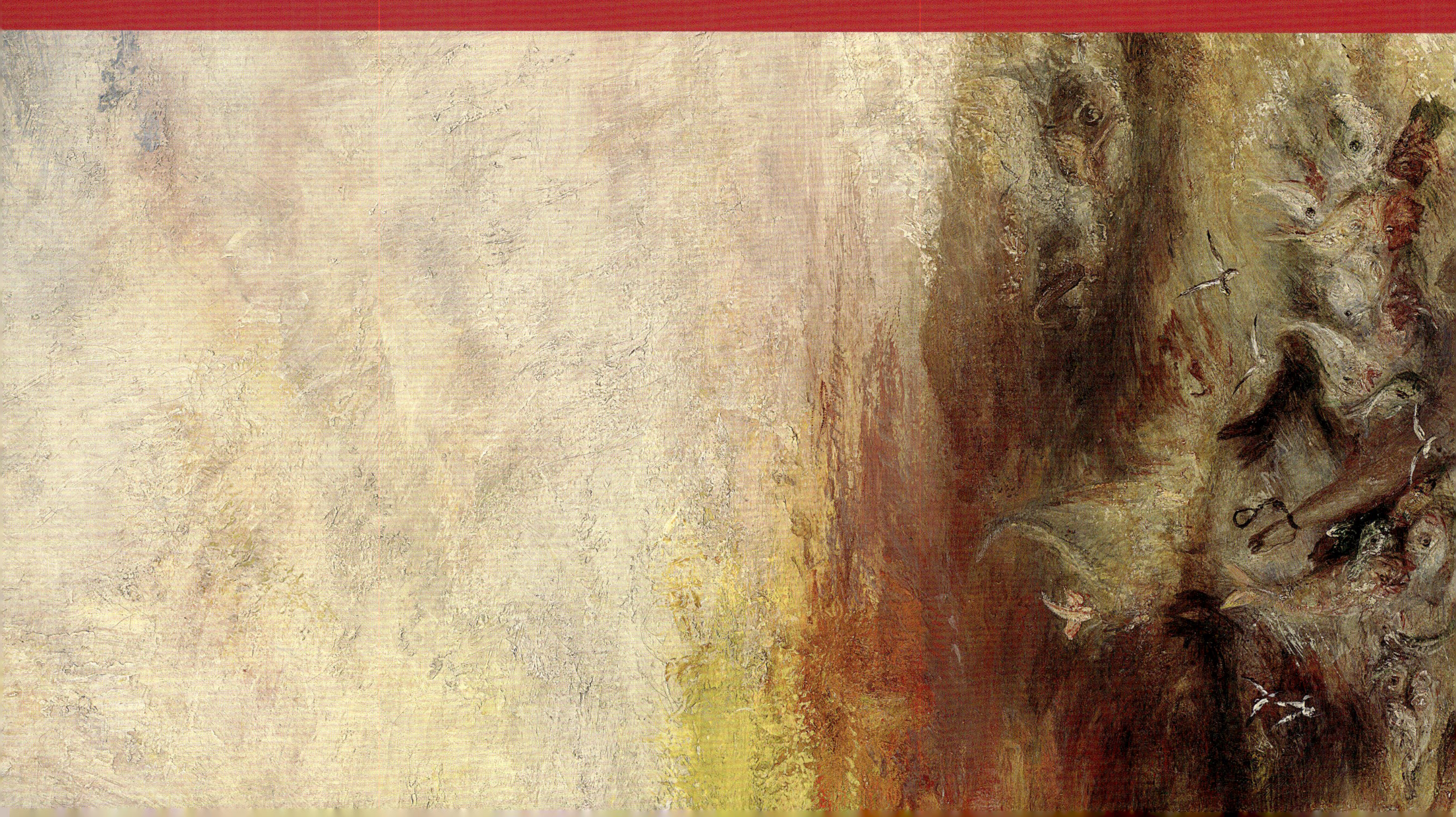

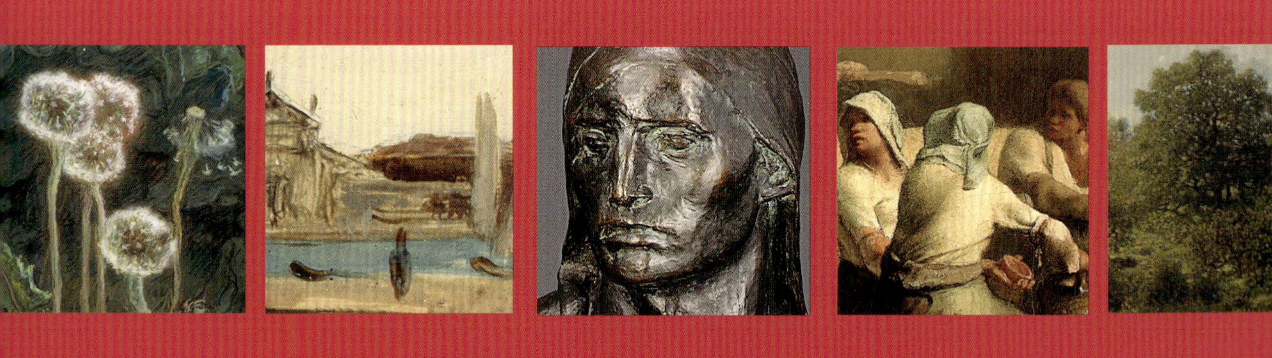

Representing Nature: Romantic Landscape and the Realist Revolution

At the turn of the nineteenth century, landscape painting lacked prestige in Europe. Ambitious artists painted scenes from history or portraits of great men. They might study a landscape as the backdrop or setting for their pictures, but they generally did not regard it as a worthy subject in its own right. All that was soon to change. The nineteenth century, an age of industrialization, which began to see the European countryside invaded by railways, mines, factories, and suburban sprawl, also witnessed a new aesthetic awakening to the natural world. As wild places disappeared, poets, painters, and the tourists who followed them flocked to nature, newly appreciative of its vanishing beauties. The Romantic landscape emerged first in England, where industrialization was rapidly advancing, and where William Wordsworth gave eloquent voice to the beauties of nature in his writings. The movement soon expanded to France, where it helped prove that artists could achieve success outside the official state system.

Romantics found in the mightiness and immensity of nature an arena for heroic self-expression, transferring from the human figure to the ocean or sky the power to elicit from viewers an emotional response. Romantic landscapists also learned to look at nature, to observe and record what they saw, with a new attentiveness. The first oil studies of clouds, of light filtered through leaves, and similar natural phenomena date to the turn of the nineteenth century, when we begin to see artists paint outdoors (*en plein air*) in increasing numbers. The shift to working outdoors was accomplished thanks to a series of technological advances. Compact paint boxes and collapsible easels and stools made the artist's studio suddenly portable. Commercially packaged paints became available in aluminum tubes from the early 1840s, drastically simplifying the formerly messy and laborious apparatus of oil painting.

The French Academy instituted a Prix de Rome—a four-year fellowship—for landscape painting in 1816, a sign of the genre's enhanced standing, but it was outside the world of the Academy and the Salon that landscape painting would achieve its true victory. In the 1830s a group of young painters settled in Barbizon, a village on the edge of the Forest of Fontainebleau, a traditional hunting preserve of the French kings. There they began to paint local landscapes—from nature, in nature—forming the so-called Barbizon School, a hinge between Romanticism and Realism in French art. The Barbizon painters' pictures of trees and streams, peasants and animals constituted both a Romantic outpouring in response to the beauty of nature and a Realist testimony to the hardships of rural life. Barbizon paintings were at first turned away by the Salon jury, but a small circle of dealers recognized the salability of such works to a new middle-class clientele. Often unversed in classical mythology and uninterested in religious or historical subject matter, these urban customers were drawn to scenes of rural life partly because of their immediate accessibility and partly out of nostalgia. The new collectors' enthusiasm for this officially scorned style demonstrated for the first time that avant-garde artists could succeed commercially without any help from the Academic system.

The case of Jean-François Millet, a relative latecomer to the Barbizon scene, exemplifies the phenomenon. Millet had trained with the Academic artist Paul Delaroche but had failed to find favor with his master or to attract positive notice through his early efforts as a history painter. Arriving in Barbizon in 1849, Millet began to paint peasants and soon struck a chord with his matter-of-fact portrayals of rural labor, dividing Salon audiences into opposing camps: avant-garde supporters and conservative opponents. Like the Realist novels of Gustave Flaubert, the paintings of Millet and his contemporary Gustave Courbet galvanized debate surrounding the purpose of art: Should it draw on classical tradition or look to contemporary life? Should it invent, or should it record? Should it evoke an ideal world, or should it represent the one in which we live? ***—E.A.B.***

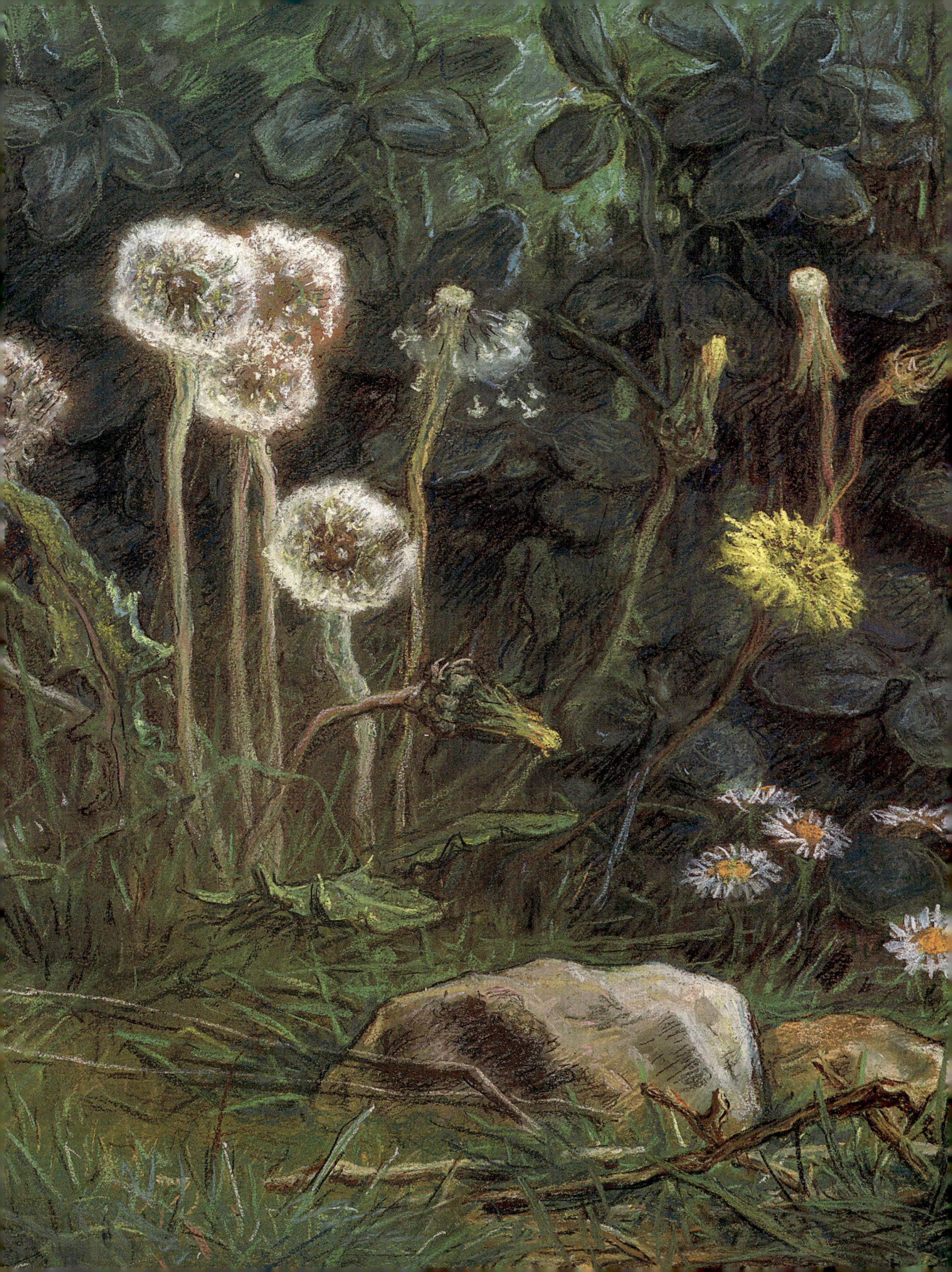

John Constable
English, 1776–1837
Stour Valley and Dedham Church, about 1815

As agricultural reforms and industrialization transformed English society at the turn of the nineteenth century, a group of Romantic artists offered a newly nostalgic perspective on the English countryside. Rather than emulate the idealized landscapes of old masters, Constable based his practice on firsthand observation, sketching out-of-doors to master light and atmospheric effects and to bring new topographic accuracy to his pictures.

The countryside that most occupied him was that of Suffolk, where he spent his youth. This painting shows a view of Dedham village—its church spire and low red roofs—with the Stour River winding its bright course through the middle

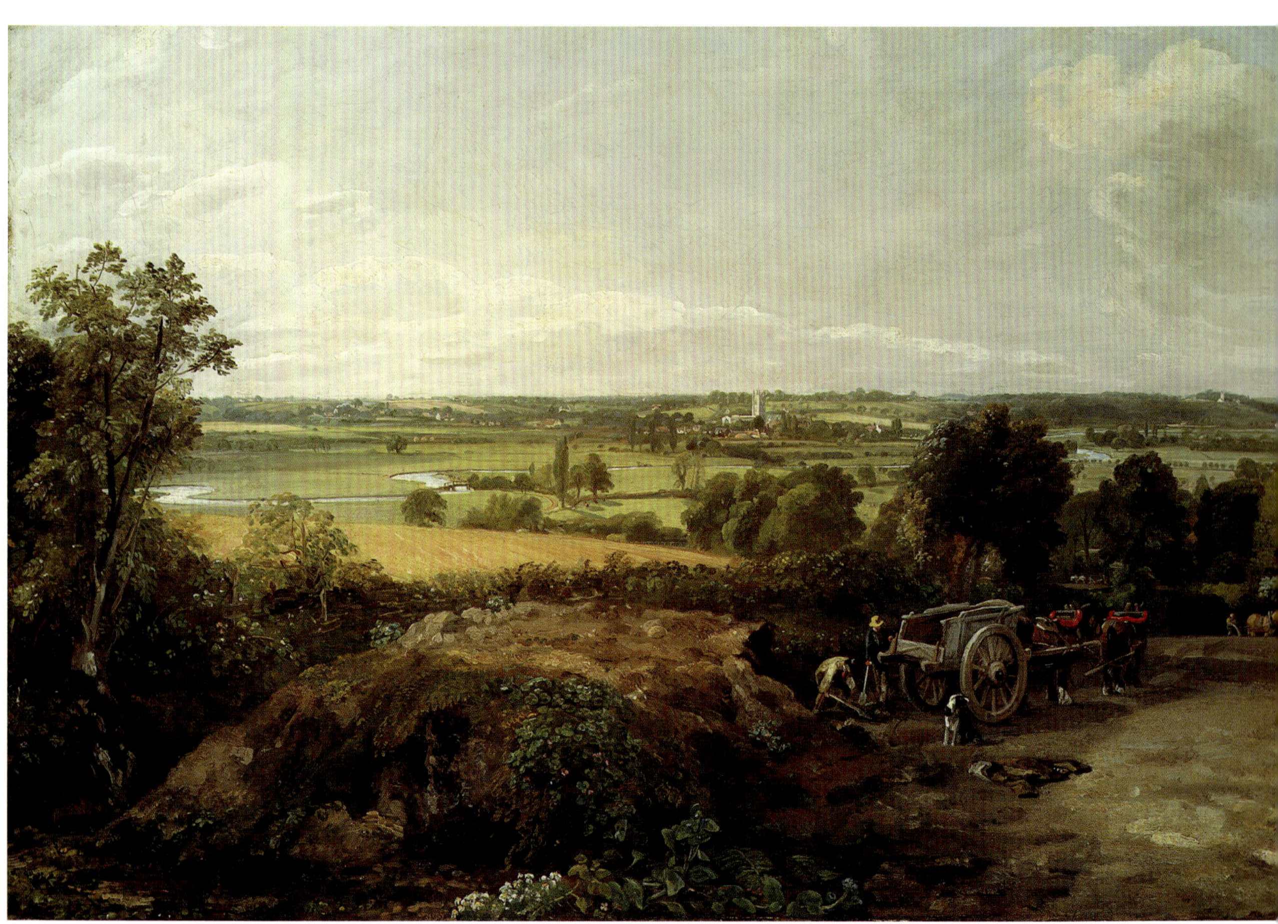

distance. The season is early fall; in the fields at right, the summer's crops have been plowed under to make way for winter wheat.

Constable devoted the foreground to a less scenic motif: a dung heap and two workers loading their cart with manure. For Romantics like Constable, all aspects of agrarian life held special significance. In an 1800 poem *The Farmer's Boy*, Robert Bloomfield had praised manure:

> Thence from its chalky bed behold convey'd
> The rich manure that drenching Winter made,
> Which pil'd near home, grows green with many
> a weed
> A promis'd nutriment for Autumn seed.

As in the poem, Constable's pile is "green with many a weed"—a promise of its efficacy as fertilizer. This promise of fertility reflects the picture's original purpose. It was commissioned by Thomas Fitzhugh as a wedding present to his bride, Philadelphia Godfrey. The image of fertile fields awaiting cultivation suggests the bridegroom's hope for a fruitful union. Constable's chosen vantage point was a hill on the estate of Miss Godfrey's family, Old Hall, the childhood home that she would leave for London following her marriage.

Oil on canvas
55.6 x 77.8 cm (21 7/8 x 30 5/8 in.)
Warren Collection—William Wilkins Warren Fund, 48.266

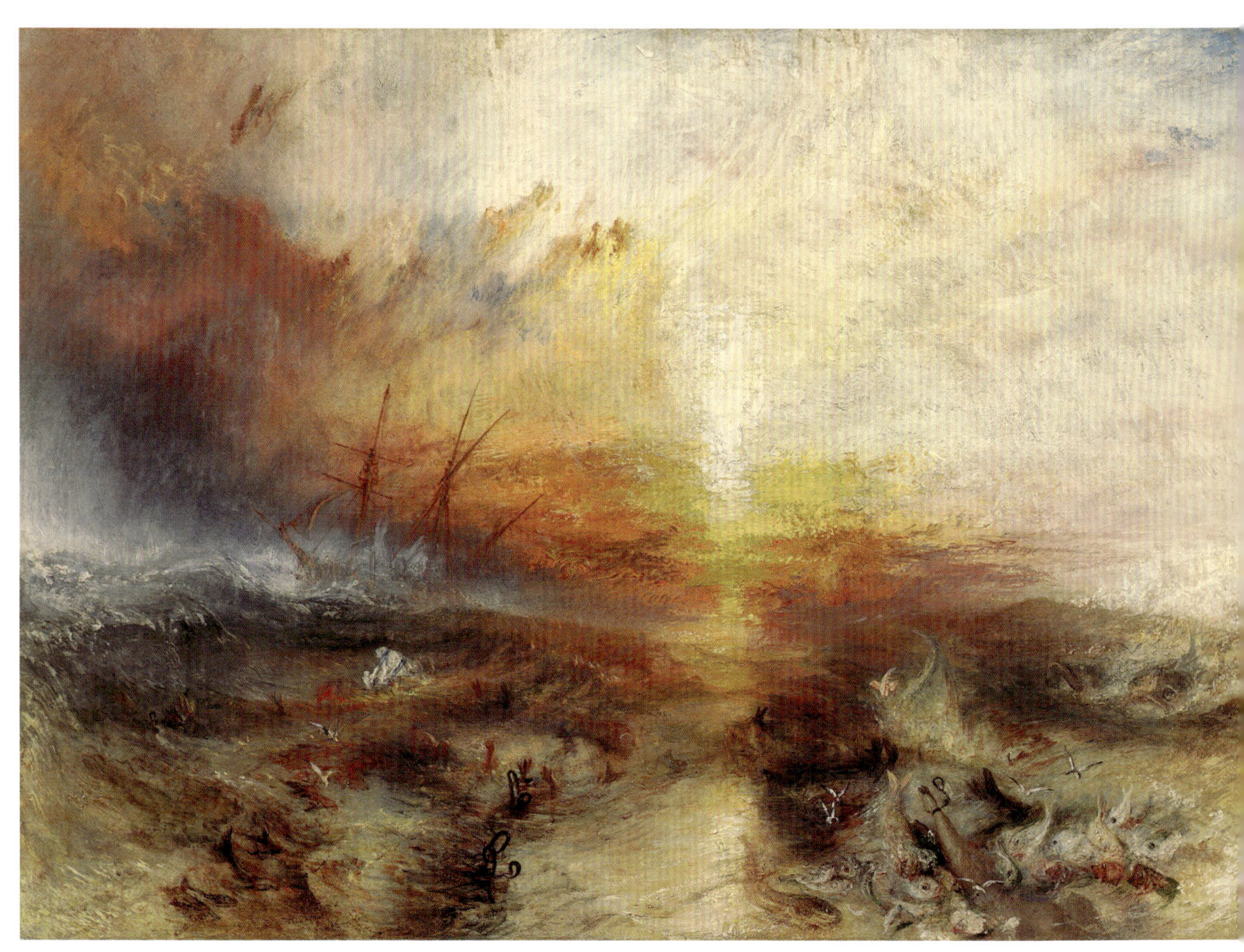

Joseph Mallord William Turner

English, 1775–1851

Slave Ship (Slavers Throwing Overboard the Dead and Dying, Typhoon Coming On), 1840

Turner was England's great Romantic painter. His fluent, virtuosic brushwork and high-keyed palette could conjure not only dazzling light and atmospheric effects but also powerful sensory and emotional experiences. In this painting, Turner used alternating layers of varnish and paint—applied in the brightest areas with a palette knife, rather than a brush—to evoke the crimson sky and sallow, turbulent sea. In the distance, a ship pitches on the waves. In the foreground, fish swarm around human bodies sinking below the surface. A length of chain at left and a shackled ankle at right tell the story: the disappearing limbs and desperate, straining hands belong to a slave ship's jettisoned human cargo.

The subject derives from an actual event. In 1783, following an outbreak of disease on the slave ship *Zong*, traders threw infected slaves overboard and reported them as lost at sea in order to claim insurance money. The horrific incident was not isolated but part of a widespread practice that persisted well into the nineteenth century. Turner revealed his subject in a poem published in the Royal Academy of Arts exhibition catalogue of 1840:

> . . . the Typhon's coming.
> Before it sweep your decks, throw overboard
> The dead and dying—n'er heed their chains . . .

Most visitors to the exhibition were unimpressed. They complained of Turner's unrealistic colors and pointed out the improbably floating chains. The critic John Ruskin, however, defended Turner staunchly, devoting the most celebrated passage of his book *Modern Painters* to this picture: The storm "gathers cold and low, advancing like the shadow of death upon the guilty ship as it labors amid the lightning of the sea, its thin mast written on the sky in lines of blood." Ruskin's book and the description it contained made Turner and his painting world famous. The critic himself owned *Slave Ship* for almost thirty years. Purchased by a Boston collector, the picture went on view in 1877 at the Museum of Fine Arts, where its abolitionist message found a sympathetic audience, epitomized by a critic for the *Boston Evening Transcript*: "It is the embodiment of a giant protest, a mighty voice crying out against human oppression."

Oil on canvas

90.8 x 122.6 cm (35¾ x 48¼ in.)

Henry Lillie Pierce Fund, 99.22

Jean-Baptiste-Camille Corot
French, 1796–1875
The Piazzetta, Venice, 1828

Corot painted this fresh oil sketch in the summer of 1828 on his way home to France from Italy. Smaller than a sheet of writing paper—just six by ten inches—the picture is a triumph of economy and precision. A thin, streaky foreground leads us into the scene, whose monuments—the church and bell tower, two freestanding columns and their long, slender shadows—are described with brisk strokes of paint. A sailboat and a human figure in the middle distance provide scale and color and help place us in our surroundings.

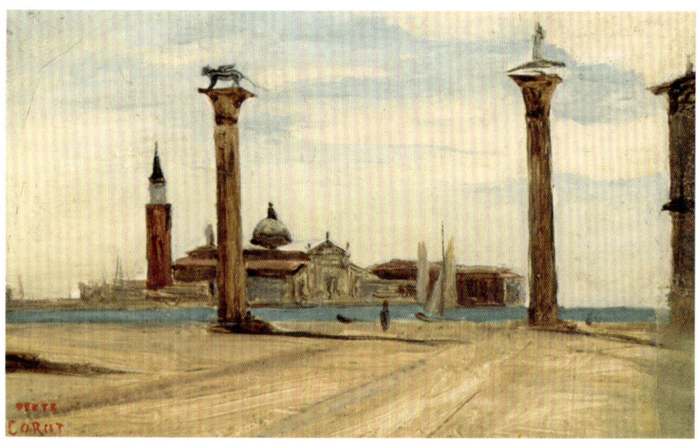

Modest dimensions, swift execution, and a paper support indicate that Corot at least began the picture—and perhaps even completed it—outdoors, standing in Saint Mark's Square and looking across the Bacino di San Marco toward the domed church of San Giorgio Maggiore. Corot had picked up the practice of outdoor oil sketching in Rome, where it flourished in the early decades of the nineteenth century, and, though he would never have exhibited a picture like this one—regarding it as a sketch or an aide-mémoire—his work in this vein came to be widely admired in the later nineteenth century, when artists move away from formal *paysages composés* (composed exhibition landscapes), painted in the studio, toward a more spontane ous outdoor approach.

Oil on paper, mounted on paperboard
15.9 x 25.1 cm (6¼ x 9⅞ in.)
Bequest of Frederick Frothingham, 94.318

Jean-Baptiste-Camille Corot
French, 1796–1875
Dante and Virgil, 1859

Corot was a landscapist. A rare literary subject in his oeuvre, this picture represents an episode from Dante's *Divine Comedy*. The Italian poet, wearing a red cap and dark cloak, recoils in terror from three wild animals that block the entrance to hell: a lion, a wolf, and a panther (to which Cor gave a tiger's striped coat). The ancient Roman poet Virgil, i a laurel wreath and white toga, comes to Dante's aide, offer ing his services as a guide to the afterlife. It is the first scen of the *Inferno*.

Corot toiled for a full year over this enormous canvas, and it created a stir when exhibited at the Salon of 1859. Among its admirers was the critic Théophile Gautier, who praised the picture's light, "which is neither the dawn nor the dusk, which comes from neither sun nor moon, a sort of extra-planetary gleam . . . the light of the other world."

"Dante," Gautier proclaimed, "has never been better understood than by this good and simple Corot." For him, the self-conscious simplicity of Corot's style was a virtue. But other viewers took issue with the artist's naïve figures. The caricaturist Bertall summarized the picture thus: "The two poets, disguised as umbrellas . . . visit a Corot landscap populated with felt animals."

Oil on canvas
260.4 x 170.5 cm (102½ x 67⅛ in.)
Gift of Quincy Adams Shaw, 75.2

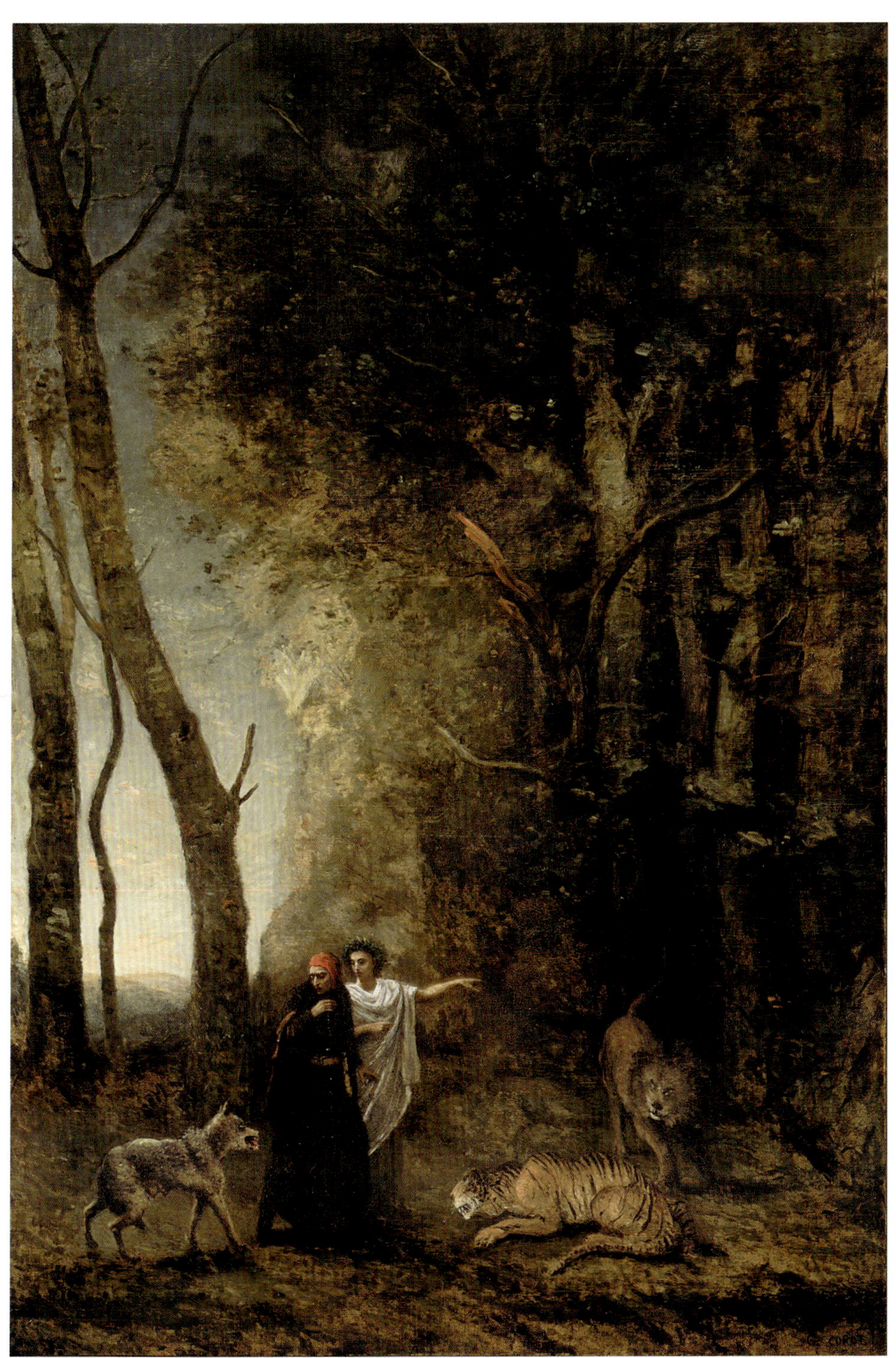

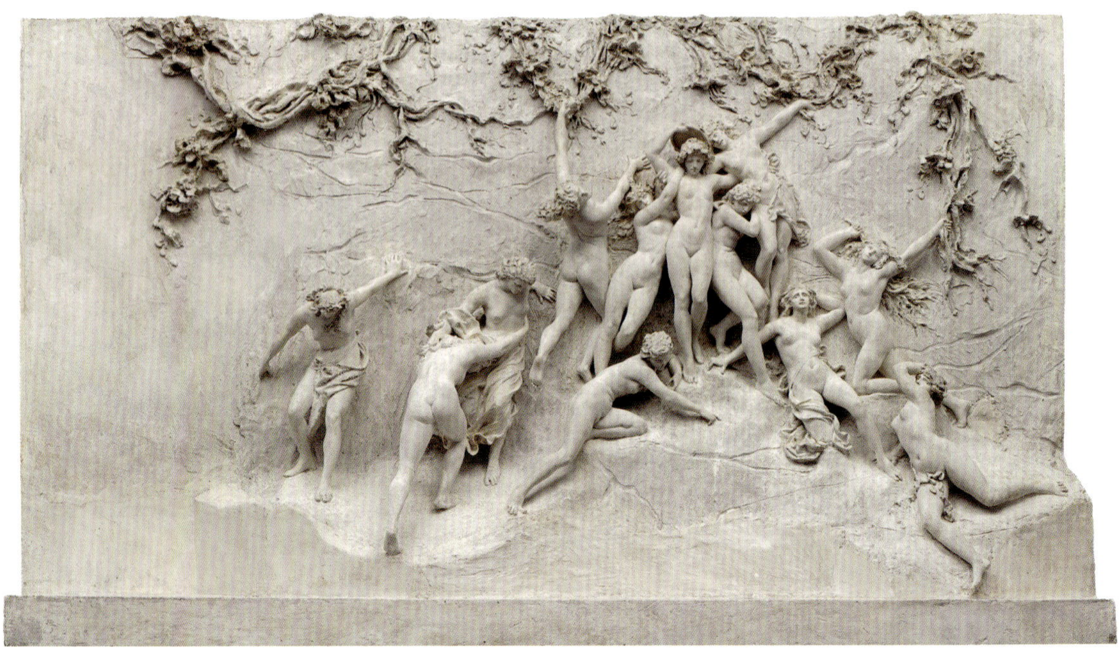

Gustave Doré

French, 1832–1883

Maenads in a Wood, 1879

This plaster relief shows a group of female nudes arranged on a hilly landscape. At the peak of the composition a woman holds a tambourine over her head. Other figures climb and gesture, reach up, stretch, and recline. Some hold on to or pull at branches and tendrils or each other. It seems an abstract ballet, with the goal of presenting the female body in a wide range of expressive and beautiful postures. The title indicates a classical source for the subject, as maenads were the female followers of the ancient wine god, Dionysus (Roman Bacchus).

Further hints at the genesis of this relief come from other works by Doré, who was better known as a printmaker and a painter. The composition is closely related to two works lost and known only through old photographs, a painting that was shown in the Salon of 1879 and a plaster relief probably made around the same time. Both represented the death of Orpheus, a story from ancient Greek mythology in which the musician and poet was torn to pieces by a group of jealous maenads. Doré does not show the dismembered body of Orpheus here, transforming the scene from a highly charged, violent celebration of death into an idyll of women cavorting in the forest. Large in scale, this work is one of Doré's most ambitious sculptures. Although plaster was often used preparatory to marble sculptures in the period, Doré signed this relief, indicating that he considered it a finished work.

Plaster

120 x 196.1 x 25.1 cm (47 ½ x 77 ⅛ x 9 ⅞ in.)

Gift of Mr. and Mrs. John L. Gardner in honor of Perry Townsend Rathbone and European Decorative Arts and Sculpture Curator's Fund, 1994.192

Narcisse Virgile Diaz de la Peña
French, 1807–1876
Bohemians Going to a Fête, about 1844

Diaz began his career as a porcelain painter but had already made a name for himself at the Salon with small nudes and Orientalist scenes by the mid-1830s. It was at this moment that he began working outdoors in the Forest of Fontainebleau with Corot, Millet, and Rousseau. The dappled light, mossy rocks, and pale, svelte tree trunks in this picture demonstrate both Diaz's close study of nature and his ties to Rousseau. The composition itself derives from an earlier—and more radical—picture by that artist of cattle descending a mountain pass. Whereas Rousseau's painting was rejected by the Salon jury in 1836, Diaz's version, which replaces cattle with more picturesque and colorful human figures, triumphed at the Salon of 1844, causing one critic to exclaim, "His pictures are like a pile of precious stones."

The French word *bohémien* originally meant "gypsy" and referred to Roma people, who were once widely believed to come from Bohemia (today in the Czech Republic). By the mid-nineteenth century, though, the word could also designate painters, writers, actors, and students—members of youthful artistic communities on the margins of bourgeois society. With its merry cascade of figures in exotic dress, this picture sums up an emerging sense of bohemian identity among artists like Diaz and his comrades in Barbizon.

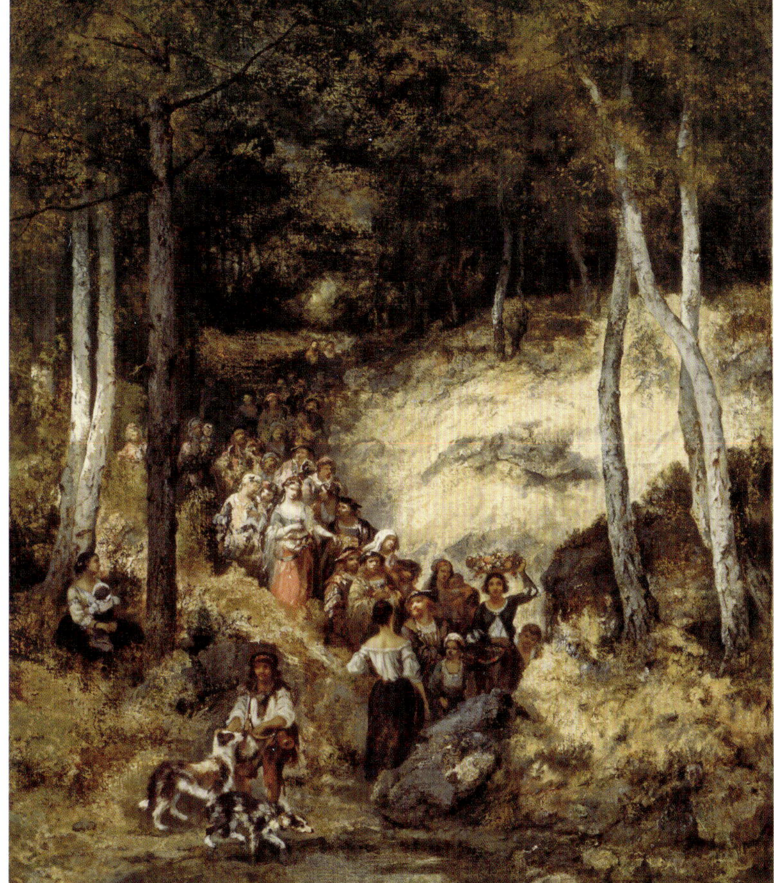

Oil on canvas
101 x 81.3 cm (39¾ x 32 in.)
Bequest of Susan Cornelia Warren, 03.600

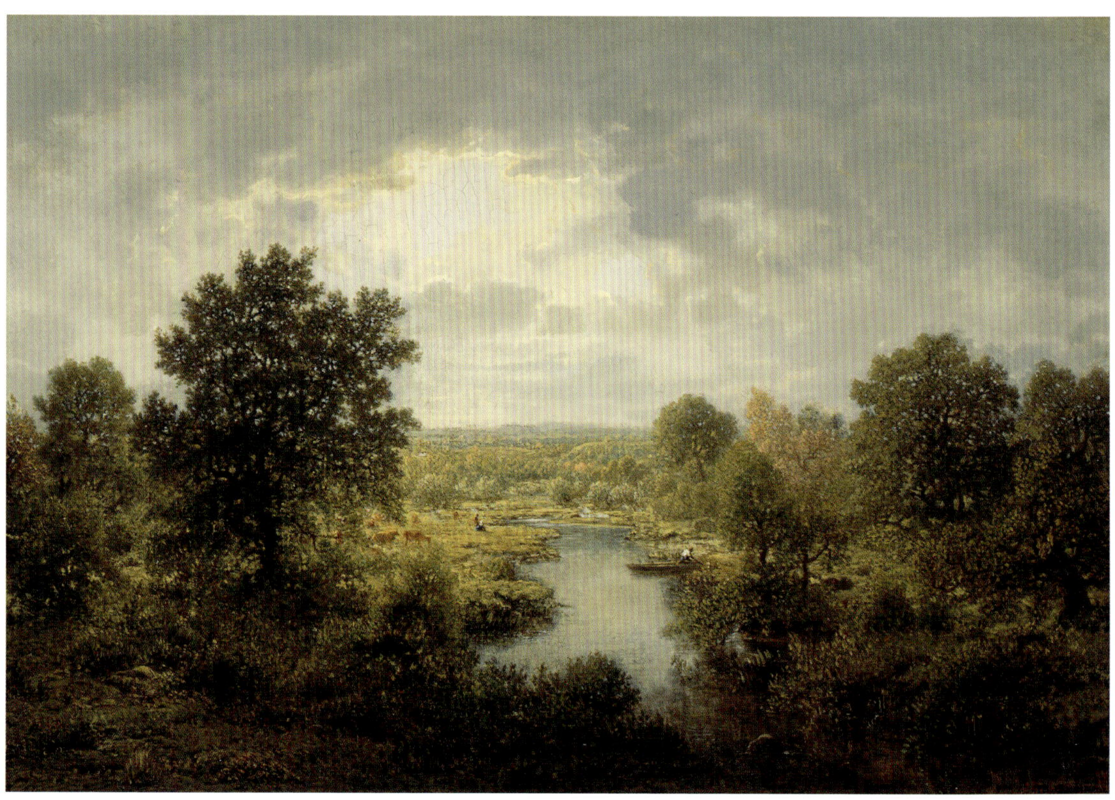

Théodore Rousseau
French, 1812–1867
Banks of the Sèvre (Vendée), 1859

Clouds part over a stream, letting sunlight pour down on its marshy banks. Sky, trees, water, and light are the subjects of this picture, engulfing and overpowering the barely visible boatman in the middle distance. Rousseau was among the first artists of his generation to paint in Barbizon and its environs. After a brief and frustrated formal training, he began to work on his own in the Forest of Fontainebleau at age eighteen, producing pictures in which the human figure seldom plays more than a peripheral role—landscapes focused on the natural world as a self-contained and timeless realm, even through its changing seasons, light, and weather.

Although Rousseau made a point of working outdoors, producing both drawings and oil sketches *en plein air*, his finished exhibition pictures, like this one, shown at the Salon of 1859, were made in his studio. Carefully composed fabrications, these paintings reveal the artist's debt to an older landscape tradition. This picture's masterful light effects—the parting clouds mirrored in a luminous expanse of water, the rugged, backlit tree—testify to Rousseau's admiration for the seventeenth-century Dutch painters Meindert Hobbema and Jacob van Ruisdael.

Oil on panel
53.3 x 74.6 cm (21 x 29 3/8 in.)
Gift of Mrs. Henry Sturgis Grew, 17.1461

Jean-François Millet
French, 1814–1875
Harvesters Resting (Ruth and Boaz), 1850–53

Combining an episode from the Bible with a scene of life in the modern French countryside, this painting was the work on which Millet lavished more attention than any other and which he considered his greatest achievement. In the biblical story, a Moabite woman, Ruth, marries into a distant tribe and, when widowed, is left to provide for her mother-in-law and herself in a strange land. She does so by gleaning—following harvesters through the fields to gather whatever grain they leave behind. On the estate of a wealthy landowner, Boaz, Ruth is invited to join the harvesters at their midday meal. Hearing her tale of fortitude and filial piety, Boaz takes Ruth as his wife.

The story had been most famously treated by the seventeenth-century painter Nicolas Poussin, whom Millet regarded as a hero and a rival across generations. To prepare his own version of the scene in which Boaz invites Ruth to eat with the harvesters, Millet produced almost fifty pages of drawings, working out each figure, each scythe, each earthenware vessel and wooden spoon, with special care. The homely props and figures (some chewing with their mouths open) reflect Millet's close observation of local peasants, and indeed his updated rendition of the story can be read as a commentary on the larger state of affairs in rural France. The right to glean—a traditional means of sustenance for the old, infirm, and destitute—had recently come under threat in a new regime of large-scale, proto-industrial farming. Against the backdrop of a growing population of rural indigents, Boaz's gesture of invitation can be read as a plea for inclusion of those left behind by the march of progress.

Oil on canvas
67.3 x 119.7 cm (26 1/2 x 47 1/8 in.)
Bequest of Mrs. Martin Brimmer, 06.2421

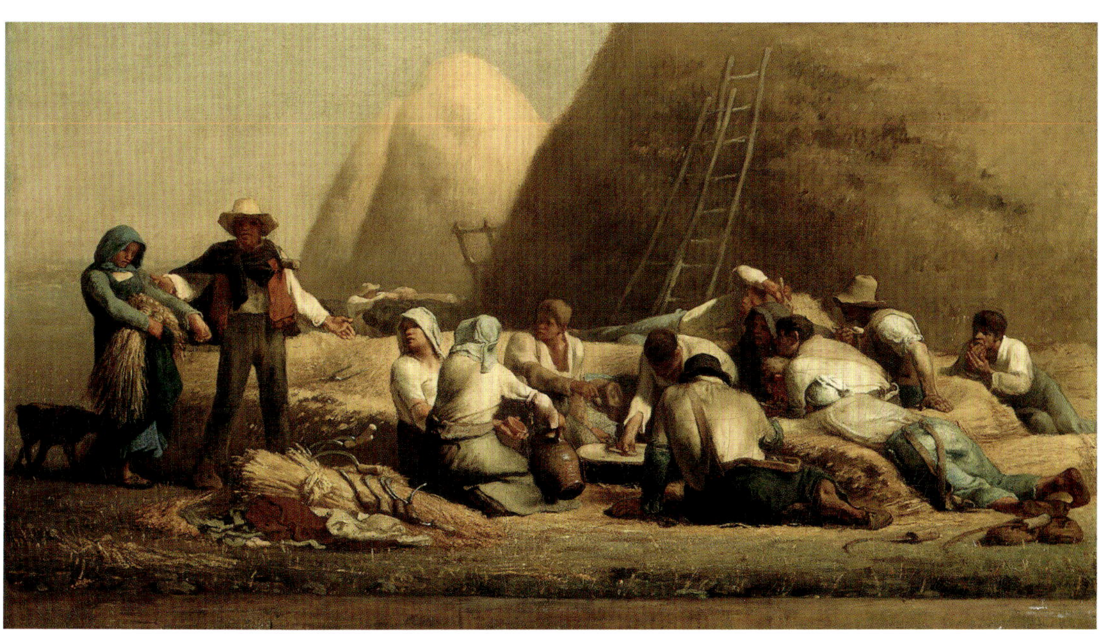

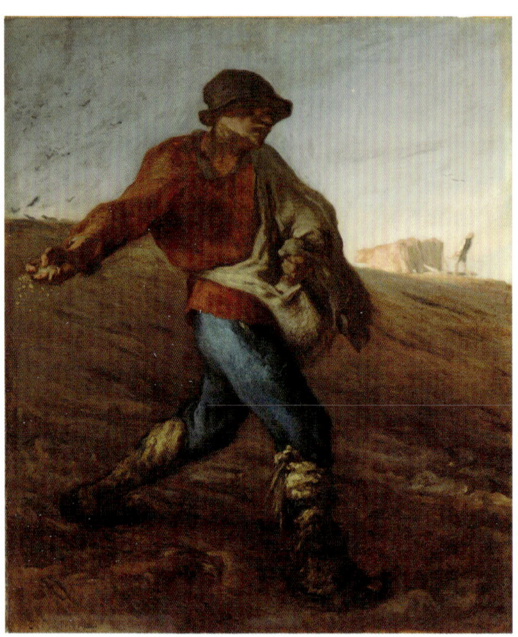

Jean-François Millet
French, 1814–1875
The Sower, 1850

This representation of a peasant sowing winter wheat was Millet's first true masterpiece. Exhibited at the Paris Salon of 1850–51, the picture attracted both praise and opprobrium and made its author famous virtually overnight. Silhouetted against the sky, the sower strides down a twilit hillside, a bag of seed slung over his shoulder. His legs are wrapped in straw for warmth. His hat is pulled down low over his eyes. It is an evening in November, the time for sowing winter wheat, and chilly work. Up the slope at right, another peasant drives an ox-drawn harrow, covering sown seeds with earth to protect them from the coming winter and wheeling birds.

For many contemporary viewers, the sower's monumental scale and dynamic pose seemed to contradict his identity as a peasant. His form recalled bodies in Michelangelo's work or in ancient Roman statuary. Never before had so anonymous a figure been treated with such dignity and drama in a Salon painting. Most critics agreed on the "beauty, poetry, and grace" of the protagonist's pose, but many objected to Millet's choice of colors and his broad, loose manner of paint application, which the belle-lettrist critic Théophile Gautier dismissed as "Millet's trowel scrapings."

The roughness of this painter's technique seemed to correspond to the roughness of his subject at a time when aesthetic anxiety about the declining classical tradition and political anxiety about the rural poor went hand in hand. Some observers denounced Millet as a socialist, but the artist insisted that his motives were apolitical. He sought only to capture the dignity of his subject, to invest with beauty—and even heroism—the labor of a nameless peasant.

Oil on canvas
101.6 x 82.6 cm (40 x 32½ in.)
Gift of Quincy Adams Shaw through Quincy Adams Shaw, Jr., and Mrs. Marian Shaw Haughton, 17.1485

Jean-François Millet
French, 1814–1875
Young Shepherdess, about 1870–73

Seated amid her flock and lost in a daydream, the young shepherdess lets her distaff fall idle in her lap. An airy landscape of fields and sky opens behind her. The sun is high and hot. The life-size of this figure is virtually unique in Millet's oeuvre; he began painting her in about 1870 on a canvas originally covered with a very different composition: *The Babylonian Captivity of the Jews*.

That picture—the artist's most ambitious history painting—had languished in his studio since 1848, when he had exhibited it at the Salon to tepid reviews. This failure helped precipitate Millet's turn away from his academic training toward the frank portrayal of rural life and labor that would make him famous. More than two decades later, the now-celebrated artist found himself short of supplies during the Franco-Prussian War, but his decision to paint this shepherdess over his grand biblical composition must have carried symbolic weight as well.

Her pose recalls older representational traditions: like a Madonna of Humility, she sits on the ground; like the harvest goddess Ceres, her knees are parted, her skin, tanned. Yet she is not a traditional object of veneration, not a goddess or a saint, but a bored adolescent with wooden shoes and a sunburn, lovingly observed by the great painter of peasants.

Oil on canvas
162 x 113 cm (63¾ x 44½ in.)
Gift of Samuel Dennis Warren, 77.249

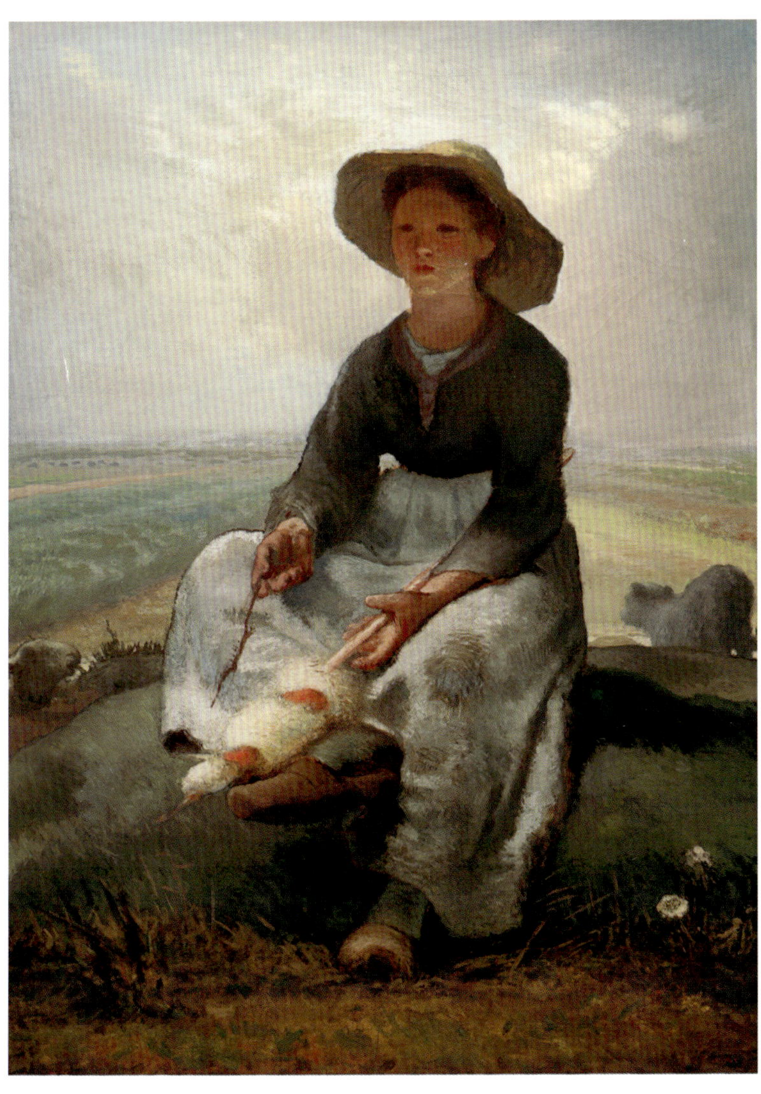

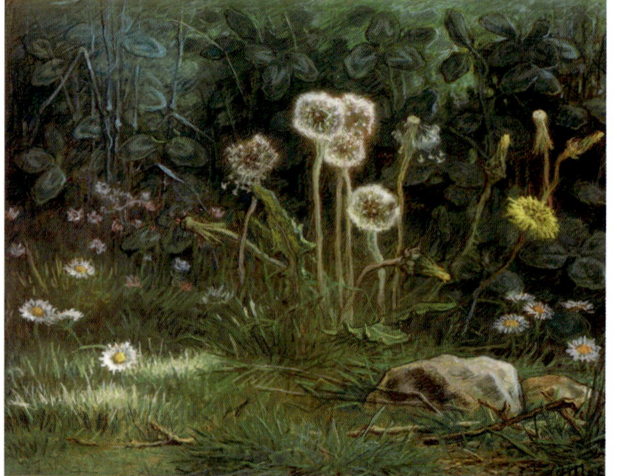

of grass, and little twigs of all kinds [are] not, in their way, the most beautiful of all . . . these poor despised things are inferior to nothing in God's creation."

Pastel on tan wove paper
40.6 x 50.2 cm (16 x 19¾ in.)
Gift of Quincy Adams Shaw through Quincy Adams Shaw, Jr., and Mrs. Marian Shaw Haughton, 17.1524

Jean-François Millet
French, 1814–1875
Dandelions, 1867–68

In the mid-1860s Millet turned to pastels, producing many of his most engrossing works in this powdery medium, from moonlit landscapes to gritty genre scenes to this bewitching, bug's-eye view of dandelions. The Museum of Fine Arts is home to the largest collection of Millet's pastels in the world: thirty-one in all. *Dandelions* is perhaps the finest example.

The scene captures every phase of the plant's growth, from bud to blossom to seed. As one early critic pointed out when he saw this picture, the great German draftsman Albrecht Dürer had set a precedent in the sixteenth century for the intimate portrayal of dandelions, but Millet's extraordinary command of the pastel medium gave his picture a unique softness and luminosity. The feathery globes of his dandelions gone to seed seem to glow with a light all their own.

A stand of weeds transfigured, the scene exemplifies Millet's larger commitment to honor beauty found in humble places. Writing to this picture's patron in 1867, he explained, "I am not sure the most modest objects, the bushes and briars, tufts

Constantin Émile Meunier
Belgian, 1831–1905
The Dock Hand, modeled 1885, cast 1905

A heroic image of a working man is not a traditional subject of monumental bronze sculpture. In nineteenth-century Europe, greater appreciation of the realities of the world, including the labor that supported social structures, led to new subjects in art. In this context, a nearly life-size figure cast in the precious metal of bronze transforms both the medium and the subject. Since the Renaissance, the single figure in bronze typically represented famous individuals, classical gods and heroes, or other characters from history and literature. Meunier rethinks such images, presenting a powerful man whose muscles are developed through hard labor. He wears his working clothes, cut just loose enough to allow ease of movement. Dock hands wore this hooded garment, possibly simply a sack, to protect their shoulders and necks as they hoisted and carried loads. His boots would keep his feet dry on the docks. He is at rest in a contrapposto stance, with weight on one leg, made both casual and more imposing through the placement of his hands on his hips. His head is turned to his right, and weariness and resignation register in his face. The figure stands on a plank set askew on the bronze base. This may be a hint at the precarious existence faced by the laborer or perhaps a nod to his ability to maintain his balance in a challenging world.

Bronze
117 x 46.4 x 45.7 cm (46⅛ x 18¼ x 18 in.)
Helen and Alice Colburn Fund, 60.235

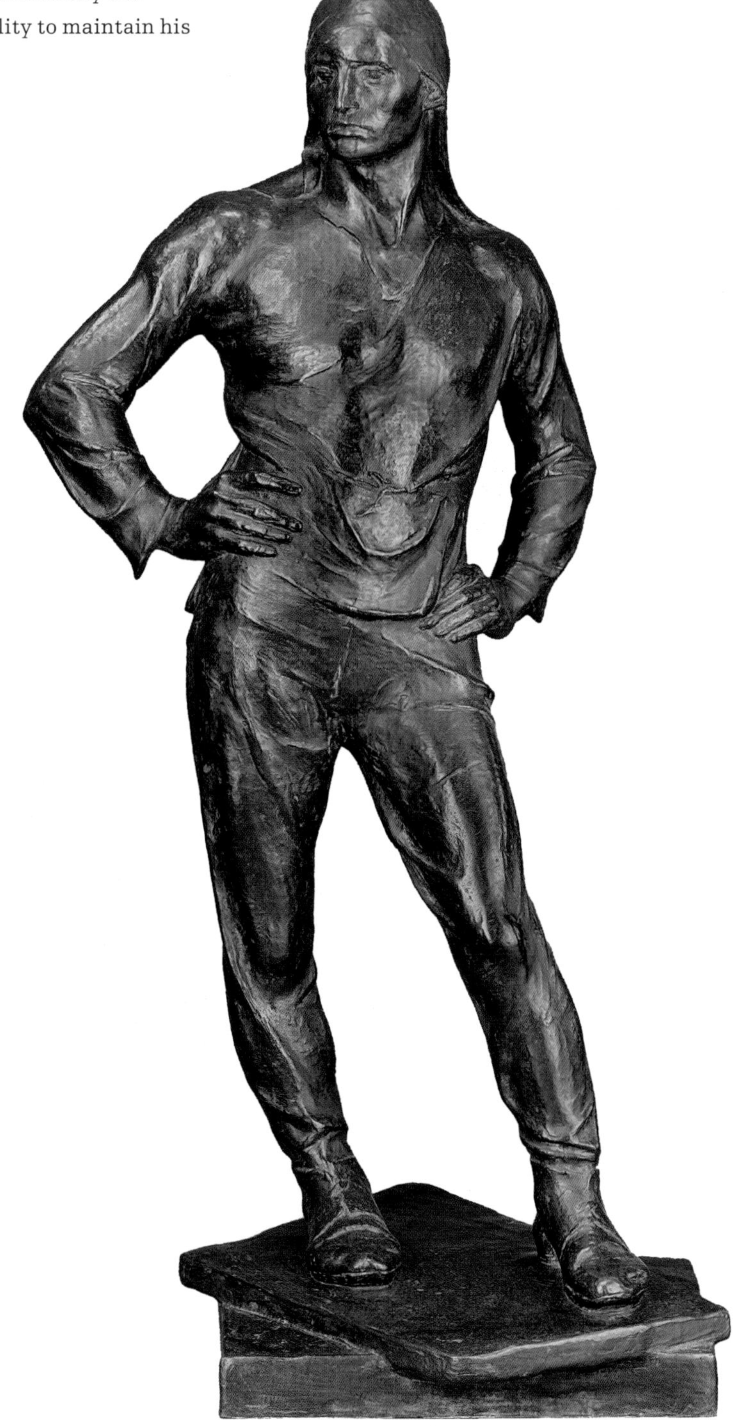

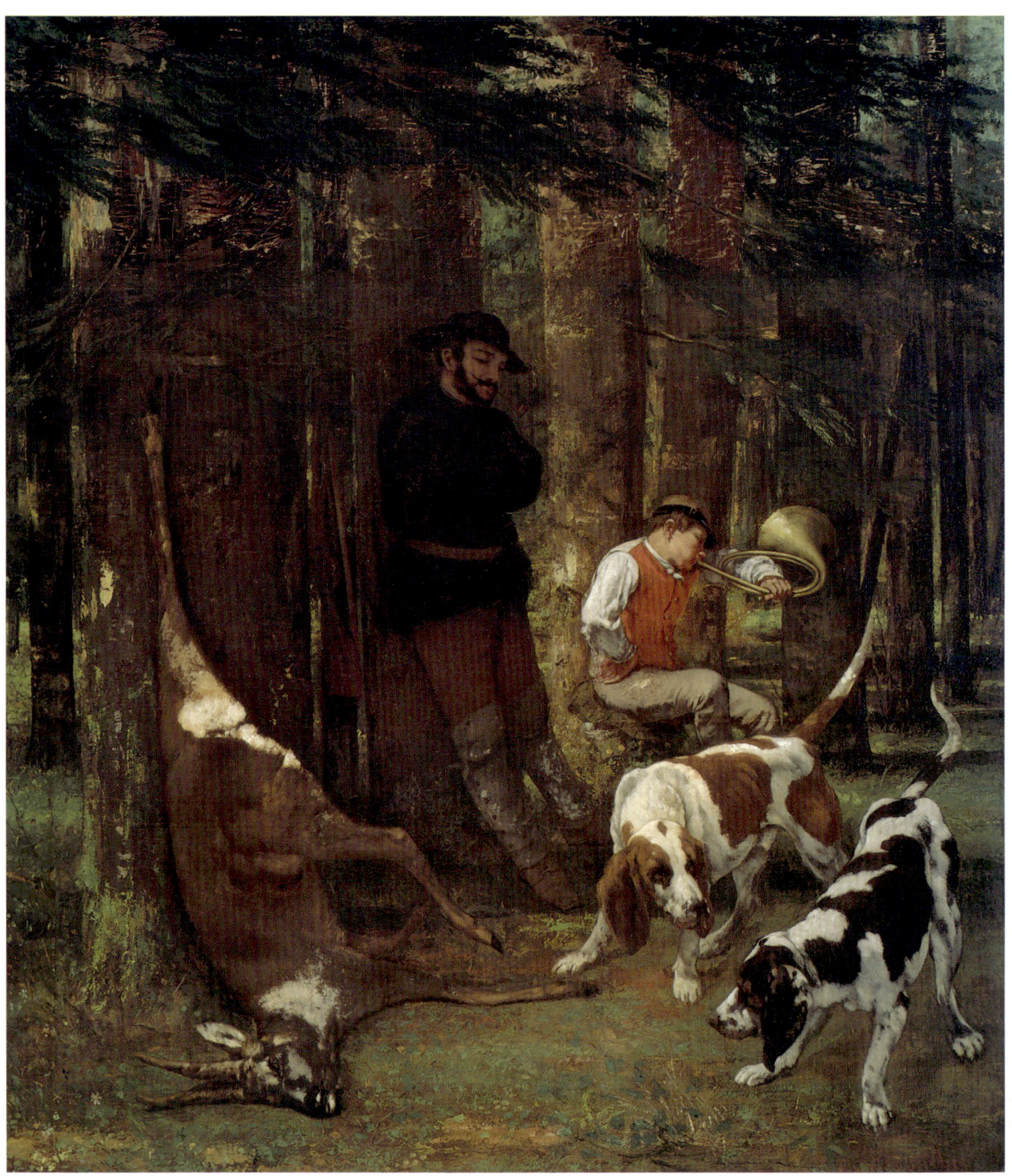

Gustave Courbet

French, 1819–1877

The Quarry (La Curée), 1856

"The hunter," Courbet once wrote, "is a man of independent character, who has a free spirit, or at least a feeling for liberty. His is a wounded soul, a heart that goes forth, into the wilderness and the melancholy of the woods, to stir up its languor." Courbet was himself an avid hunter, pursuing game throughout western France, Switzerland, and Germany. For him the hunter and the artist were one: wounded souls, seekers, solitaries. In this monumental composition, he portrayed himself as a melancholic hunter, leaning against a tree beside his quarry. Behind him, a young companion sounds his hunting horn, while two dogs in the foreground snarl at each other before tearing into the carcass.

Both the deer and the dogs are painted with mesmerizing naturalism. The deer's nose glistens, still moist; its lifeless body has a convincing softness and heft. Every muscle stands out beneath the dogs' fur; their anatomy and their antipathy are both shrewdly observed. Yet the spatial relationships between the dogs, the carcass, the hunter, and his companion are oddly disjointed. Each form remains a discrete unit not fully integrated with its surroundings. This effect is the result of Courbet's additive approach to the composition. He began with a single canvas, representing the hunter and his prey and then added four panels, expanding the composition to include trumpeter, dogs, and treetops. Critics were thrilled with the monumental result and, at the Salon of 1857, awarded the painting higher praise than any other work by the artist to date.

Oil on canvas

210.2 x 183.5 cm (82¾ x 72¼ in.)

Henry Lillie Pierce Fund, 18.620

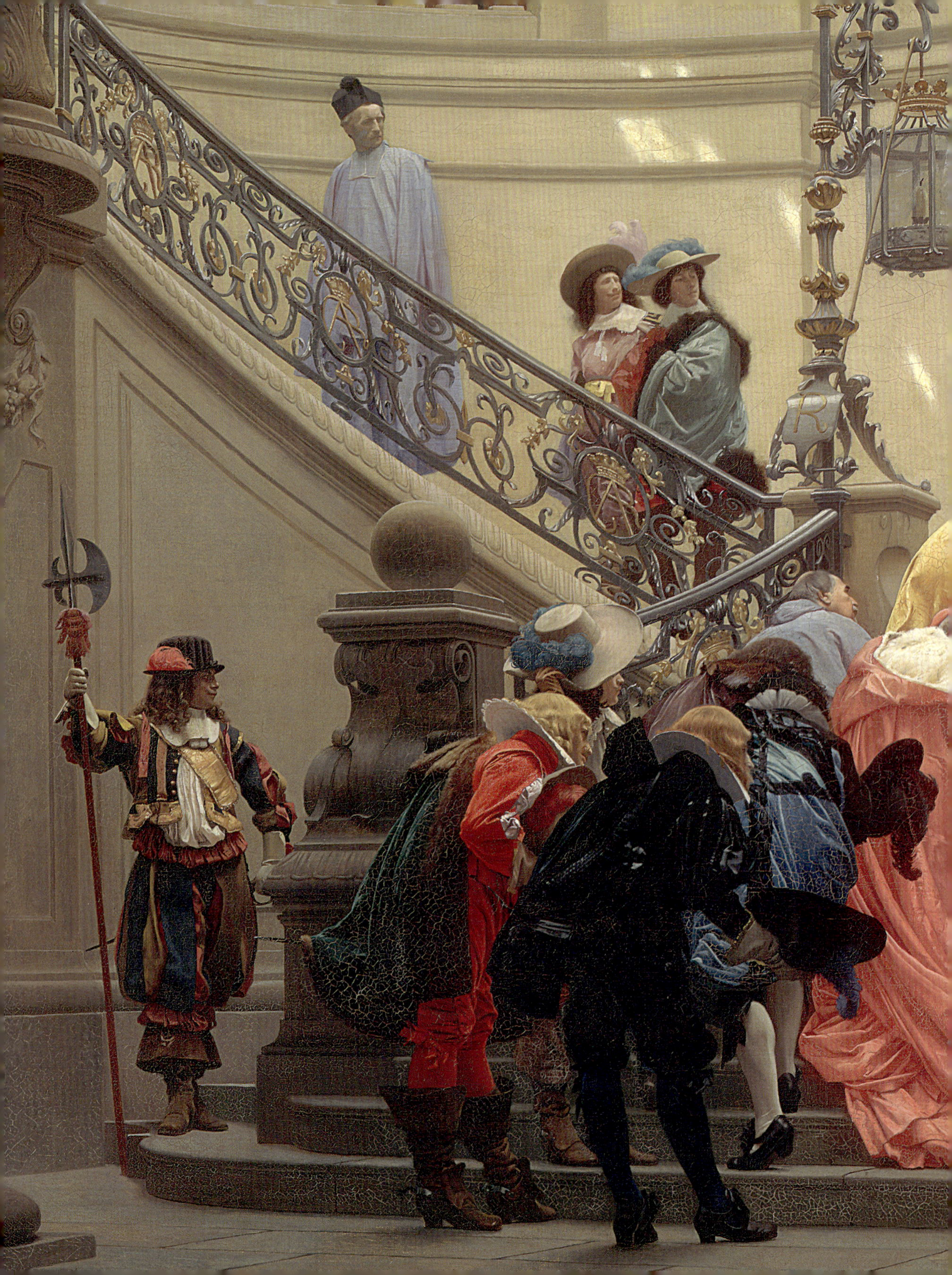

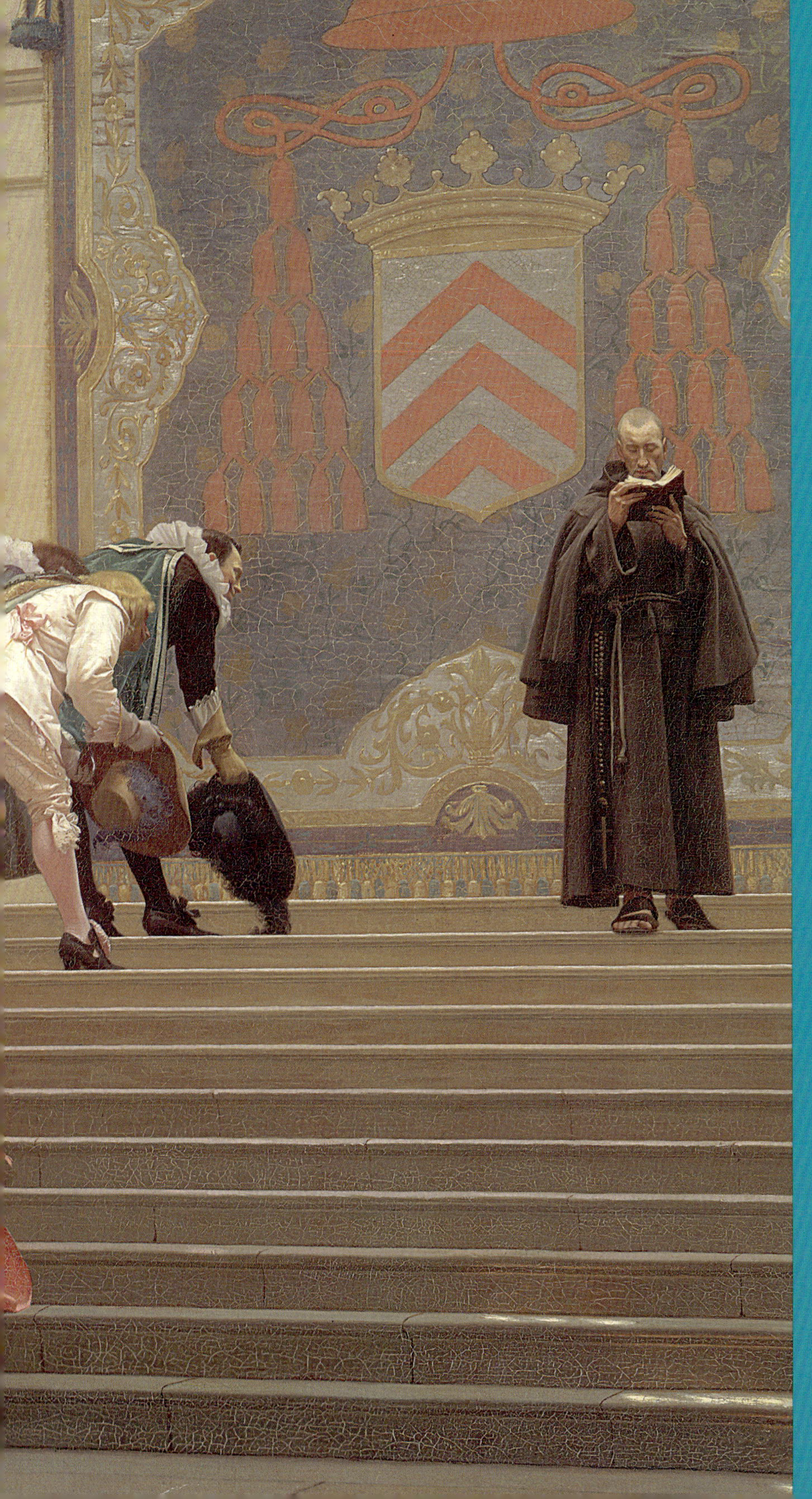

3 ACADEMIES AND OFFICIAL ART

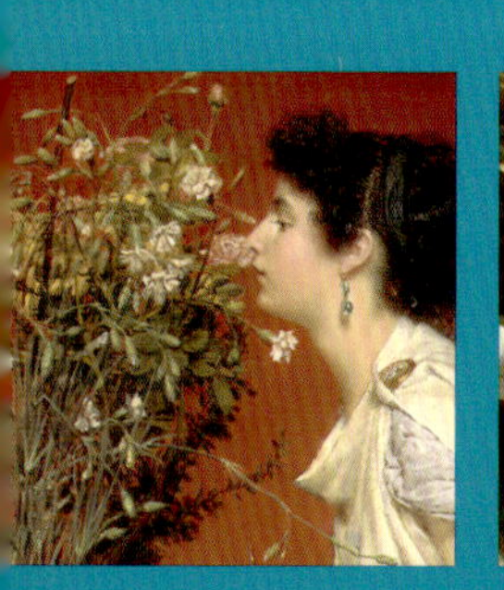
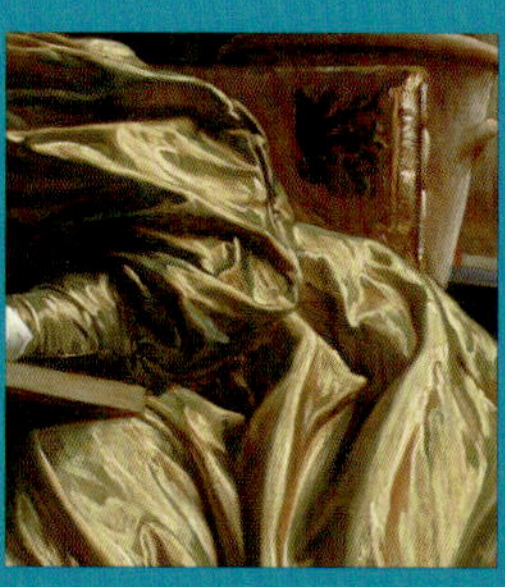
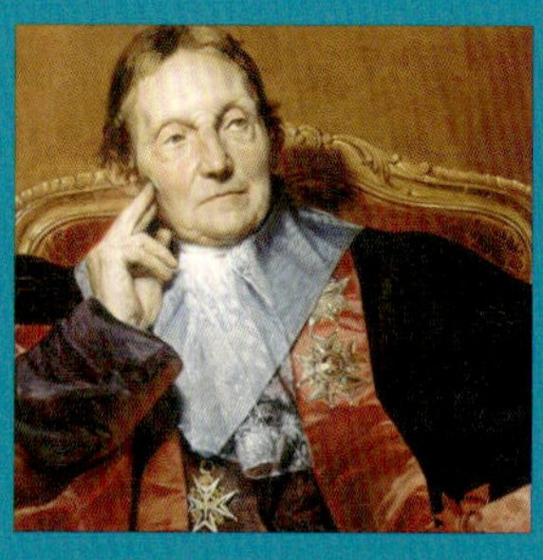
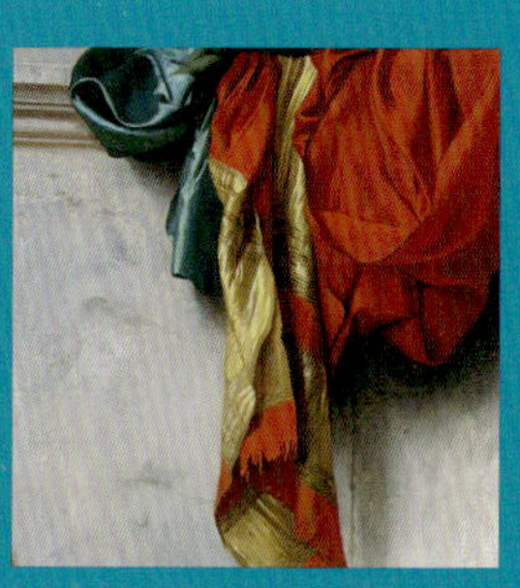
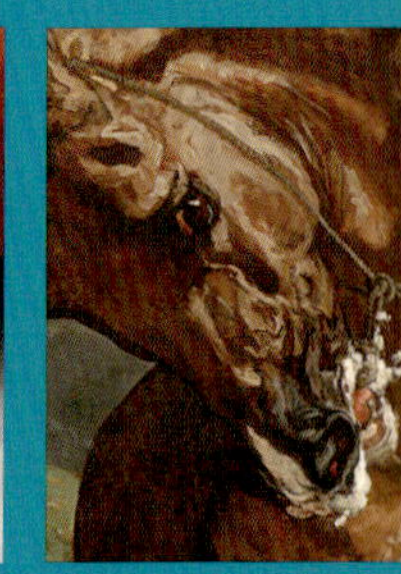

Academies and Official Art

Founded under royal patronage in the seventeenth and eighteenth centuries, state-sponsored academies continued to dominate art instruction across Europe through the end of the nineteenth century. Perhaps the most powerful among these institutions were the Académie des Beaux-Arts in Paris and the Royal Academy of Arts in London, though equivalents existed in cities from Antwerp to Vienna and Düsseldorf to Madrid. Academies oversaw art schools, sponsored scholarship competitions, and juried annual or semi-annual exhibitions—displaying hundreds, or even thousands, of works—that could determine the success or failure of an artist's career.

Academic schools promoted drawing, particularly drawing after the human figure, as the building block of both painting and sculpture, the preliminary stage of all artistic invention. Students generally began by copying prints, moved on to drawing plaster casts of antique statues, and finally graduated to study of the live model. This programmatic education encouraged pupils to see the world around them through the lens of classical tradition, to temper the real with the ideal—whence the curious combination of naturalism and classicism we often find in nineteenth-century Academic art.

As a general rule, it was only after he (for most of the nineteenth century, art academies across Europe excluded women) had learned to draw that a student was permitted to try his hand at painting or sculpting, usually working in the studio of an established Academy member, learning the master's methods and absorbing his style. Making a finished work generally entailed the production of countless studies—drawings, oil sketches, clay models. Each mature artist had his own formula for the order and number of such preparatory works, but the expected result was generally an object so seamlessly finished as to betray no clue of its making. Not a brushstroke, not a fingerprint, not a chisel mark: no trace of the artist's hand.

Academies also promoted a clear hierarchy of subject matter, sometimes called the hierarchy of the genres. Most highly valued were works portraying "historical" subjects, narratives drawn from classical literature or mythology, from the Bible, or from the distant past. Telling such stories required an impressive command of classical tradition, a mastery of the human figure, an ability to orchestrate complex action and to elicit an emotional response from one's audience. History painting, the early Academicians believed, was an intellectual achievement as much as a technical feat, a task performed with one's mind, not just one's hands. Historical subjects set art apart from craft.

Next in the hierarchy came so-called genre subjects: episodes from everyday life. Though they did not demand the same kind of erudition as historical subjects, genre scenes still required an ability to use human figures to tell a story, preferably one with an affecting or edifying moral. As the nineteenth century wore on, the line between history and genre increasingly blurred; artists looked beyond heroic episodes from history and literature toward everyday scenes from an imagined past, bringing history closer to the lived experience of ordinary viewers.

After history and genre came portraiture. Though less complex than a historical or genre scene, a portrait required not only skill at rendering likeness but insight into the sitter's character and condition in life. Over the course of the century, as church and state commissions for historical and religious art dried up, portraits became an ever more important source of income for many Academic artists. After portraiture came landscape, whose focus on the natural world, rather than the human figure, limited its potential intellectual content in the eyes of early Academicians. Nonetheless, landscape painting's fortunes rose swiftly in the 1830s and 1840s, when a growing middle class emerged as the primary market for works of art. Like landscape, still life—which originally occupied the bottom rung of the ladder—grew in prestige and value. Originally scorned by Academic artists as mere copying, still-life painting became, by the end of the century, an important avenue for formal experimentation.

The changing art market was in large part responsible for the transformation and ultimate demise of the Academic tradition in the nineteenth century, but so too were shifting ideas about the identity of the artist, increasingly defined in terms of provocation, heroic suffering, and bohemianism: the values of the avant-garde. The Academies' insistence on patient study and apprenticeship, classical learning and professional hierarchy came to seem far removed from the realities of modern life. By the early twentieth century, the notion of measuring an artist's success by his membership in an official academy was beginning to seem as outmoded as the French Academicians' elaborate uniforms—complete with sash and sword—which earned them the derisive nickname *pompiers*: firemen. ***—E.A.B.***

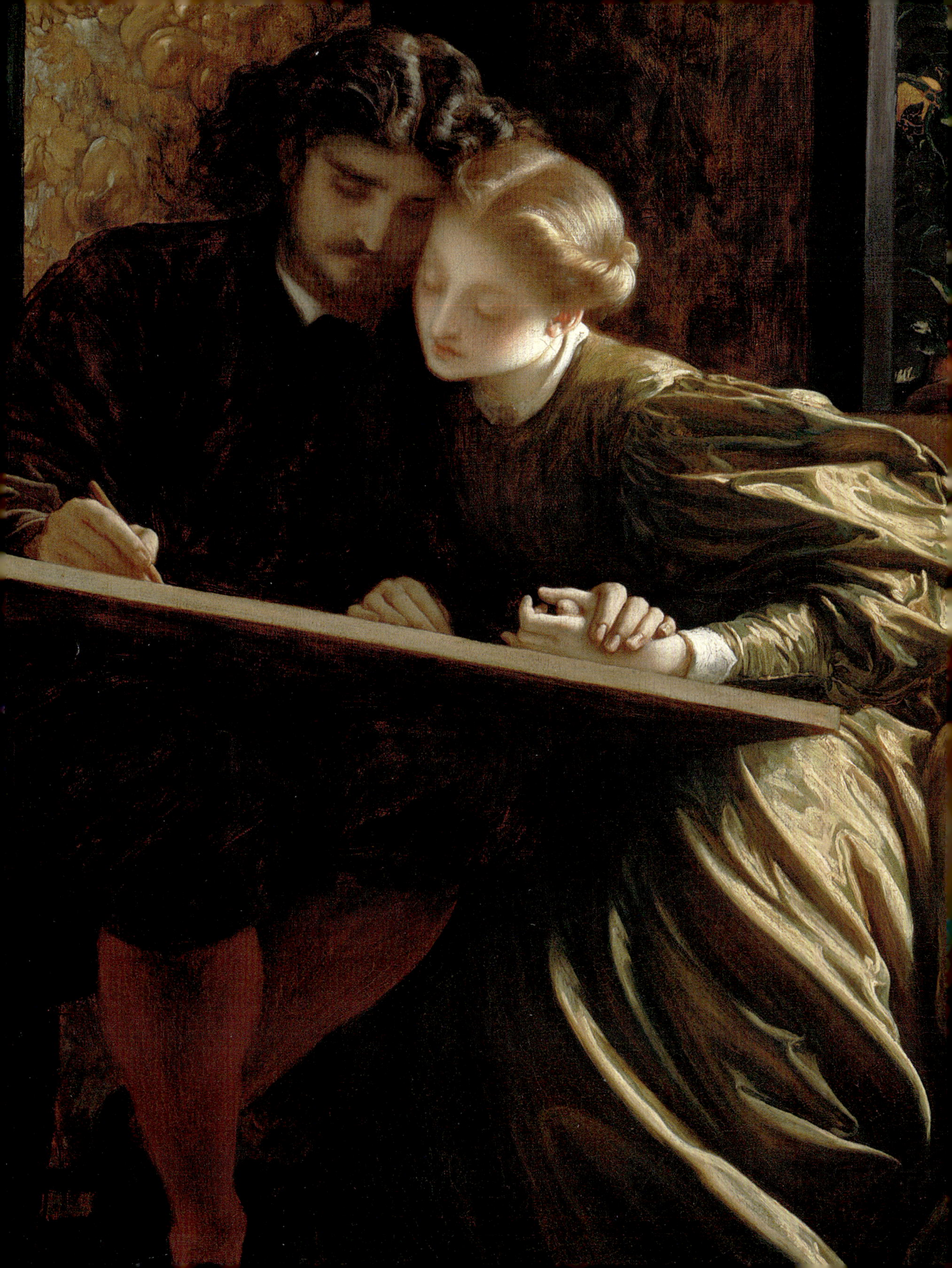

William-Adolphe Bouguereau

French, 1825–1905

Fraternal Love, 1851

Bouguereau was perhaps the defining example of the Academic artist in late nineteenth-century France. A pleasing blend of classical restraint and tender naturalism made his work wildly popular—and ubiquitously reproduced—during the period. With its graceful seated figure and its masterful treatment of the boys' pudgy bodies, *Fraternal Love* exemplifies the artist's approach.

Bouguereau's path to official success began in 1850, when he won the French Academy's Rome Prize. He began this picture in Rome, during the first of four years' study there. He quickly fell under the spell of the Italian Renaissance master Raphael, whose influence is strongly felt in the soft contours and serene pyramidal composition of this painting. So powerful was Raphael's imprint on this picture that its subject was long mistaken for a Madonna and Child with the infant Saint John, one of Raphael's great subjects. The original title, however, under which Bouguereau exhibited this work at the Universal Exposition of 1855 was *Amour fraternel (Fraternal Love)*, indicating that the artist intended the painting not as a devotional image but as a secular allegory in step with the liberal political atmosphere of France around 1850.

Oil on canvas

147 x 113.7 cm (57⅞ x 44¾ in.)

Gift of the Estate of Thomas Wigglesworth, 08.186

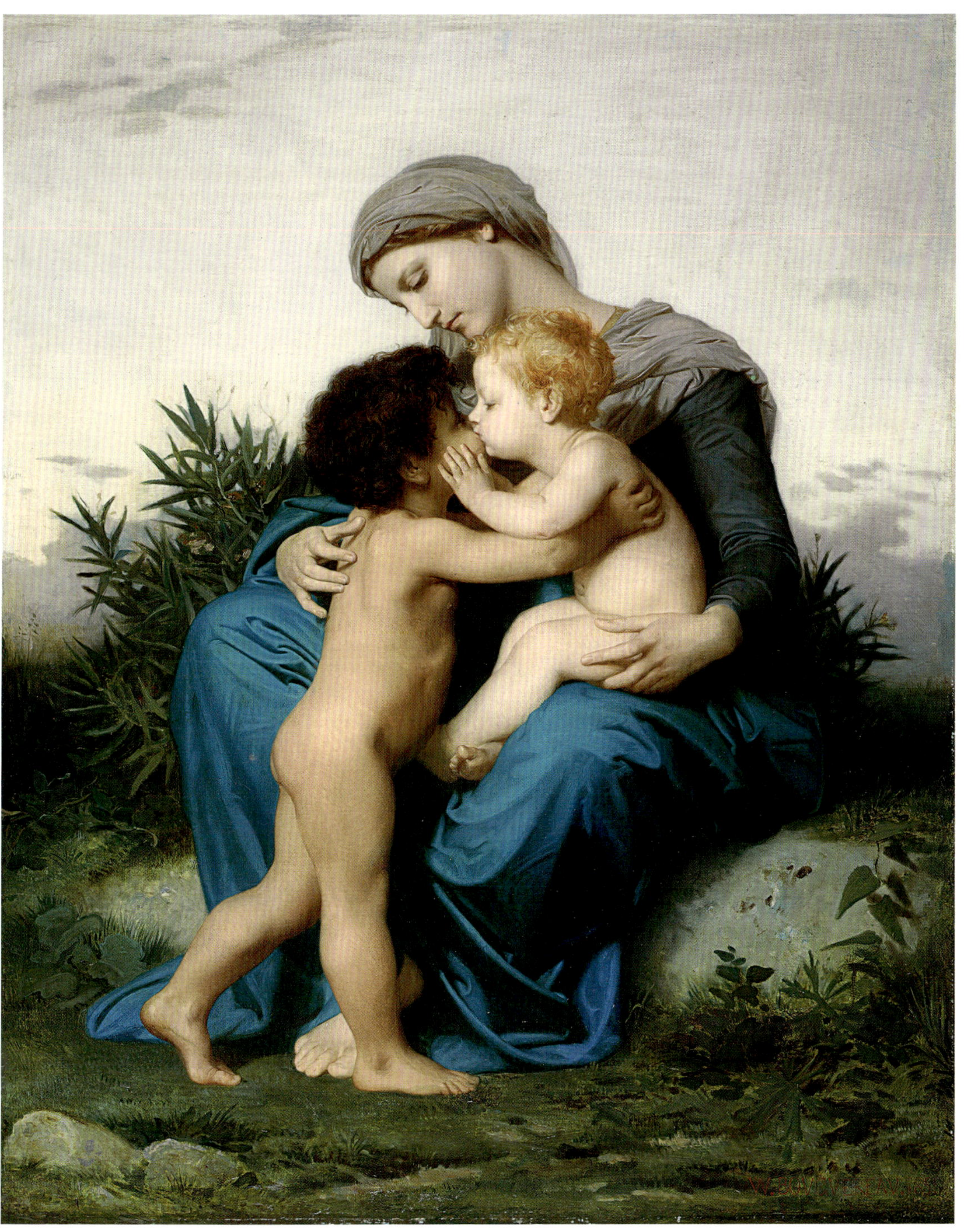

Jean-Baptiste (Auguste) Clésinger
French, 1814–1883
Head of Christ, 1867

Clésinger is best known for a titillating marble sculpture of a reclining nude woman bitten by a serpent, which caused a scandal when it was shown at the Salon of 1847 because it was cast from life. This practice flouted every rule of good Academic art and artistic practice, which required careful study from life through drawing and modeling, and the gradual development of the skill required to create a naturalistic nude figure. Life casting was condemned for requiring no artistic skill, and the painter Delacroix called Clésinger's work a "sculpted daguerreotype." Yet Clésinger also produced strikingly moving religious images, including this bust of Christ crowned with thorns. Like many nineteenth-century sculptures, the bust was reproduced in a variety of materials. The original version was carved in marble in Rome, where Clésinger would have seen the Baroque sculptures that inspired it. The rich brown color of the bronze and its high, reflective polish add a disconcerting sensuousness to the image. As in many images of Christ, who was believed to have suffered and died but then rose from the dead, there is an interplay between lifelikeness and death. With eyes nearly closed and head inclined, Christ may or may not be represented here as dead. Soft curls fall over his shoulders, in sharp contrast to the aggressive and naturalistic crown of thorns. The wound in Christ's side, displaced here to his upper torso, drips blood; its inclusion recalls the incident in the Crucifixion narrative when Christ's side was pierced with a sword. Such details, and the larger-than-life scale of the figure, confront the viewer with the physical and spiritual presence of the subject.

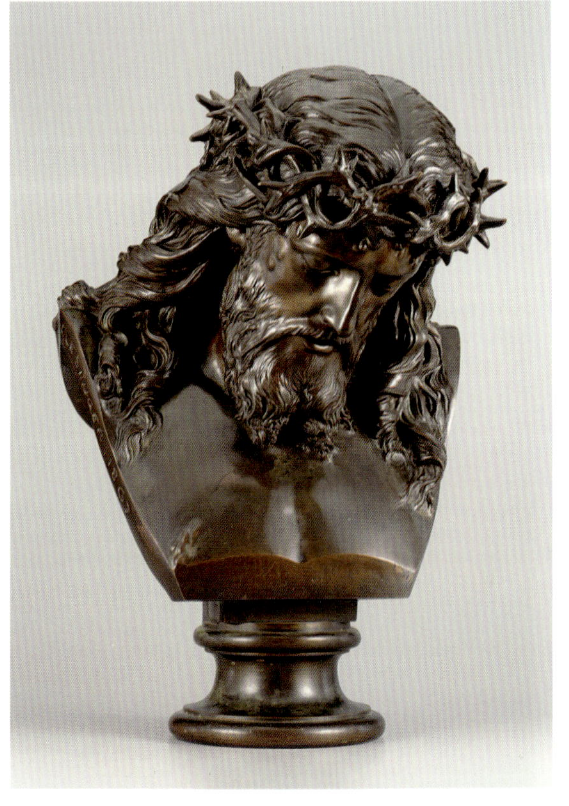

Bronze
63.2 x 40 x 46.7 cm (24⅞ x 15¾ x 18⅜ in.)
Gift of Patricia Learmonth, to the memory of her husband, Raoul H. Fleischmann, 1983.158

Frederic, Lord Leighton
English, 1830–1896
Painter's Honeymoon, about 1864

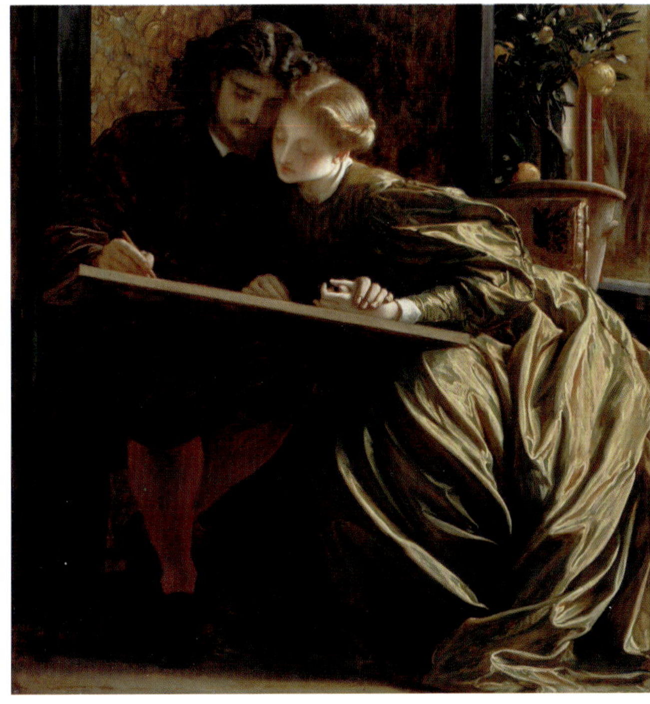

With a sketching board propped on his knees and his bride seated beside him, Leighton's painter appears engrossed in his work. The couple's clasped hands, which mark the center of the composition, epitomize a newly sentimental attitude toward marriage in Victorian society. The wash of golden light, the potted lemon tree, and the picture's bohemian hero may conjure Leighton's own memories of Italy, where he spent several formative years studying classical and Renaissance art.

At once naturalistic and heavily idealized, this picture demonstrates Leighton's extensive and diverse academic training, which began in Florence in the winter of 1845–46. His family was English but spent most of the artist's early life traveling on the Continent; after less than a year's instruction at the Academy of Fine Arts in Florence, Leighton moved with his parents to Germany, where he continued his studies at the State Academy in Frankfurt. Six years later he returned to Italy, setting up his studio in Rome and remaining there from 1852 to 1855. He spent the late 1850s in Paris, where he met Jean-Auguste-Dominique Ingres and absorbed the influence of Ary Scheffer. Indeed, when Leighton returned at last to London in 1859, his pictures were widely considered too French, too foreign; they were routinely rejected by the exhibition jury of the Royal Academy. *Painter's Honeymoon* may have been one of two submissions turned away in 1864; the picture was accepted and exhibited, however, in 1867, when Leighton's fortunes began to improve. Admitted as a member of the Royal Academy the following year, he rose quickly through its ranks and was elected president in 1879.

Oil on canvas
83.8 x 76.8 cm (33 x 30¼ in.)
Charles H. Bayley Picture and Painting Fund, 1981.258

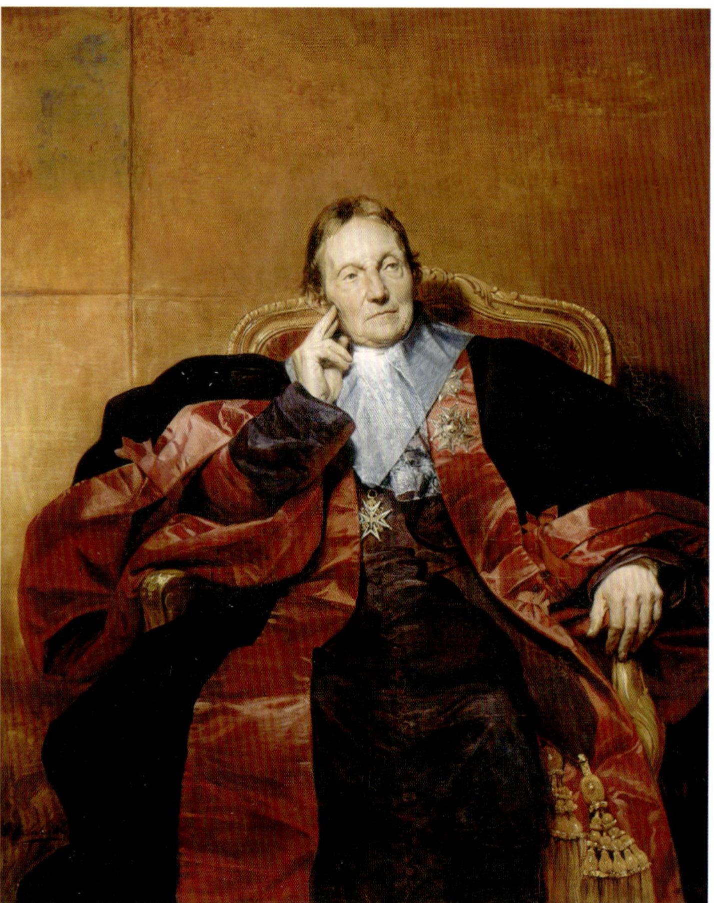

Paul Delaroche
French, 1797–1856
Marquis de Pastoret, 1829

Combining the dramatic light effects and psychological penetration of a Romantic likeness with the immaculately finished surface and sumptuous costume of a pre-Revolutionary portrait, this painting points to the delicate positions and split allegiances of both Delaroche and his sitter in 1829. Restored to the throne after the defeat of Napoleon in 1815, the Bourbon kings ruled France until the Revolution of 1830. Among the highest officials at the Bourbon court, the Marquis de Pastoret was appointed Chancellor of France in 1829 and immediately commissioned Delaroche to paint this portrait in his new robes of office.

The artist originally included Pastoret's family coat of arms, in gold, at the upper left, as well as an inscription identifying the sitter at right. With the Revolution of 1830 and the collapse of the Bourbon government, however, Pastoret was disgraced; the arms and inscription (now visible only as smudges) were painted over—either by Delaroche or a subsequent owner of the painting—in an attempt to conceal Pastoret's identity.

The artist fared better than his sitter in those tumultuous times, in part because his style was not easily identified with a particular political point of view. Perhaps the most influential member of the French Academy in the second quarter of the nineteenth century, Delaroche charted a course between the high color and emotion of the radical Romantics and the smooth linearity and aesthetic conservatism of the late Neoclassical school. Delaroche's style, sometimes known, like that of Ary Scheffer, as the *juste milieu* (happy medium), was a compromise, offering something for everyone. His work found a broad, popular audience through reproductive prints.

Oil on canvas
155.3 x 122.6 cm (61⅛ x 48¼ in.)
Susan Cornelia Warren Fund and the Picture Fund, 11.1449

Franz Xaver Winterhalter
German, 1806–1873
Wienczyslawa Barczewska, Madame de Jurjewicz, 1860

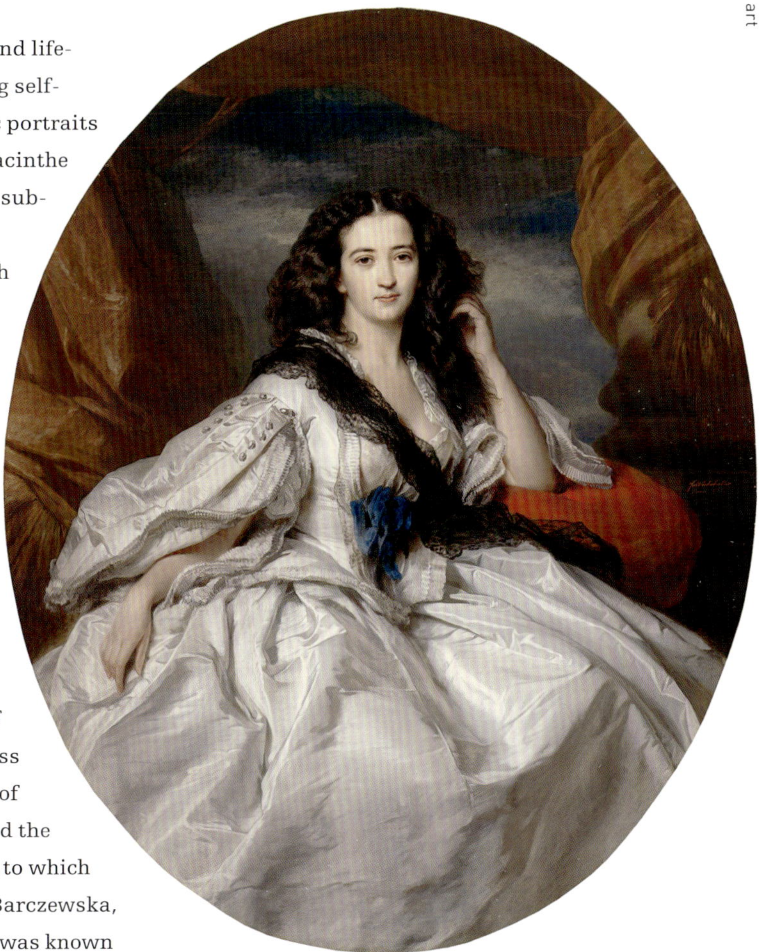

With its sumptuous, billowing draperies and life-size, half-length composition, this painting self-consciously references French aristocratic portraits of the ancien régime by such artists as Hyacinthe Rigaud and Nicolas de Largillière. But the subject's seductively disheveled tresses place this picture squarely in the mid-nineteenth century: a post-Romantic glamour portrait of the kind that made Winterhalter the most celebrated portraitist of his age.

With a brilliant, pan-European clientele, an eye for fashion, and a virtuosic talent, Winterhalter made his name in Second Empire Paris. The artist, it was claimed, could paint a portrait directly on the canvas from start to finish without preparatory drawings or sketches. He painted the crowned heads of Europe (Queen Victoria of England, Empress Eugénie of France, Queen Maria Hendrika of Belgium, Empress Elizabeth of Austria) and the glittering reaches of Parisian high society, to which the sitter for this portrait, Wienczyslawa Barczewska, belonged. A Polish aristocrat, Barczewska was known in Paris as *La Maréchale* for her husband's rank as marshal in the Russian Imperial Army. Like many members of the Polish nobility, the couple lived as expatriates in France, where Winterhalter continued to work until compelled to leave at the outbreak of the Franco-Prussian War.

Oil on canvas
156.1 x 124 cm (61½ x 48⅞ in.)
Museum purchase with funds bequeathed by Genevieve Gray Young in memory of Patience Young and Patience Gray Young, 1998.396

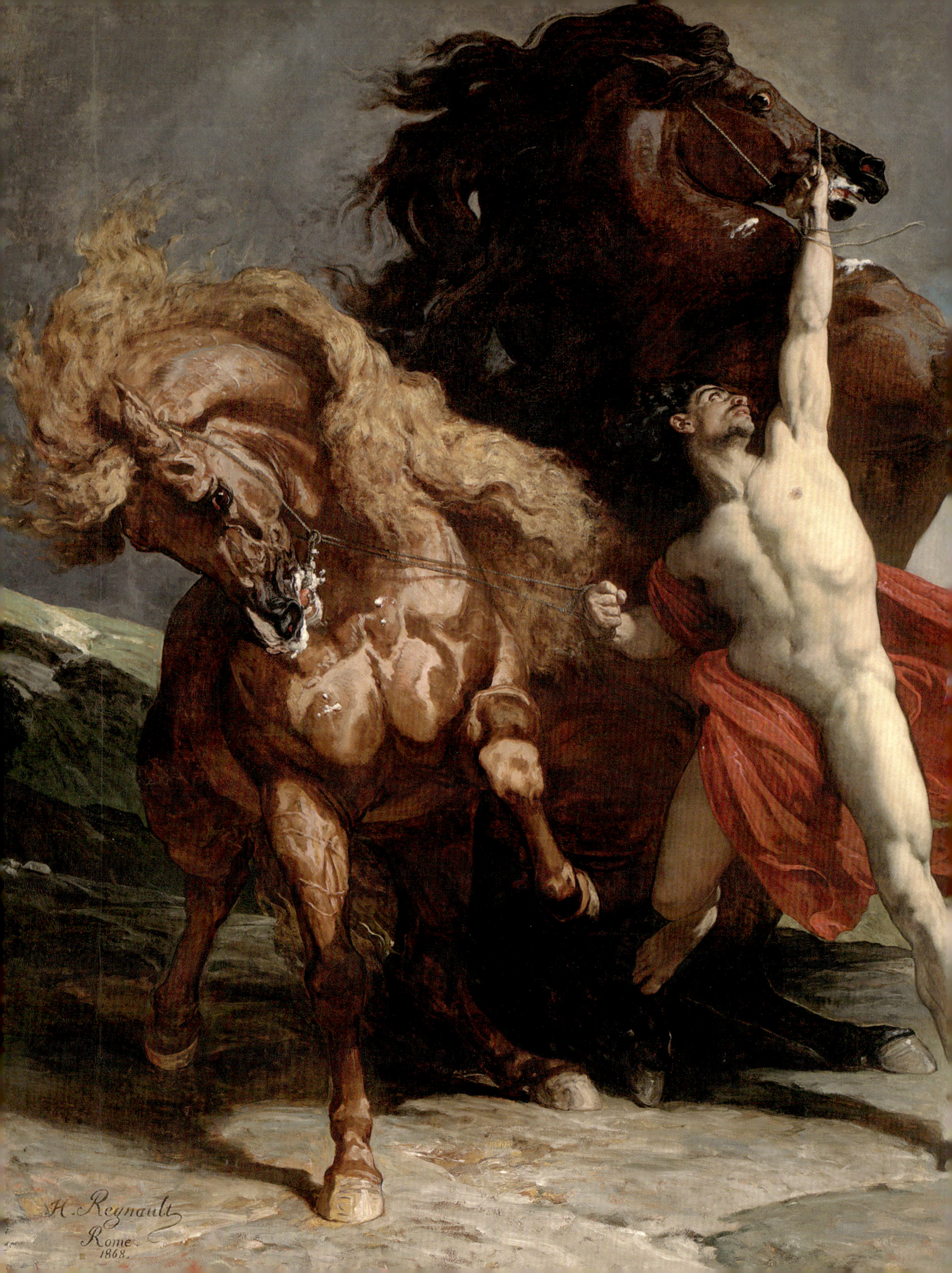
H. Regnault
Rome
1868.

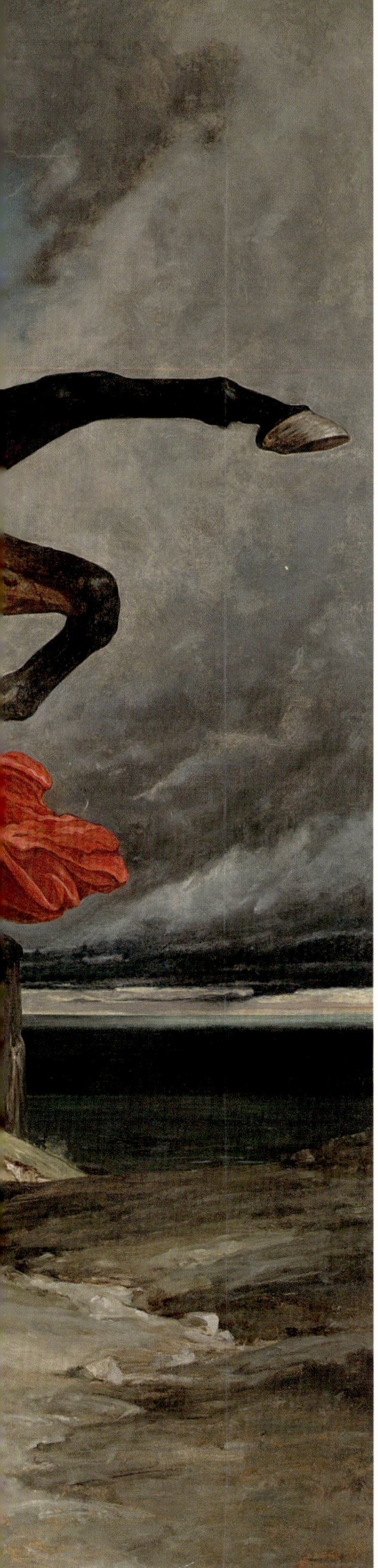

Henri Regnault

French, 1843–1871

Automedon with the Horses of Achilles, 1868

Worked up from numerous studies, Regnault's giant painting is nonetheless extraordinarily free in its execution, with broad, rapid strokes contributing to its breathless energy. The subject comes from Homer's epic poem the *Iliad*: the Greek hero Achilles instructs Automedon to harness his horses, Xanthos and Balios, but the animals sense their master's impending death and shy away, straining against their bridles.

Regnault won the French Academy's Rome Prize in 1866. The terms of this award required the young painter to send home one picture each year, demonstrating progress made abroad to his professors back in Paris. The first of these submissions was to be a modest single-figure nude, displaying the student's mastery of anatomy. Instead, Regnault sent this larger-than-life composition, with its foaming stallions and windblown hero.

Academic officials grumbled at the brash gesture, but Regnault never lived to follow or flout their guidance. He enlisted in the French army at the outbreak of the Franco-Prussian War and was fatally shot in 1871. His precocious talent and untimely death made him a French national symbol and an international art icon, driving interest in his paintings to feverish heights by 1881, when this one came up for sale in New York, perhaps the most famous work of contemporary art west of the Atlantic. The picture attracted a following among students at the School of the Museum of Fine Arts, who took up a public collection to buy it for the Museum in 1890.

Oil on canvas

315 x 329 cm (124 x 129½ in.)

Museum purchase with funds donated by contribution, 90.152

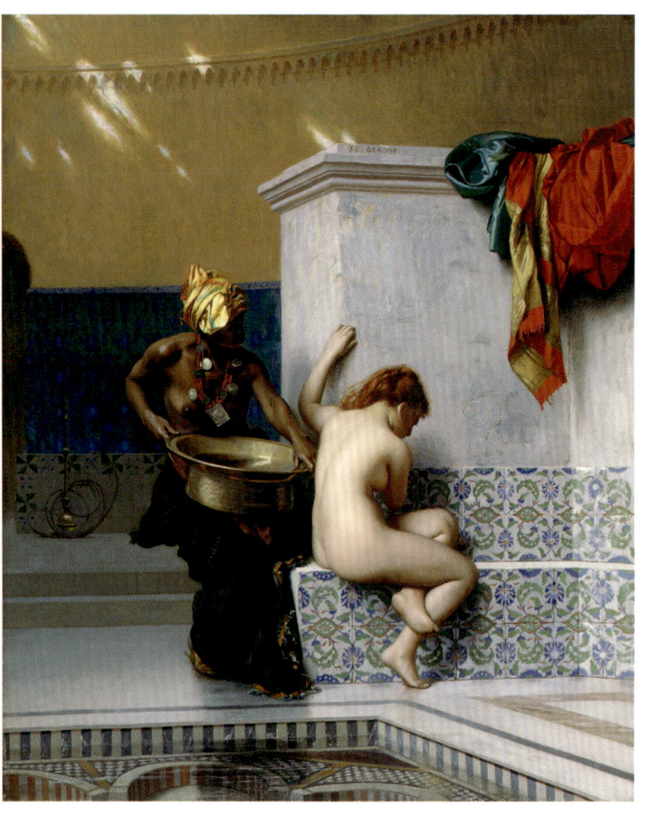

Jean-Léon Gérôme
French, 1824–1904
The Moorish Bath, 1870

Among the most commercially successful artists of the nineteenth century, Gérôme built his reputation as an Orientalist, painting scenes of an imaginary place that combined characteristics of North Africa and the eastern Mediterranean with the artist's own fantasies and inventions. Here Gérôme afforded his viewer a glimpse into the private world of a women's bathhouse, a scene he surely never witnessed. The pale, red-headed nude—perhaps meant to suggest a Circassian slave from the far reaches of the Ottoman Empire—forms a striking contrast to her African attendant.

The nude's sleek flesh and complex pose echo the famous bathers of Jean-Auguste-Dominique Ingres, a reigning Orientalist of the preceding generation. Unlike Ingres, though, Gérôme actually traveled to North Africa and Asia Minor some dozen times between 1852 and 1880, making hundreds of sketches and bringing back photographs, costumes, and a wide range of props to help stage scenes like this one in his Paris studio. The results can be as convincing as dreams, stitching together narrow observation and blithe fabrication with a seamless, photographic realism. In his numerous bathing scenes, Gérôme's scholarly, ethnographic interest gives way to frankly erotic fantasy. His virtuosic technique heightens the sensuality of these pictures; their enamel-smooth surfaces were frequently described by contemporary critics as *léchés*: licked.

Oil on canvas
50.8 x 40.6 cm (20 x 16 in.)
Gift of Robert Jordan from the collection of Eben D. Jordan, 24.217

Jean-Léon Gérôme
French, 1824–1904
L'Éminence Grise, 1873

Gérôme was the unrivaled master of historical genre, a new kind of history painting invented in the nineteenth century. Whereas traditional history painters celebrated grand, heroic events, historical genre painters sought instead to capture the material and psychological experience of the past, to place their viewers *inside* history.

A pool of light on stone steps, the glint of a nobleman's spurs, the well-thumbed pages of a breviary: from such seemingly incidental details this picture conjures a whole world. We stand at the foot of a staircase in the seventeenth-century palace of Cardinal Richelieu, the royal counselor who effectively ruled France during the childhood and early reign of Louis XIII. Above the stairs, a tapestry bearing the cardinal's arms announces his dominion. At right, a monk in gray robes and sandals descends, lost in his book, while richly dressed courtiers and clergymen bow before him.

The monk is François Le Clerc du Tremblay, the Capuchin friar who served as confessor and adviser to Richelieu. Known as L'Éminence Grise—the Gray Eminence—for the color of his robes and his notorious influence at court, Le Clerc du Tremblay became a symbol of covert authority: the power behind the throne. Gérôme suggests the courtiers' mingled fear and contempt for the Gray Eminence as they bow and scrape but cast resentful looks in his wake.

The artist owned a vast collection of historical costumes in which he liked to pose models as he made drawing after drawing to prepare a composition like this one. Rigorous preparation allowed him to produce famously "tight" paintings, in which brushstrokes are all but invisible. The mirror-smooth surface of this canvas enhances the illusion that we are looking through a window, witnessing the scene depicted at firsthand.

Oil on canvas
68.6 x 101 cm (27 x 39¾ in.)
Bequest of Susan Cornelia Warren, 03.605

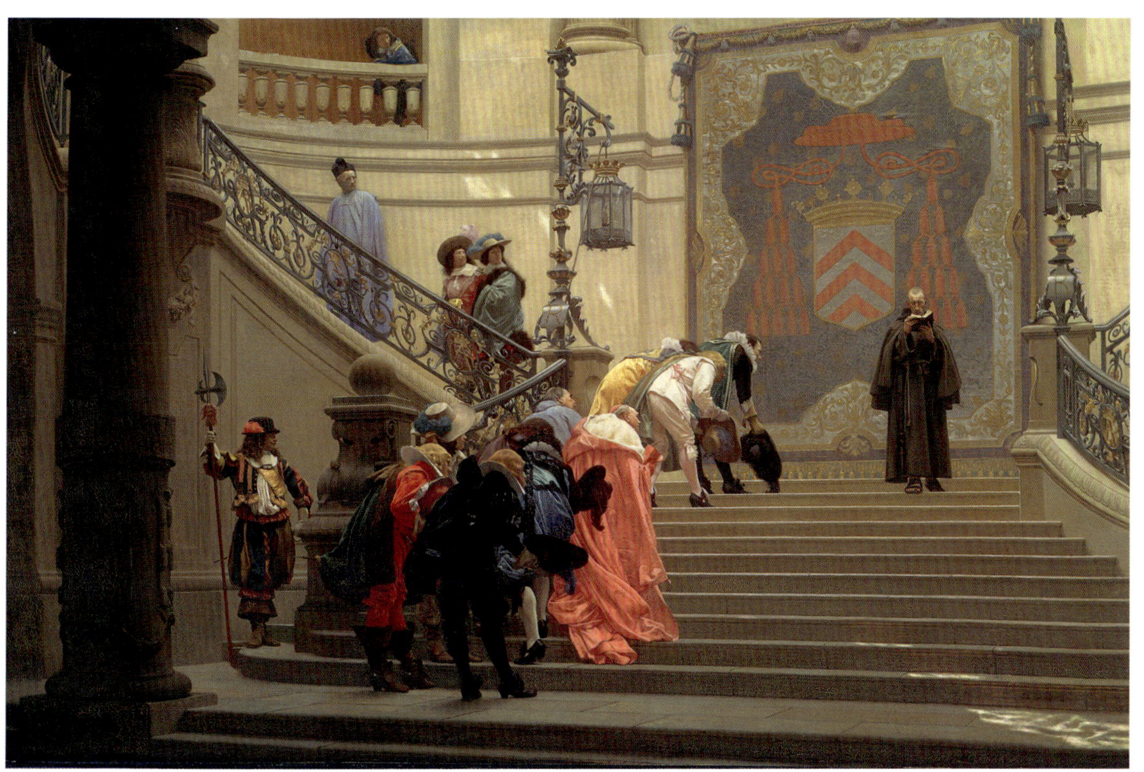

Sir Lawrence Alma-Tadema

Dutch (active in England), 1836–1912

Woman and Flowers, 1868

One of the most successful and admired artists of the 1860s and 1870s, Alma-Tadema specialized in precious, small-scale scenes of everyday life in ancient Rome. In this painting, for which the artist was awarded the Order of the Dutch Lion in 1868, a Roman matron sets aside her embroidery to smell the blossoms of her potted plants. Her costume and jewelry, like the bronze table and mosaic floor, impart a convincing archaeological flavor to the scene, but the dark-haired model (likely Alma-Tadema's first wife) is unmistakably a Victorian lady.

The Alma-Tademas took their 1863 honeymoon in Italy, where the artist compiled a collection of sketches, photographs, and ancient objects to furnish future genre scenes with period detail. Yet, for all their reference to the ancient world, the artist's pictures remain rooted in contemporary concerns—notably those of the bourgeois home. He denigrated Realist painters, whom he associated with "the hollow notion that you must paint your own time," and insisted that their pictures, "in reality, never . . . give us any feeling of our own." Though crowded with antique artifacts, it is precisely "a feeling of our own time" that Alma-Tadema's little scene conveys, speaking eloquently to the modern age—its domestic pleasures and its longing for a vanished past.

Oil on panel

49.8 x 37.2 cm (19⅝ x 14⅝ in.)

Gift of Edward Jackson Holmes, 41.117

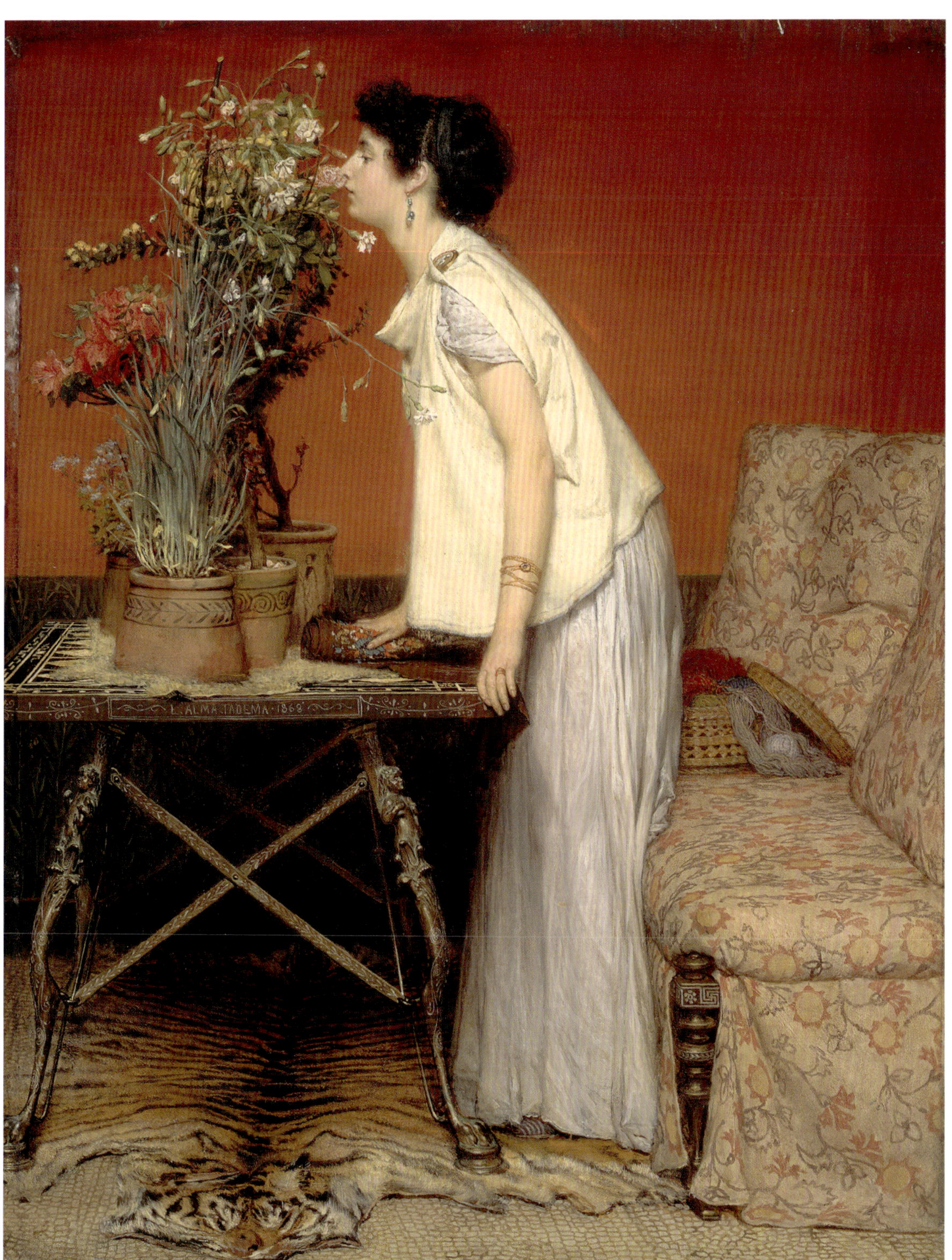
L. ALMA TADEMA · 1868

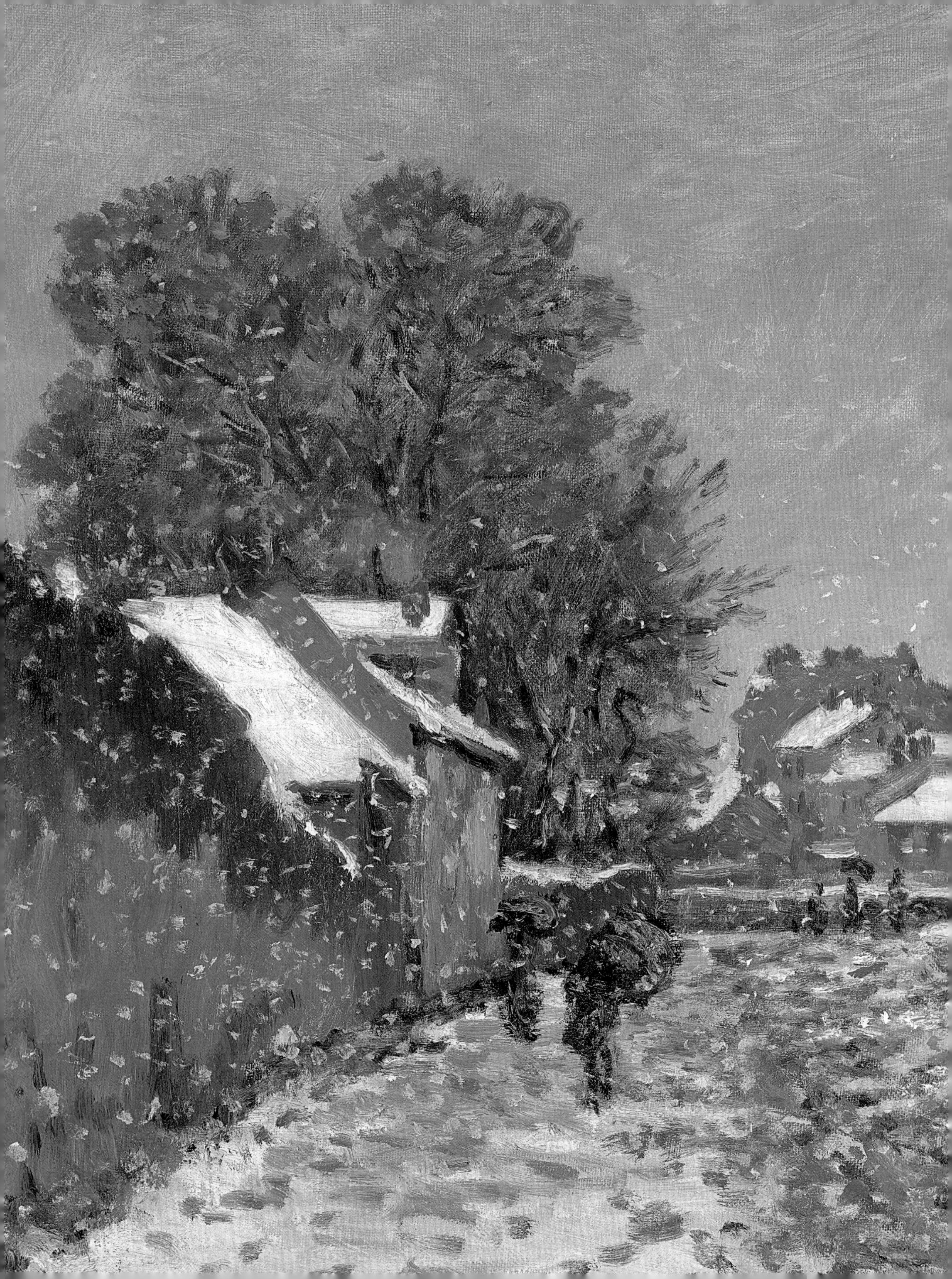

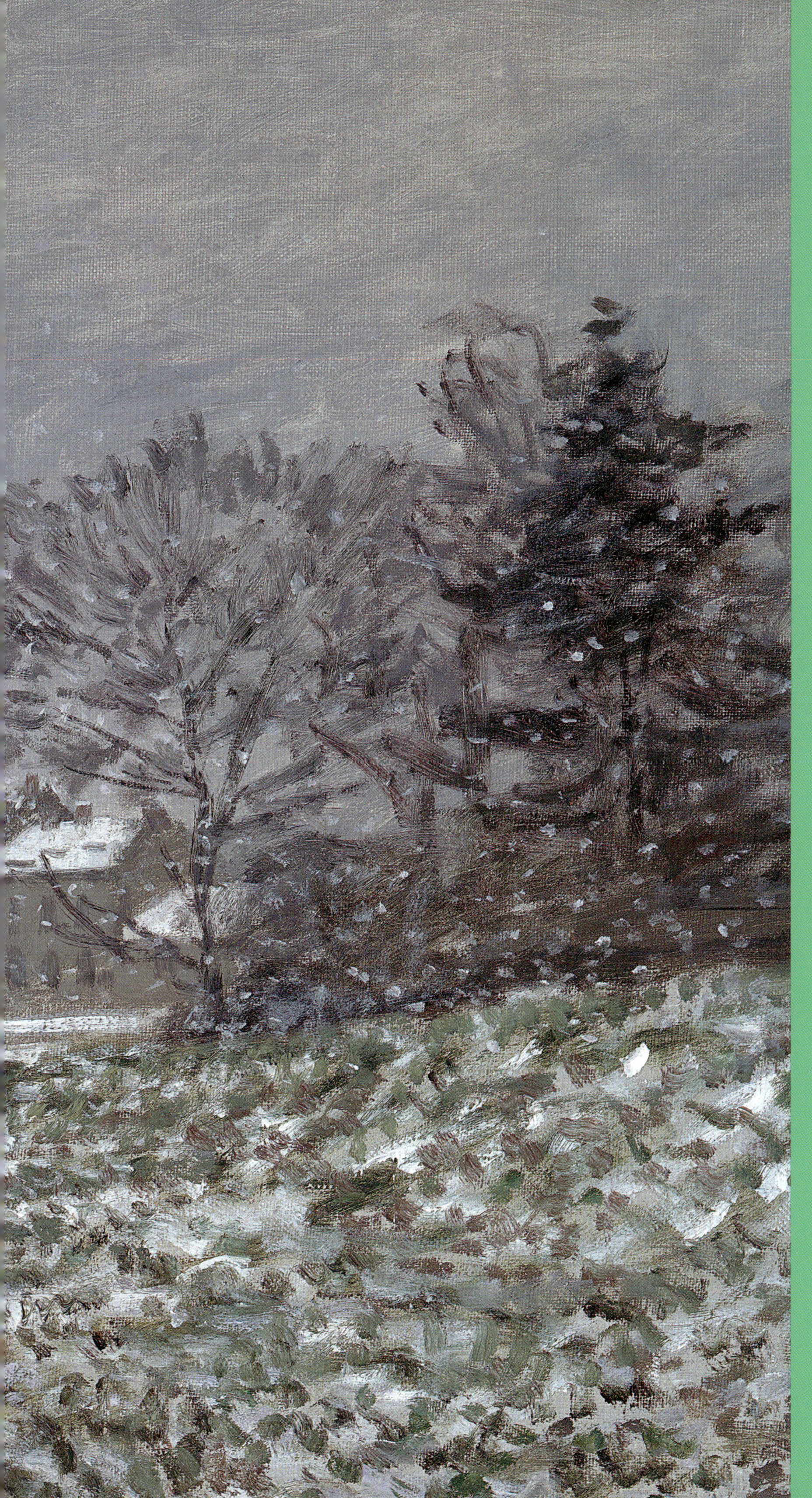

4 TOWN AND COUNTRY: naturalism and impressionism

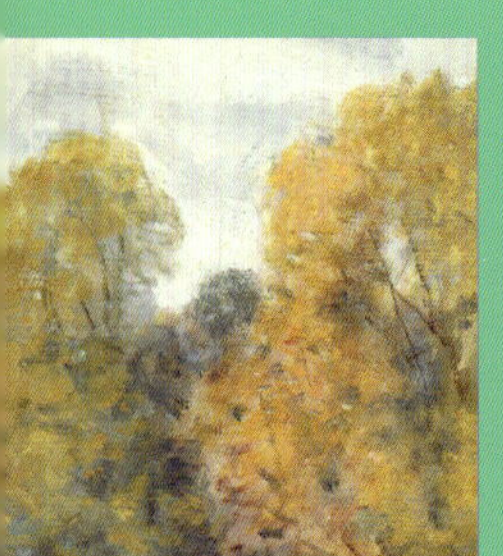
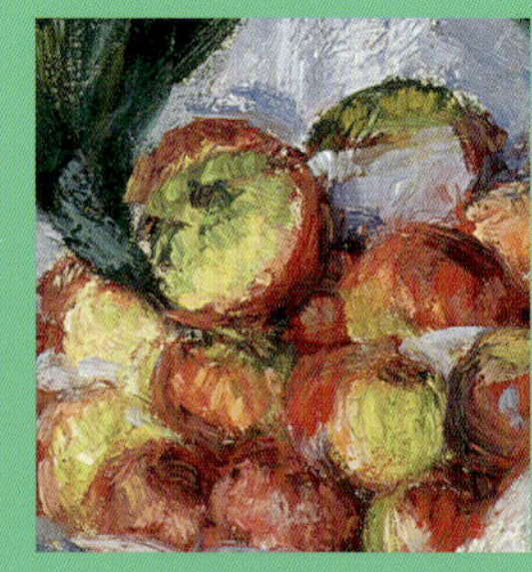
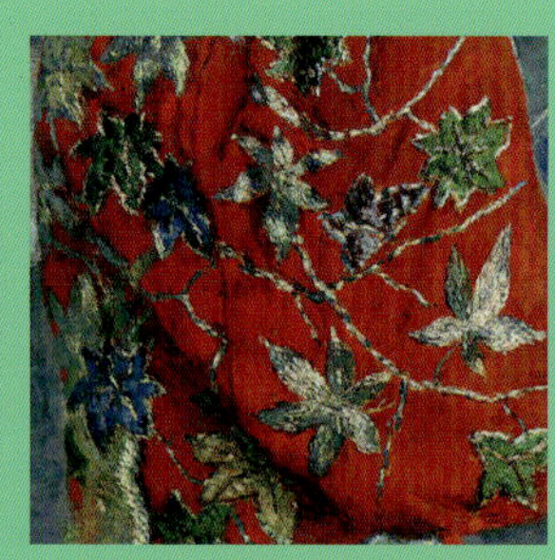
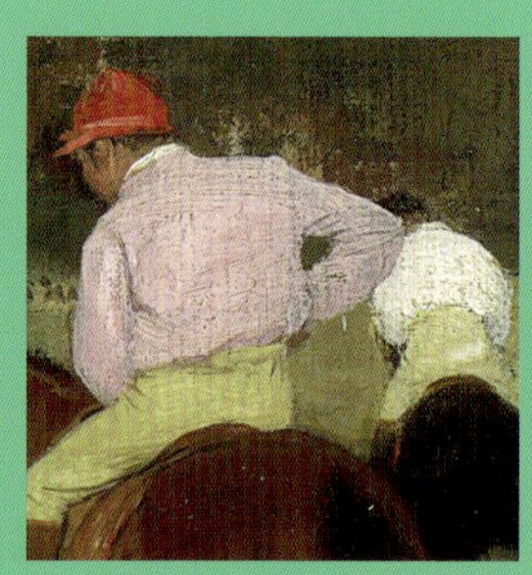
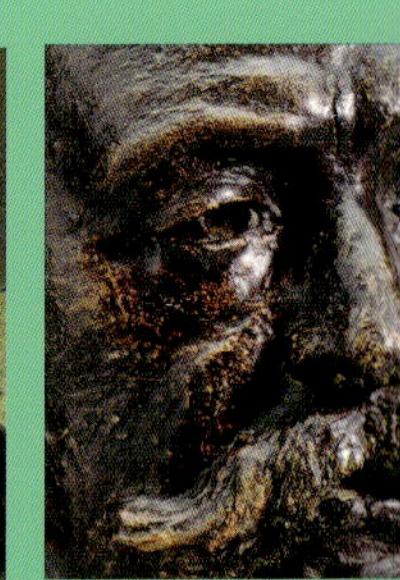

Town and Country: Naturalism and Impressionism

In April 1863 the jury of the official Paris Salon rejected more than two thousand paintings, a solid and unprecedented majority of the works submitted. Artists were outraged. Yielding to their protests, Emperor Napoleon III proposed the poisoned compromise of a secondary exhibition, where members of the public could judge for themselves the merit of works scorned by the jury. Christened the Salon des Refusés (Salon of Rejects), this exhibition furnished the conservative press with a source of snide merriment but nonetheless marked a watershed moment in the history of modern art.

Luncheon on the Grass, one of Édouard Manet's contributions to the show, presented two gentlemen in modern dress picnicking with a nude woman. Lacking any clear narrative or mythological pretext for its nude, the picture caused a scandal. Ladies are said to have fainted in the gallery where it was displayed. Critics deplored not only the painting's supposed indecency but also its apparent lack of finish. Manet's summary style, his harsh lighting and abrupt modeling, pointed to a larger trend in French art revealed by the Salon des Refusés: the emerging aesthetic of the *ébauche* (sketch), a frank, unfinished quality on the rise among young artists.

Manet quickly became the hero of the *ébauchistes*, the standard-bearer of a "new manner in painting," as the writer Émile Zola called it. Manet and Zola most likely met in the early 1860s at the Café Guerbois, unofficial headquarters of the Parisian avant-garde, where Naturalism was born. Naturalists did for the city essentially what their Realist predecessors had done for the countryside, treating familiar figures from the streets of Paris with a new, aggressive honesty. Whereas Realists had tended to proselytize and moralize, however, Naturalists took a more laconic approach—presenting (or seeming to present) only the facts and letting them speak for themselves. Like the novels of Zola, Joris-Karl Huysmans, and the brothers Goncourt, the early paintings of Manet and Edgar Degas shocked their contemporaries by presenting uncomfortable realities of life in the capital—prostitution, for example—in brisk, dispassionate terms.

In the 1870s and 1880s Naturalism was gradually domesticated, adopted, and co-opted by less radical artists. The young painters who so admired Manet took their work in a different direction, launching a movement of their own. Pooling their resources, thirty artists—including Degas, Claude Monet, Auguste Renoir, Paul Cézanne, Berthe Morisot, Camille Pissarro, and Alfred Sisley—rented a photographer's studio at 25 boulevard des Capucines in April 1874. There they showed an array of brilliantly colored, breezily executed pictures to an uncomprehending public. One, by Monet, titled *Impression, Sunrise*, gave the movement its name, when a sneering critic dubbed the painter and his colleagues *Impressionnistes*. The name, however, was apt, since the Impressionists sought to capture fleeting perceptions and experiences, whether in nature or the modern city: impressions of the world around them.

Several artists in the group—notably Monet, Pissarro, and Sisley—worked almost entirely outdoors, applying color in pure, unblended strokes to capture the play of light on water or the shifting shadows of leaves on a lawn. Rather than the progressive shades of gray conventionally used to describe three-dimensional form, light, and shade, the Impressionists used bright (often chemically manufactured) pigments—purple, blue, acid green, lemon yellow. The movement was not monolithic, however; the eight Impressionist group exhibitions (1874, 1876, 1877, 1879, 1880, 1881, 1882, and 1886) showcased diverse approaches, presenting the sunlit river views of Monet alongside Cézanne's stern, lapidary landscapes; Renoir's bright, lyrical scenes of suburban courtship alongside Gustave Caillebotte's muted portrayals of ordinary Parisians; Degas's velvety pastels alongside the same artist's scandalous sculpture, the *Little Fourteen-Year-Old Dancer*.

The group's diversity was also a source of conflict; Monet and his faction favored bucolic landscape; Degas and his favored scenes of city life. Some members of the group continued to submit work to the annual Salon; others refused to do so on principle. In the 1880s the Impressionists drifted apart, held together chiefly by their shared dealer, Paul Durand-Ruel, who provided several members of the group with their sole source of income and ultimately launched their successful solo careers. Durand-Ruel's policy in the early 1880s of organizing monographic exhibitions—most notably for Monet and Renoir—helped these artists gain a following but also encouraged them to pursue ever more highly individualized stylistic experiments.

The late series paintings of Monet began as an Impressionist project—rapid, firsthand observations of changing light and weather—but they quickly evolved into something more personal and inward, canvases clotted with paint, objects concerned with their own making. Their affinity with the contemporary sculptures of Auguste Rodin is powerful. The image and the material from which it is fashioned—paint in Monet's case, bronze or marble, in Rodin's—are magically conjoined by the masterful and everywhere evident touch of the maker. ***—E.A.B.***

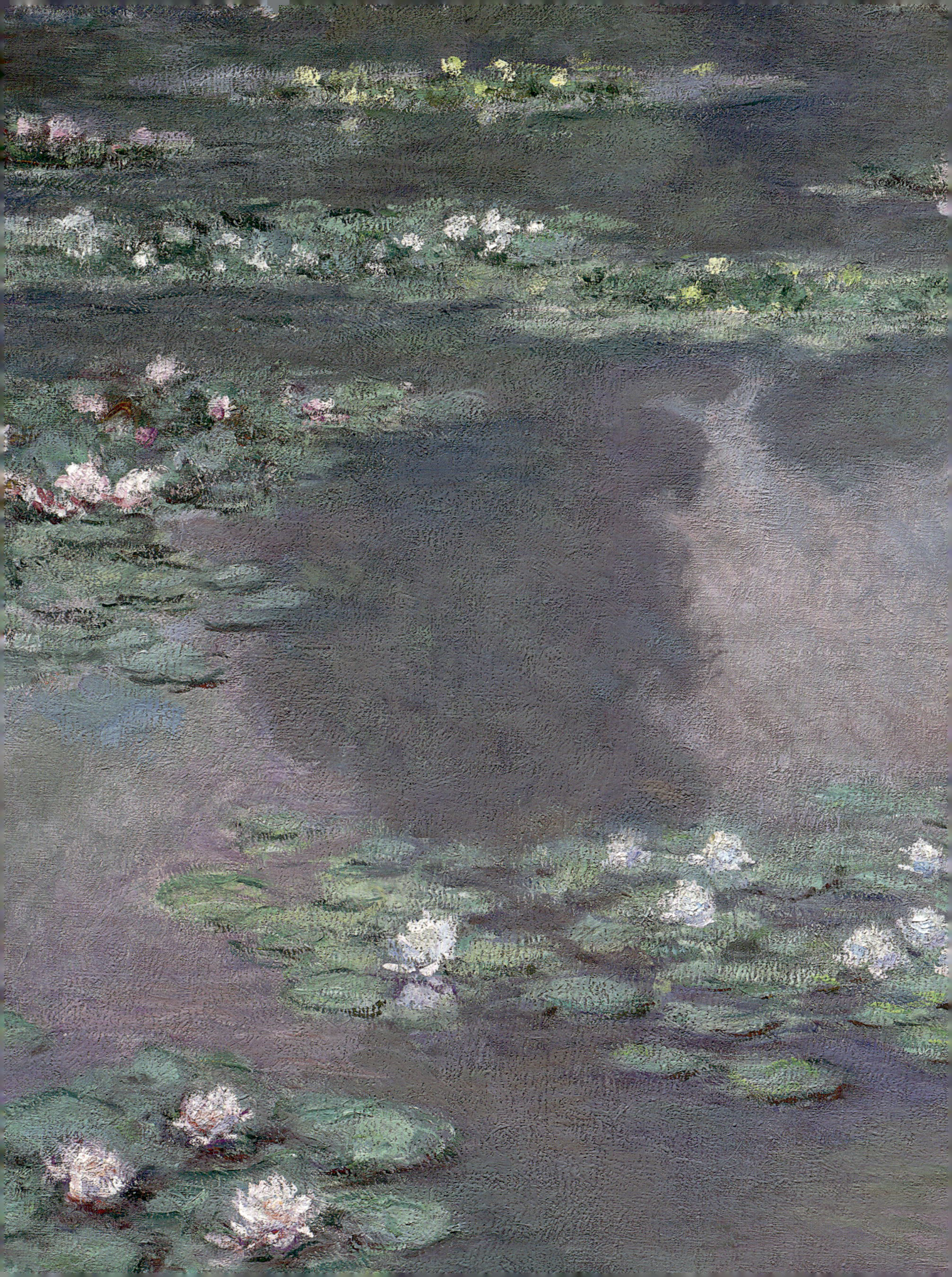

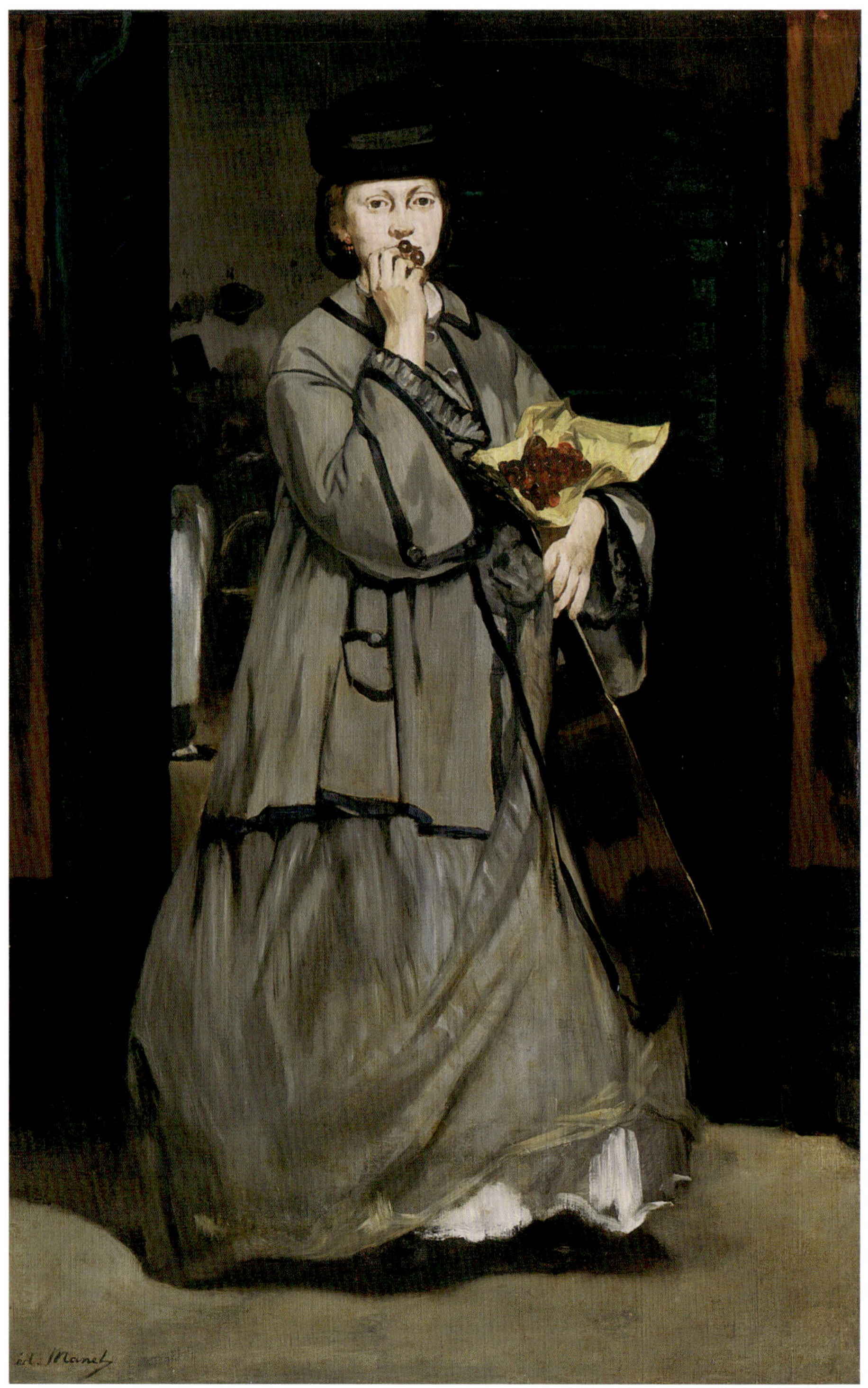
éd. Manet

Édouard Manet

French, 1832–1883

The Street Singer, about 1862

When he first saw this painting, Manet's friend and critical ally Émile Zola wrote, "In it nature seems analyzed with an extreme simplicity and precision . . . one feels the harsh search for truth, the conscientious work of a man who wishes, above all, to state frankly what he sees." What *we* see is a young musician just leaving a seedy café, perhaps having performed for its patrons or taken some refreshment herself. With one hand, she hefts her guitar and hitches up her skirt. With the other, she grabs a fistful of cherries from the parcel tucked under her arm.

In the social landscape of nineteenth-century Paris, this woman is a performer, not a respectable lady: a lady would not frequent such an establishment, would not eat in a public street, and certainly would not hitch up her skirt in this way, revealing the rapidly brushed hem of her petticoat. Yet this garment itself—like all of her clothing—tells a different story and provides our first clue that the scene is not, as Zola would have it, a frank statement of what Manet saw but, rather, a fiction carefully orchestrated in his studio. For the singer's outfit, with its piped jacket and hoop skirt, is far too chic for its indigent wearer.

Another of Manet's friends, Antonin Proust, provided a different account of the painting's genesis. He wrote that Manet had witnessed the scene on a Paris street, had asked the singer to pose for him, and, when she declined, had shrugged, saying, "There's always Victorine." He meant Victorine Meurent, his great model and muse of the 1860s, the face of the modern city in Manet's early work. He posed her in his studio as the street singer, dressing her in a fancy costume that tears the illusion of a moment caught on the fly. Among Manet's most celebrated works, this picture is not a scene observed but an object made with the artist's hands and mind.

Oil on canvas

171.1 x 105.8 cm (67 3/8 x 41 5/8 in.)

Bequest of Sarah Choate Sears in memory of her husband, Joshua Montgomery Sears, 66.304

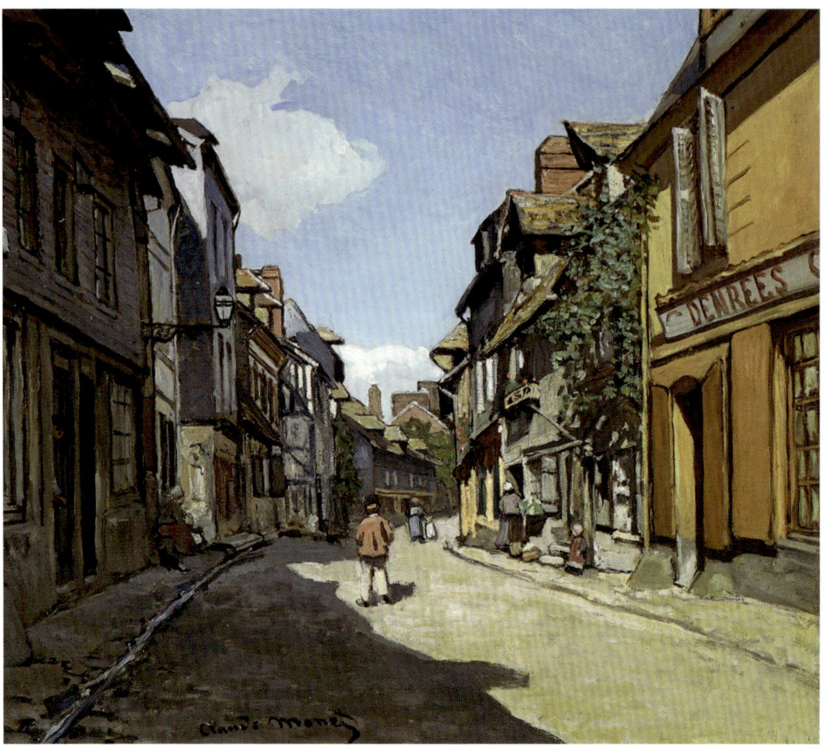

Claude Monet
French, 1840–1926
Rue de la Bavole, Honfleur, about 1864

Monet likely painted this view of a quiet street in the town of Honfleur during an 1864 visit to Normandy. A blue sky and deep shadows—punctuated here and there by tiny orange nasturtiums—convey the sense of a bright summer day. Before evolving his mature Impressionist manner in the early 1870s, the artist painted in a style heavily influenced by Édouard Manet. With its bold modeling and crisp shadows, this scene exemplifies that early style.

Raised in Le Havre, Monet returned to Normandy for summer visits throughout the 1860s. In 1864, he was joined on one such expedition by Frédéric Bazille, whom he had befriended in the studio of Charles Gleyre. The young painters had bonded over a shared dislike for their academic instruction; along with Auguste Renoir and Alfred Sisley—fellow alumni of the Gleyre atelier—they began to paint together outdoors in 1863, forming the tight, collaborative kernel of the future Impressionist group. Bazille, who was independently wealthy and acquired several pictures by his friends, may have been the first owner of this painting. Writing to him in 1864, Monet voiced their shared ambition "to struggle, scrape, begin again, for one can do what one sees and what one understands . . . it seems to me, when I see nature, that I am going to do it all."

Oil on canvas
55.9 x 61 cm (22 x 24 in.)
Bequest of John T. Spaulding, 48.580

Edgar Degas

French, 1834–1917

Racehorses at Longchamp, 1871, possibly reworked in 1874

Under a twilit sky, jockeys and their mounts mill about beside a racetrack on the outskirts of Paris. The rooftops of the fashionable sixteenth arrondissement are just visible above the treetops, and a few remaining onlookers disperse in the distance. Horse racing, a luxury sport imported from England, enjoyed a vogue in nineteenth-century Paris. Built on the western edge of the city in 1857, the Longchamp racetrack drew fashionable spectators, including Degas, who produced his first studies of horses in the 1860s, and whose love for these animals was matched only by his attachment to the ballet.

Like ballet dancers, racehorses combined ungainliness and grace, animal energy and supreme discipline. Degas made a systematic study of the movements of both dancers and horses, but his pictures convey an impression less of bodies in motion than of movement arrested, captured and contained by rigorous outline and broad zones of color. The results are far removed from the breezy sense of motion we associate with his fellow Impressionists' work.

Degas never claimed, as Monet did, that his pictures were made *sur le motif*—in the presence of the things they depicted. He worked and reworked his compositions in his studio; X-ray images of this painting reveal that Degas moved and repainted whole figures and groups to achieve the picture's seemingly casual, balanced asymmetry.

Oil on canvas

34 x 41.9 cm (13 3/8 x 16 1/2 in.)

S. A. Denio Collection—Sylvanus Adams Denio Fund and General Income, 03.1034

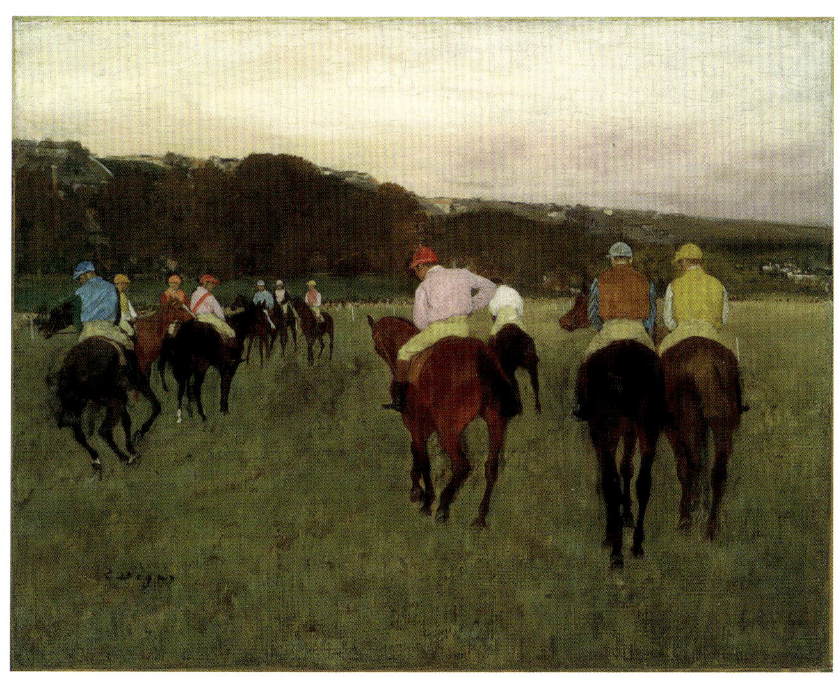

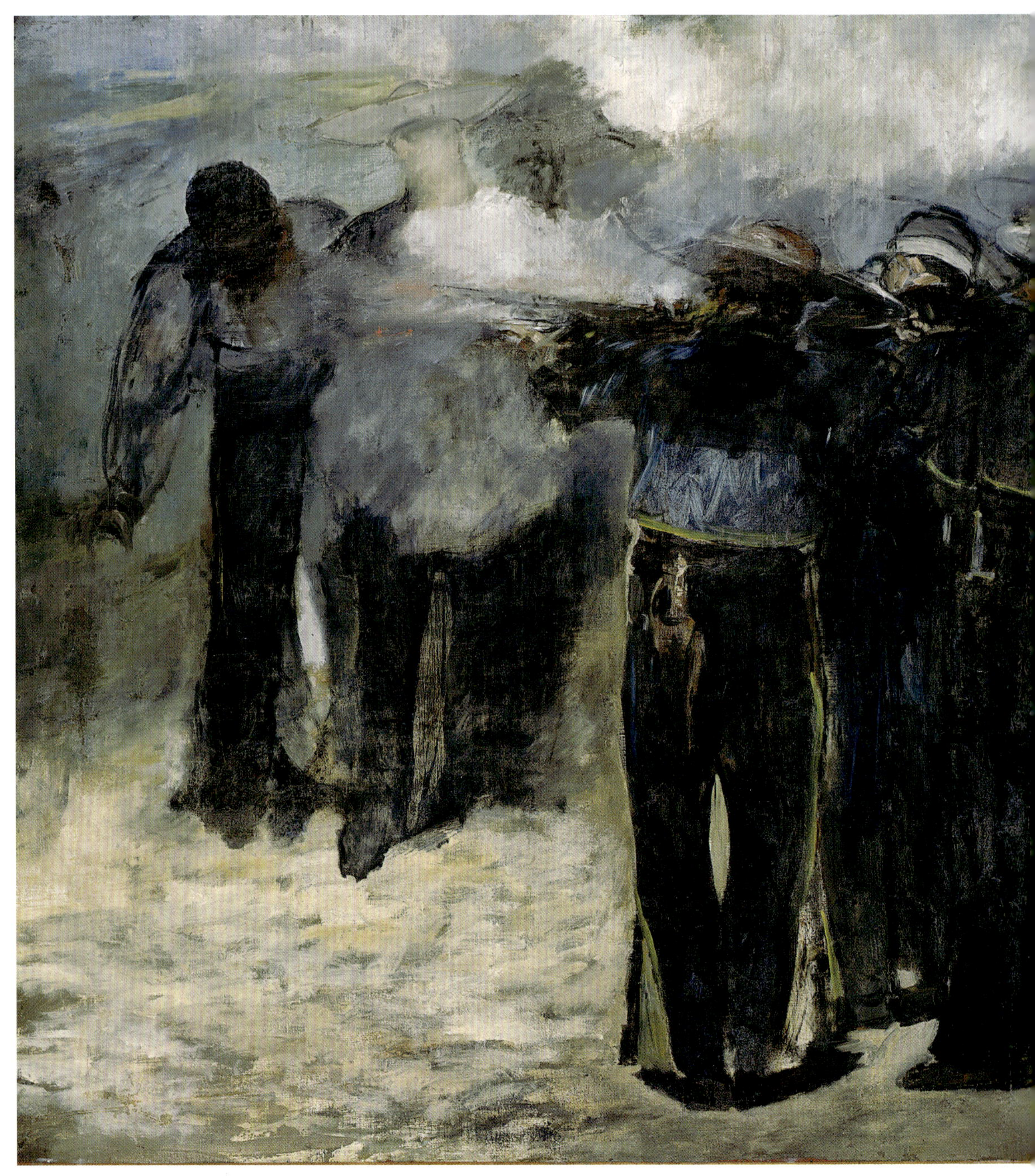

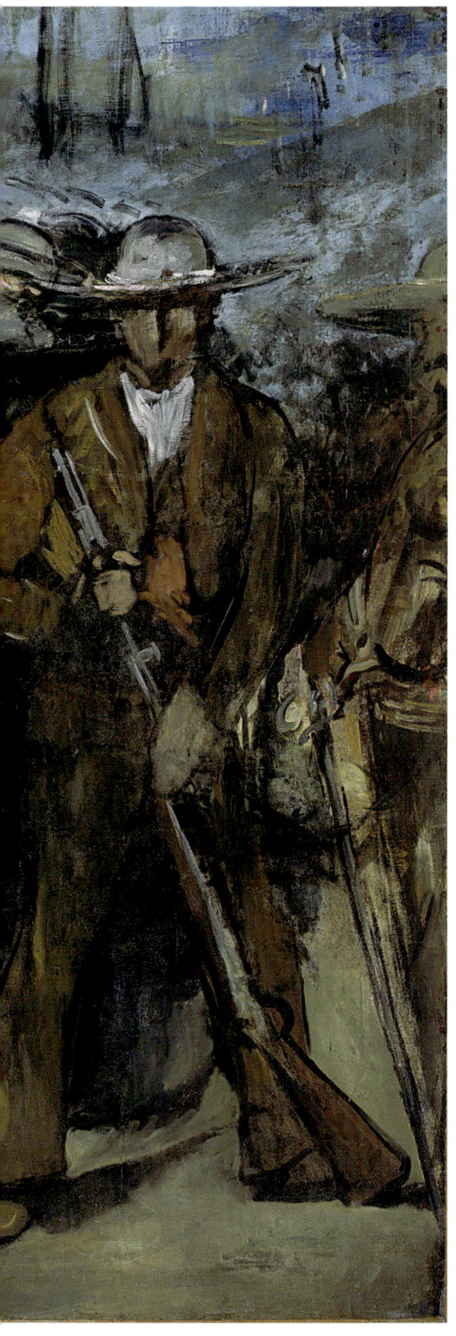

Édouard Manet

French, 1832–1883

***Execution of the Emperor Maximilian*, 1867**

Through a confusion of gunsmoke and early morning light, we make out soldiers in a firing squad, their weapons just discharged. At left, a figure slumps, apparently shot. Beside him, another stands erect. This is the unlikely emperor of Mexico: Maximilian I, an Austrian prince installed on the throne by French troops. Under the government of its elected president, Benito Juaréz, Mexico had fallen into debt to European powers, and in 1863 Spanish forces arrived to collect, reinforced by France. The following year, Ferdinand Maximilian Joseph, younger brother of the Austrian emperor, was crowned Maximilian I, emperor of Mexico. France withdrew military support from his puppet regime three years later, and Juaréz quickly regained command of the Mexican army, wresting control of the government from Maximilian, who was executed on June 19, 1867.

Manet likely set to work on this canvas—the largest he had ever painted—just days after news of the execution reached Paris. It is the first of four versions he painted of the event, and its account is somewhat muddled: the soldiers, for example, who were in fact regular uniformed members of the Mexican army, are depicted as guerrilla fighters, dressed in the sombreros and wide-legged trousers of farmhands. After reading more thorough reports, Manet abandoned the canvas, leaving it unfinished.

Its very incompleteness gives the picture a frightening, piteous effect, which is amplified by its composition: the anonymous executioners at right and brightly lit victims at left are borrowed from another celebrated painting of contemporary events, Francisco Goya's *The Third of May, 1808*, which Manet had seen two years earlier in Madrid. Even before he completed his final version of the subject, the artist was informed that it would be banned from the Salon. Its political content was deemed too explosive for public consumption.

Oil on canvas

195.9 x 259.7 cm (77 ⅛ x 102 ¼ in.)

Gift of Mr. and Mrs. Frank Gair Macomber, 30.444

Albert-Ernest Carrier-Belleuse

French, 1824–1887

Self-Portrait, about 1875

This sculpture presents the artist with his head turned, his glance averted, caught in an intimate moment of introspection. Modeled when he was about fifty years old, it is unflinching in the sculptor's naturalistic rendering of the bags below his eyes, the furrows between his brows, and the loose flesh of his cheeks, creating distinct ridges beside his broad nose. The full mustache masks the shape of his mouth, and tufts of unruly hair accentuate his high forehead. The malleable clay medium allowed Carrier-Belleuse to excavate deeply into the clay to create strong shadows, for example around the eyes and mouth, adding character and mood. The lower portion of the bust retains impressions of the artist's fingers and tool marks in the clay, revealing his sculpting process and leaving it fresh, as if unfinished. The coating of the surface, in contrast, evokes the permanent medium of bronze, adding color and shine as well as preserving the clay. This emphasis on the act of sculpting eschews the sense of the decorative that sometimes characterizes this artist's work, and in the context of a self-portrait such emphasis is an aspect of self he specifically chooses to present. The sculptor's student Auguste Rodin was inspired by this self-portrait when he made a bust of his teacher for production by the Sèvres porcelain factory, where Carrier-Belleuse was director.

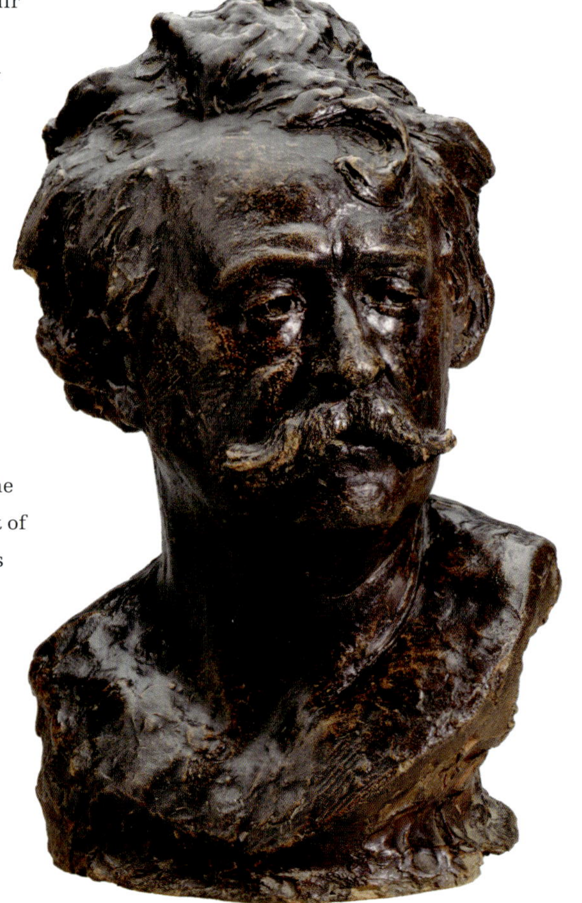

Terracotta with patination

43.2 x 27.9 x 20.3 cm (17 x 11 x 8 in.)

John H. and Ernestine A. Payne Fund, 1982.285

Auguste Rodin
French, 1840–1917
Bust of Jules Dalou, modeled 1883, cast about 1889

The sculptor Jules Dalou, a lifelong friend of Rodin, is presented with his head held high, his expression intense, proud, even haughty. Rodin delineates the muscles and tendons in Dalou's neck with great accuracy, revealing the stress required to hold one's head in such a position. The traditional form of the portrait bust is both acknowledged and transformed in one of Rodin's greatest portraits, which brings out the essential qualities and character of artist and sitter alike. Rodin shows Dalou bare-chested, evoking sculptural forms reaching back to classical antiquity, but modeled with an energy that transforms the flesh into a kind of expressive landscape. No surface is completely smoothed out: the impression of the worked clay is preserved in bronze, catching and reflecting light and selectively revealing anatomy.

The two sculptors had been students together in Paris in the 1850s. They grew apart, as they competed for commissions and diverged in their approaches to their profession, with Dalou seeking honors and Rodin pursuing his own artistic ideals over professional acceptance. This portrait was made just after Dalou attained his greatest success at the Salon of 1883, where he was awarded the Medal of Honor. The bust, in turn, was shown at the Salon of 1884 and was considered one of the best works in the exhibition, preferred by most critics to Rodin's portrait of Victor Hugo, shown at the same time.

Bronze
52.1 x 41.9 x 20.3 cm (20½ x 16½ x 8 in.)
Museum purchase with funds donated by contribution, 12.332

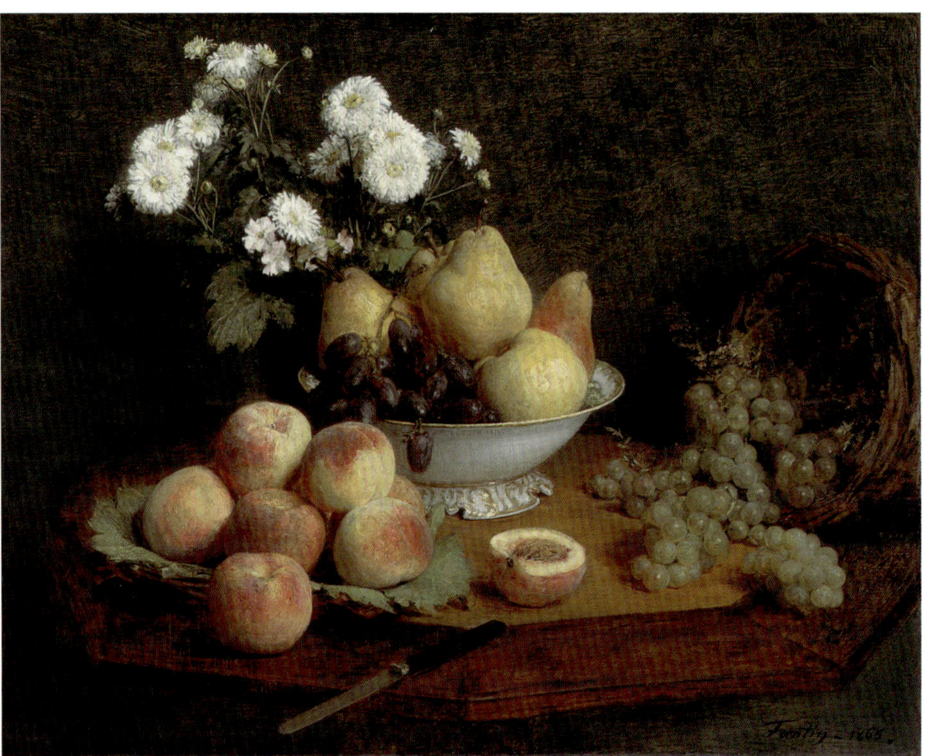

Henri Fantin-Latour
French, 1836–1904
Flowers and Fruit on a Table, 1865

Fantin-Latour was among the greatest still-life painters of the nineteenth century. A pupil of Courbet, a friend of Manet, and an ally of the Impressionist avant-garde, he nonetheless courted official favor and scored immediate critical success with sumptuous compositions like this one.

A sense of artful disorder makes this arrangement one of the most spatially ambitious in Fantin's oeuvre. At center sits a bowl of fruit: pears, an apple, a clump of heavy grapes. Behind this group a spray of white chrysanthemums stands out against the dark background. At left, a pile of peaches rests in a basket lined with leaves. More grapes tumble from another basket onto the table, enclosing the scene at right.

The picture is full of cues to touch and taste: the moist gleam of the grapes, the peaches' velvet sheen, the glinting lip of the porcelain bowl, the beckoning angle of a knife, canted off the table. A few green grapes have already been plucked, and a peach appears split open in the center foreground. Fantin borrowed several of these motifs—as well as his rapt, attentive mode of portraying them—from the eighteenth-century painter Jean-Siméon Chardin, whose work had been rediscovered by critics and collectors in the 1850s and 1860s.

Oil on canvas
60 x 73.3 cm (23 5/8 x 28 7/8 in.)
Bequest of John T. Spaulding, 48.540

Alfred Sisley
British (active in France), 1839–1899
Grapes and Walnuts on a Table, 1876

Sisley first met Monet in the studio of Charles Gleyre, an academic painter from whom both received their early training. Sisley painted just nine still lifes over the course of his career, most likely undertaking this unaccustomed genre at Monet's urging. The modest composition, with its inventory of fruit, plate, nuts, knife, and nutcracker, exhibits all the hallmarks of an Impressionist still life. The gleaming grapes, furrowed walnut shells, and bright, impasted nutcracker are all clearly painted from life and in natural light. Ranged across the snowy expanse of the tablecloth—its topography rendered with brisk strokes of blue and white—these objects take on the character of a landscape. Sisley contributed to the Impressionists' joint exhibitions of 1874, 1876, 1877, and 1882. The group's dealer, Paul Durand-Ruel, purchased this painting from the artist in 1881 and retained it in his private collection for nearly fifty years.

Oil on canvas
38.1 x 55.2 cm (15 x 21¾ in.)
Bequest of John T. Spaulding, 48.601

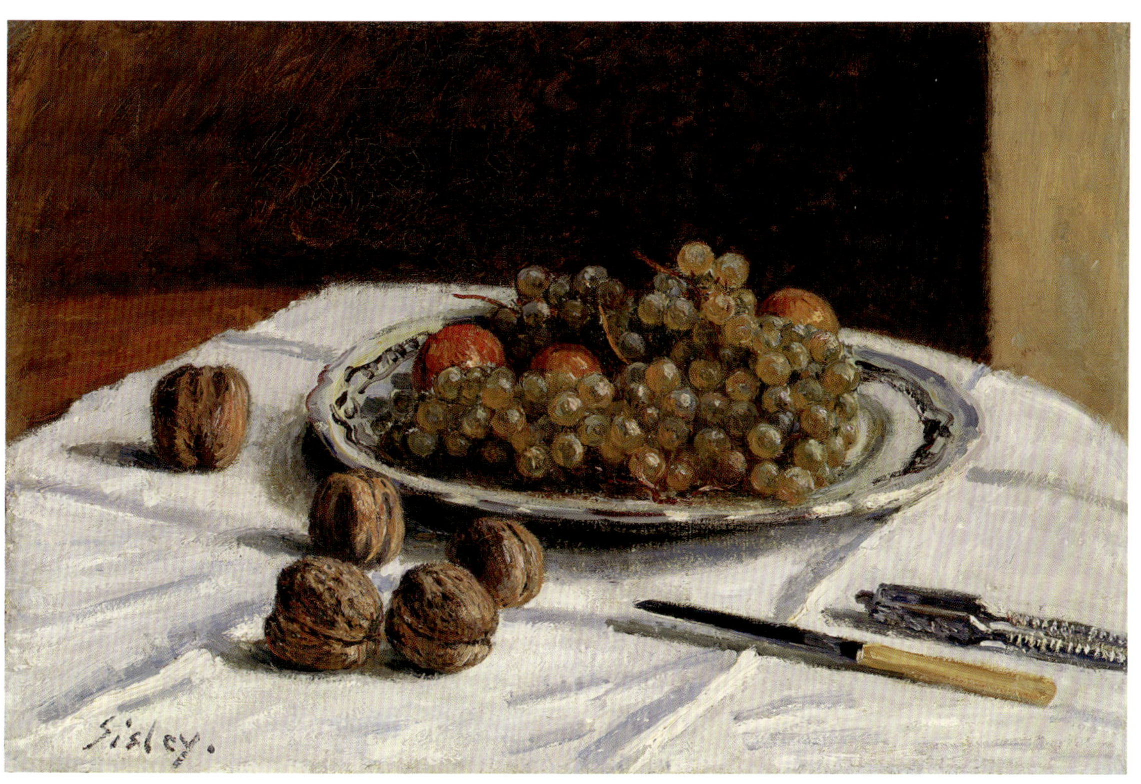

Gustave Caillebotte

French (1848–1894)

Fruit Displayed on a Stand, about 1881–82

The traditional setting for still life was domestic—either the kitchen table or the dining table—but with this painting Caillebotte signaled a change of venue from home to marketplace, from a realm of possession and satiety to one of display and desire. The produce displayed— strawberries, oranges, apples, pears, figs, grapes, and tomatoes— comes from different climates and seasons and reflects the development of hothouse agriculture and rapid rail transport in the late nineteenth century. These technologies could bring agricultural goods from near and far to the central market of Paris, Les Halles, where Caillebotte's fruits nestle in their white paper wrappings.

The Naturalist writer Émile Zola, an early supporter of the Impressionist movement, had taken Les Halles as the subject of his novel *The Belly of Paris* in 1873. With its bright strokes of unblended pigment and bold, geometric composition, Caillebotte's painting shares with Zola's book a frank, vivid approach to the business of food in the modern city. Another progressive writer, Joris-Karl Huysmans, admired the painting when it was first exhibited at the Impressionists' group show in 1882: "His fruits are extraordinary, set out against white paper beds. Juice pricks up under the peels of his pears, showing green and pink scars on their skin. A vapor darkens the seeds of his damp grapes." Huysmans compared the picture favorably with more conventional still lifes by painters like Fantin-Latour, characterized by "inflatable, impermeable fruit."

Oil on canvas

76.5 x 100.6 cm (30⅛ x 39⅝ in.)

Fanny P. Mason Fund in memory of Alice Thevin, 1979.196

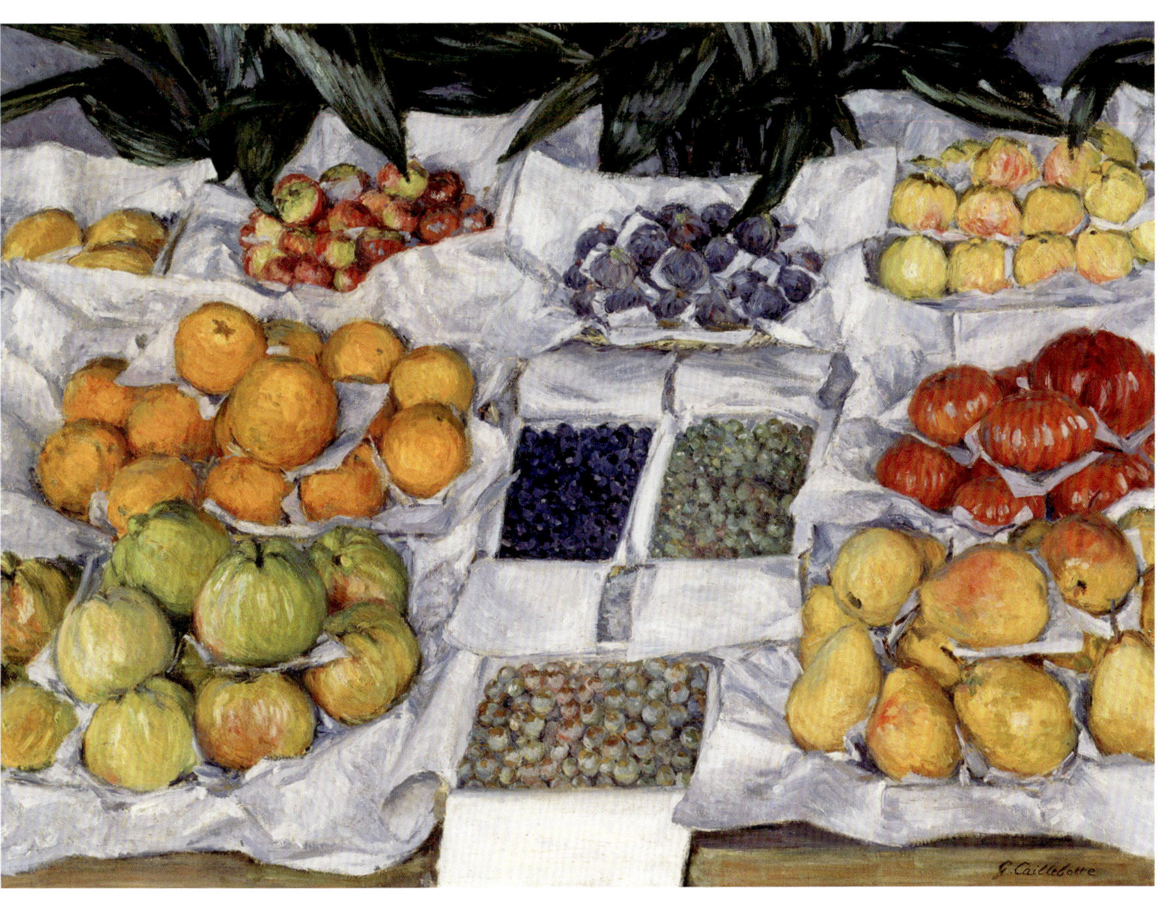
G. Caillebotte

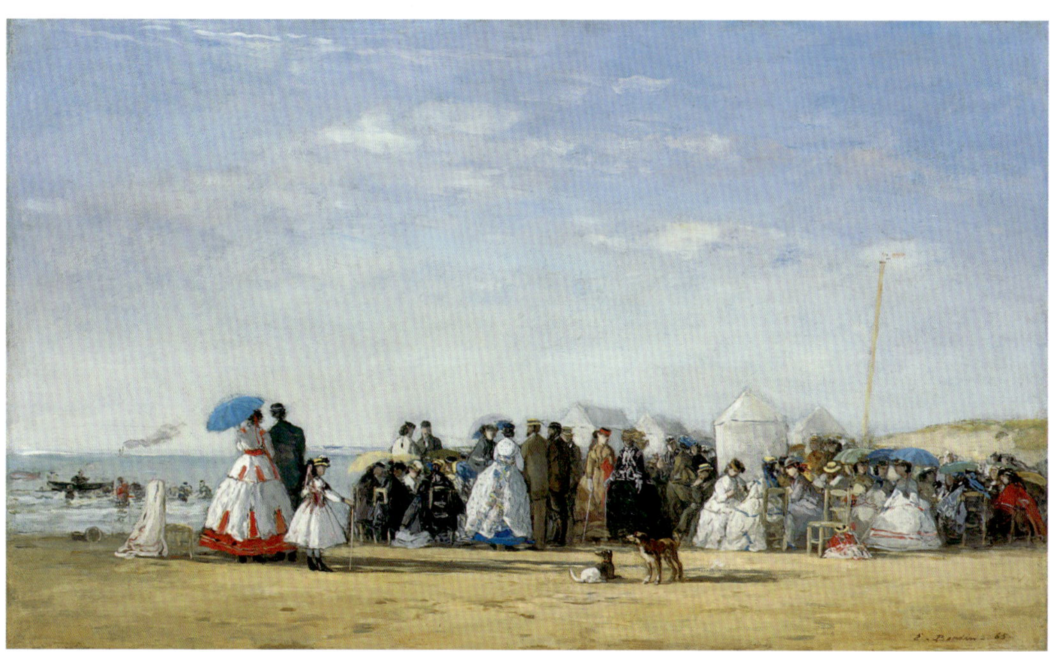

Eugène Louis Boudin
French, 1824–1898
Fashionable Figures on the Beach, 1865

The advent of train travel in the 1850s brought seaside holidays within reach for middle-class Parisians, who flocked to resort towns like Trouville, on the Normandy coast. Boudin began painting fashionable beachgoers in 1862 and found a steady market for airy, lighthearted pictures like this one. The scene is likely a weekday at the beach, where smartly dressed women and children predominate, their husbands and fathers presumably still in town on business. A stand of white bathing machines (modesty shelters used by nineteenth-century ladies to change clothes and wade into the water) gives this group the air of an elegant encampment, and such captivating details as the dogs at center and the little girl at left—a miniature lady in her hoop skirt and straw hat—add to its charm.

Though such pictures provided Boudin with a steady income, he confessed in a letter to a friend two years after he painted this scene, "This beach at Trouville that until recently delighted me, now . . . seems merely a ghastly masquerade. [When] one comes back to this band of gilded parasites who look so triumphant, one pities them a little, and also feels a certain shame at painting their idleness." Boudin's real interest in painting on the beach was to capture ephemeral effects of light and weather most pronounced at sea. He was among the earliest artists to work *en plein air* on the Normandy coast, and he encouraged the young Claude Monet to do the same.

Oil on canvas
35.5 x 57.5 cm (14 x 22⅝ in.)
Gift of Mr. and Mrs. John J. Wilson, 1974.565

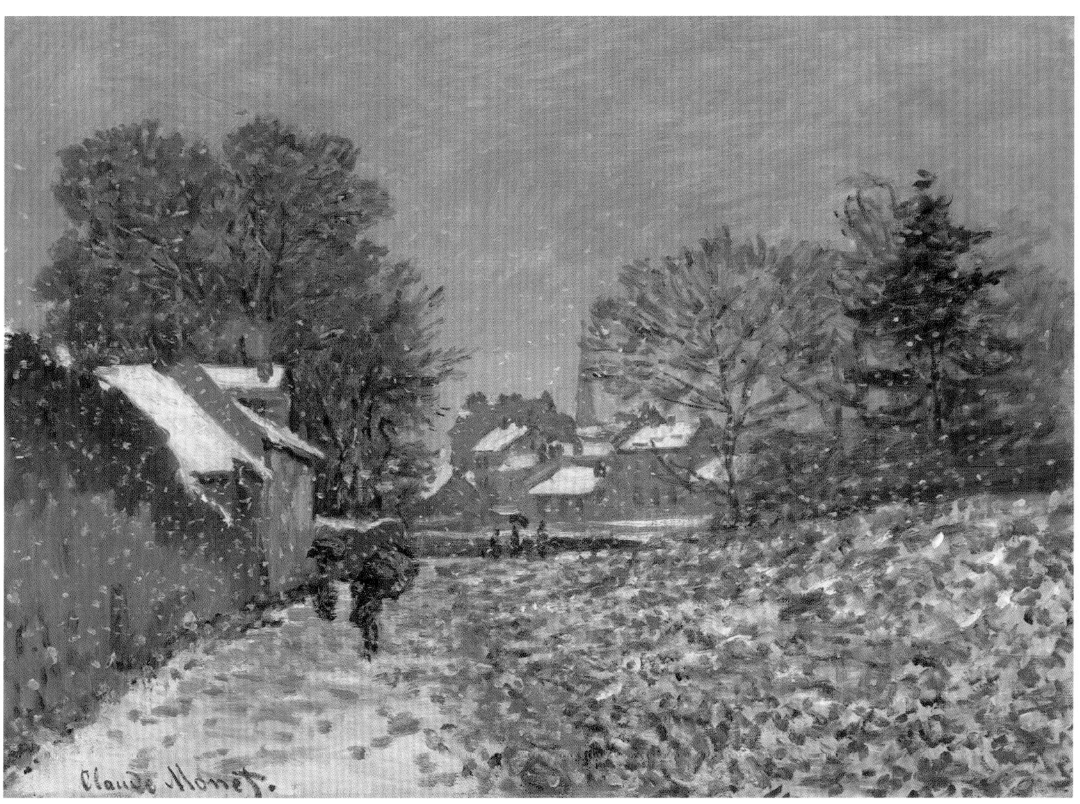

Claude Monet
French, 1840–1926
Snow at Argenteuil, about 1874

Monet sat out the tumult of the Franco-Prussian War and the Paris Commune in London. When he returned to France, Manet helped him find a house in Argenteuil, a village about ten miles north of Paris fast becoming a commuter suburb. There he remained for seven years, painting the town and the river Seine in a new style that would come to be known as Impressionism. His colors brightened. His brushwork loosened. Black virtually disappeared from his palette. He painted outdoors in all weather, working rapidly to capture fleeting effects of light and atmosphere. It was while living at Argenteuil, too, that Monet began buying Japanese woodblock prints in earnest, eventually amassing a large collection of work by Hokusai, Hiroshige, and Utamaro.

Likely inspired by the prints of Hiroshige, this scene of a road near Monet's house is unusual for its depiction of actual snowfall: a screen of drifting flakes, the twilight effect of a snowstorm. He probably began the composition outdoors, priming his canvas with pale gray (still visible between the darker strokes in the sky), and then painting the snowy roofs and bare trees with a more heavily laden brush.

Oil on canvas
54.6 x 73.7 cm (21½ x 29 in.)
Bequest of Anna Perkins Rogers, 21.1329

Alfred Sisley
British (active in France), 1839–1899
Waterworks at Marly, about 1876

Although born into a comfortably middle-class family, Sisley was forced to rely on his earnings as a painter after his father's unexpected death in 1870, a situation made the more difficult by the innovative—and often misunderstood—nature of his work. Sisley moved his young family frequently in the 1870s, always in search of inexpensive lodgings on the outskirts of Paris. From 1874 to 1877 the Sisleys lived in Marly-le-Roi, a small town a dozen miles northwest of Paris along the Seine.

It was at Marly that he painted this view of a pumping station, an engineering marvel built in the 1850s to draw water from the river to pleasure ponds at the Châteaux of Versailles and Marly. Bright foliage fills the right background, and a modern brick building at left houses the pump. A lone figure fishes off the dock in the middle distance, but the real subject of Sisley's picture is the river itself, which reflects the cloudy sky, the autumn leaves, the docks and waterworks on its glittering, uneven surface. To capture its ripples and reflections, Sisley employed the Impressionist technique he helped pioneer, laying down strokes of unblended color side by side.

Oil on canvas
46.5 x 61.8 cm (18¼ x 24⅜ in.)
Gift of Miss Olive Simes, 45.662

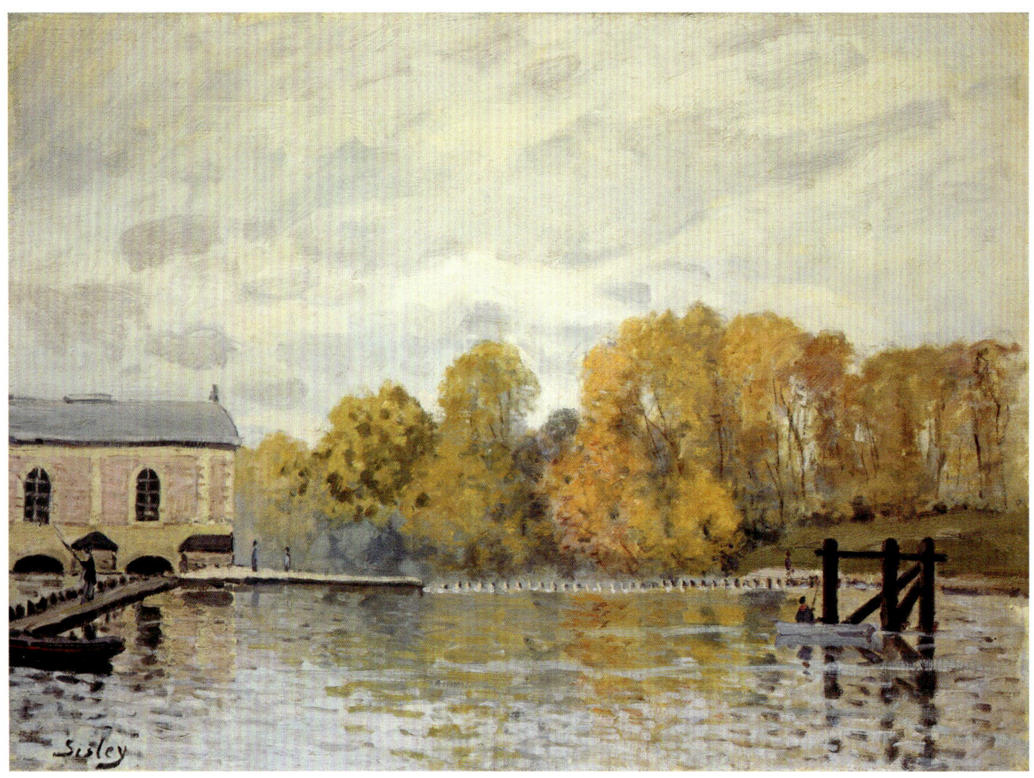

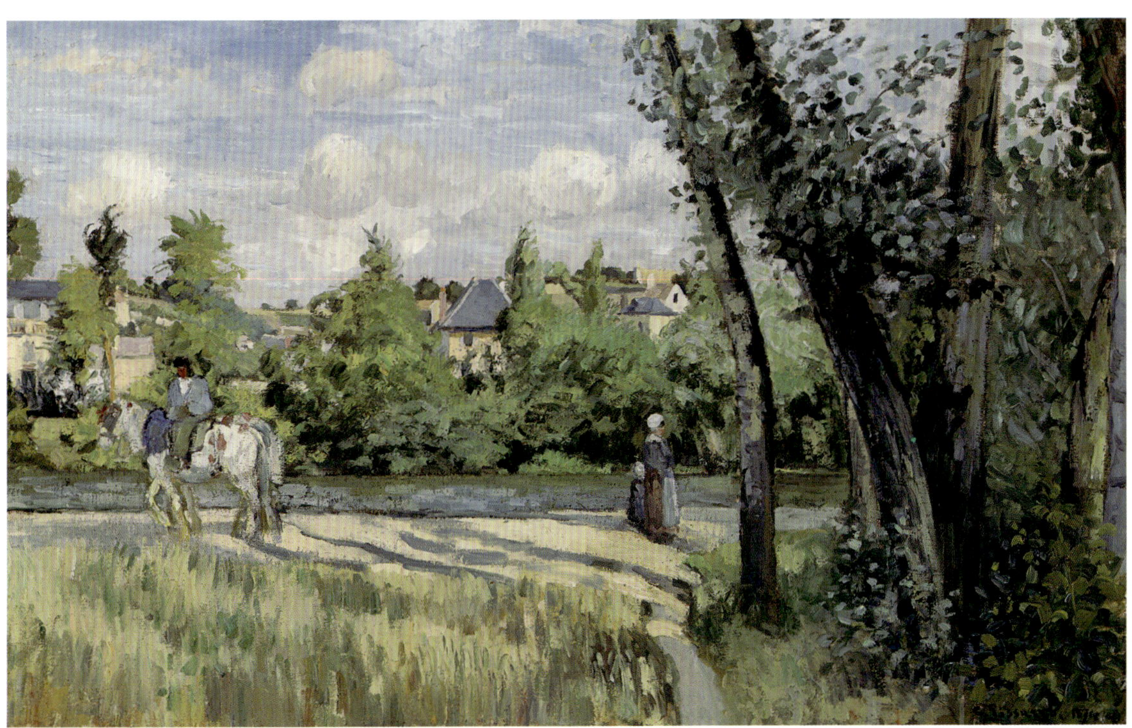

Camille Pissarro
French (born in the Danish West Indies), 1830–1903
Sunlight on the Road, Pontoise, 1874

Pissarro was the oldest member of the Impressionist circle and among its boldest innovators. He moved to Pontoise, a town on the Oise River some twenty miles from Paris, in 1872, initiating a period of close collaboration with the younger painter Paul Cézanne, who settled in the village that same year. Both artists worked outdoors, painting landscapes directly from nature in a range of cool, blonde colors. But while Cézanne increasingly explored the gap between three-dimensional space and its two-dimensional representation, Pissarro strove to open up his canvases to a natural world awash in light.

Unlike other Impressionist landscape painters, Pissarro retained an interest in the human figure throughout his career. Here a woman and child walk along the sunny riverbank, where a rider pauses with two horses, probably awaiting the arrival of a barge. The artist's treatment of these figures is as free and summary as that of the low clouds, fluttering leaves, and shadows on the path. All are elements of a landscape unified through Pissarro's deployment of horizontal zones—the sky, the far bank, the river, and the path—a compositional device that came to define his pictures from the Pontoise period.

Oil on canvas
52.4 x 81.6 cm (20 5/8 x 32 1/8 in.)
Juliana Cheney Edwards Collection, 25.114

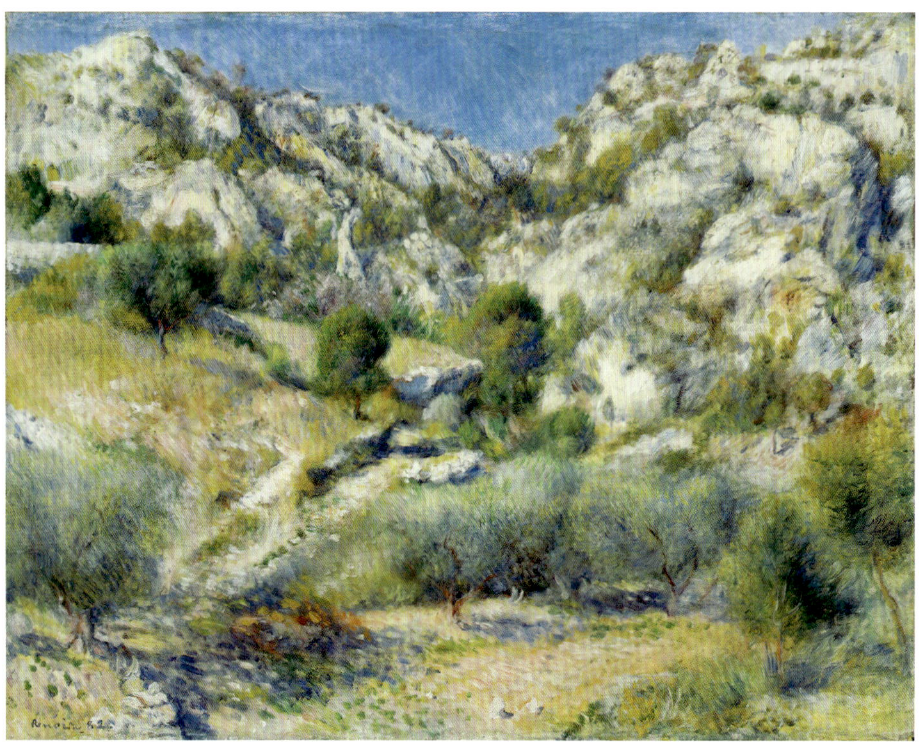

Pierre-Auguste Renoir
French, 1841–1919
Rocky Crags at L'Estaque, 1882

Under a sky of fierce, undifferentiated blue, a dirt path winds up into the hills, their rocky shoulders bare beneath scant vegetation. Olive trees cast feathery shadows in the foreground. The sun is bright. The earth is dry. We are in the South of France, outside the fishing village of L'Estaque, where Renoir set up his easel in January 1882.

A year earlier, the dealer Paul Durand-Ruel had begun buying Renoir's pictures in significant numbers, granting the artist a degree of financial stability that allowed him to travel for the first time in his life. He visited Italy that fall, where his mind was opened to Italian Renaissance painting. Passing through Provence on his return trip, he stopped at L'Estaque to visit Cézanne, who had worked there regularly since the 1860s, painting views of the town, the harbor, and their rugged environs.

The four pictures Renoir made at L'Estaque betray the depth of his admiration for Cézanne, whose work was not widely known or appreciated at the time, and whose somewhat severe, architectonic treatment of rock this painting emulates. Writing to a patron while at work on the landscape, Renoir declared, "I have ended up by not bothering anymore with small details."

Oil on canvas
66.4 x 81 cm (26 ⅛ x 31 ⅞ in.)
Juliana Cheney Edwards Collection, 39.678

Paul Cézanne
French, 1839–1906
Turn in the Road, about 1881

For a decade, from 1872 to 1882, Cézanne worked closely with Pissarro in and around the village of Pontoise. But compared with Pissarro's bright, populous scenes of towns along the Oise River, Cézanne's views of the same surroundings often have a chilly, uninhabited quality.

In this picture, which may represent the neighboring village of Valhermay, no humans are present. Save for three rectangular windows floating in the middle distance at right, the houses are virtually featureless, a tumble of geometric shapes. The road that sweeps through the foreground is fairly swallowed up by the landscape, vanishing into the grass and wall at the center of the composition. We are at once invited in and kept at arm's length. There is something forbidding in this scene.

Cézanne's struggle with fore- and background and his radical exploration of three-dimensional shapes—their perception and their representation—impart to the picture a cerebral quality. We sense it is less a window on the world than a window onto the artist's mind. Of the original Impressionist group, Cézanne was the most roundly dismissed by contemporary critics. He was a painter's painter, and his work was at first admired only by his colleagues. This landscape, for example, once belonged to Claude Monet.

Oil on canvas
60.6 x 73.3 cm (23⅞ x 28⅞ in.)
Bequest of John T. Spaulding, 48.525

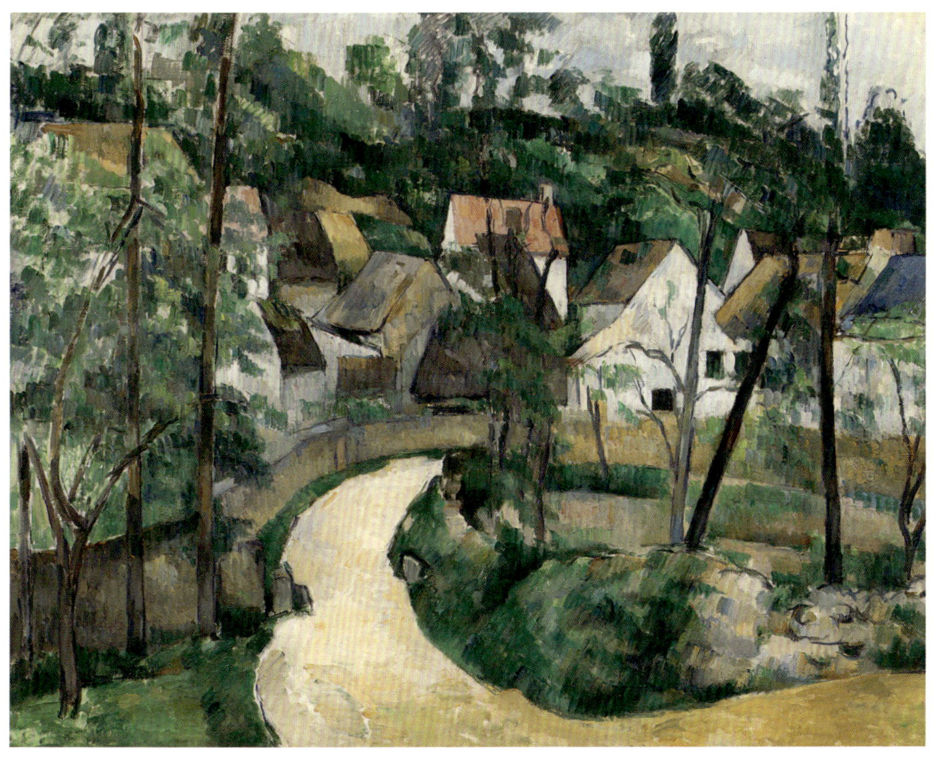

Edgar Degas
French, 1834–1917
The Duchesa di Montejasi with Her Daughters, Elena and Camilla, about 1876

Degas was a deeply private individual, and the portraits he painted of his family members are among his most private works. Never sold during his lifetime, some of them remained in his studio until his death; others, like this one of the formidable Stephanina Carafa, Marchesa di Cicerale, Duchesa di Montejasi—known to the artist as Aunt Fanny—were most likely given as gifts to their sitters. During the 1870s Degas seems to have spent considerable time with his aunt and her daughters at their elegant house on the Piazza d'Ovidio in Naples. He painted them on multiple occasions, capturing them here in black mourning weeds.

Degas was descended from a noble French family. He changed his name from the aristocratic "de Gas" to the more pedestrian "Degas" when he became a painter. Utterly distinct from the kind of formal portrait a hired artist might have painted of such an august sitter, this intensely personal portrayal of the artist's grieving, aging aunt is all the more poignant for its apparent deadpan. Isolated from her more lively daughters by an expanse of empty wall, the duchess appears profoundly alone. For all her outward composure—her folded hands and stiff pose—her eyes suggest a quiet depth of sorrow.

Oil on canvas
66 x 97.8 cm (26 x 38½ in.)

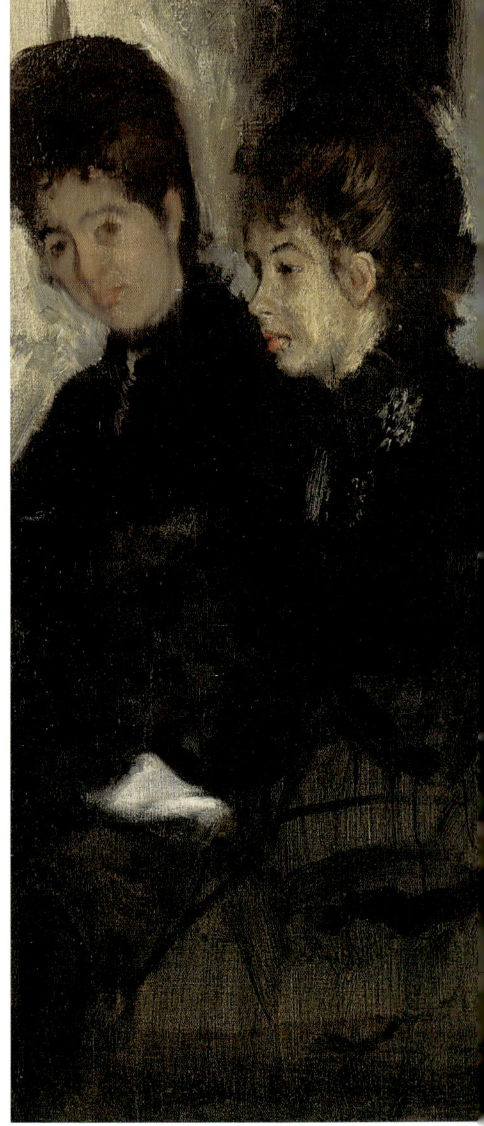

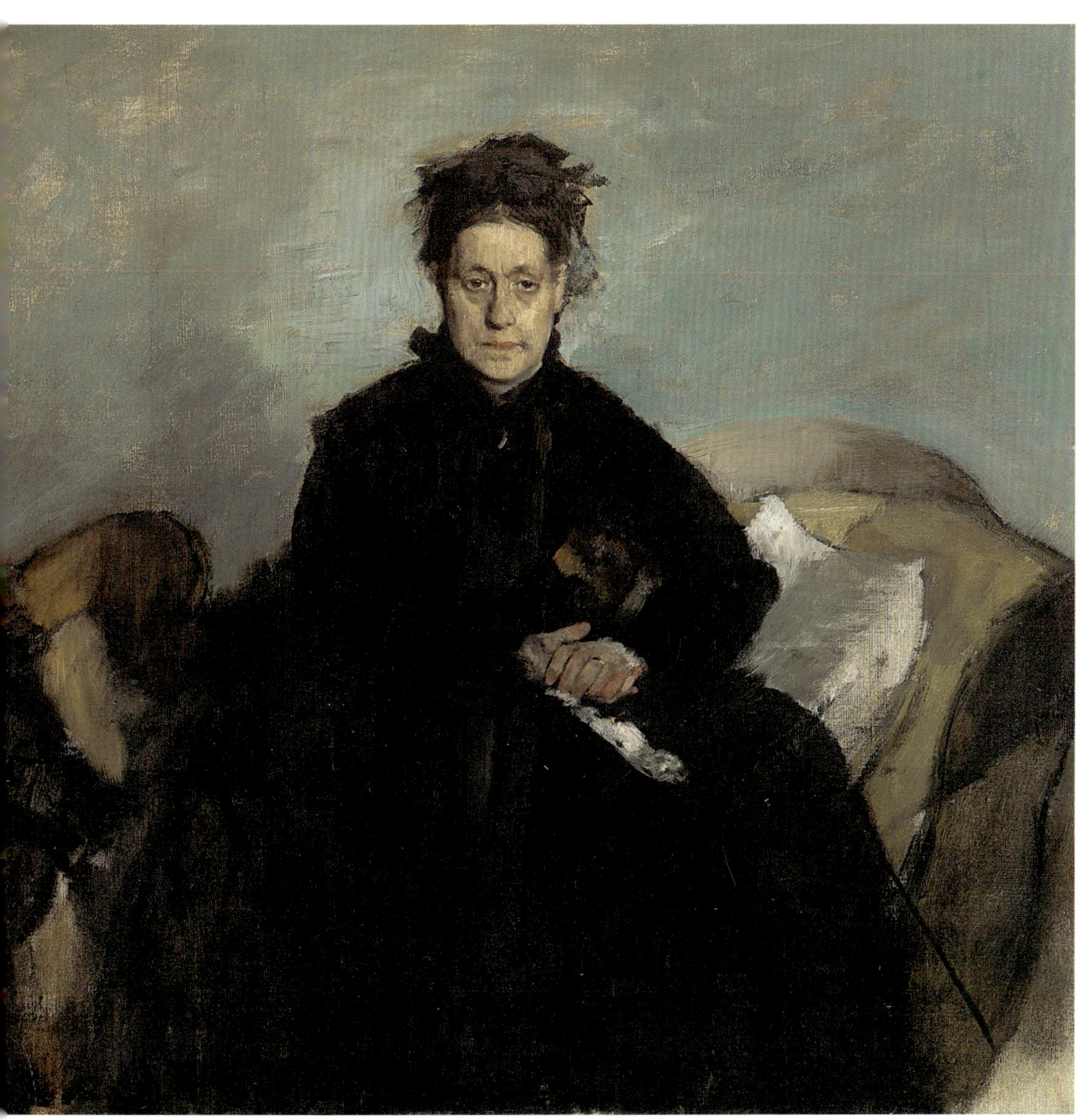

Museum purchase with funds by exchange from the Tompkins Collection—Arthur Gordon Tompkins Fund, a Gift of Mrs. Robert B. Osgood in memory of Horace D. Chapin, and a Gift in memory of Governor Alvan T. Fuller by the Fuller Foundation; and from the Charles H. Bayley Picture and Painting Fund, William Francis Warden Fund, Frank B. Bemis Fund, James E. Neill Memorial Fund, Fanny P. Mason Fund in memory of Alice Thevin, Mary S. and Edward Jackson Holmes Fund, Tompkins Collection—Arthur Gordon Tompkins Fund, Ernest Wadsworth Longfellow Fund, Frederick L. Jack Fund, Seth K. Sweetser Fund, M. Theresa B. Hopkins Fund, Harriet Otis Cruft Fund, Gift of Jessie H. Wilkinson—Jessie H. Wilkinson Fund, Lucy Dalbiac Luard Fund, Grant Walker Fund, Helen B. Sweeney Fund, and European Paintings Deaccession Fund, 2003.250

Pierre-Auguste Renoir
French, 1841–1919
Woman with a Parasol and a Small Child on a Sunlit Hillside, about 1874–76

As young men, Monet and Renoir were close friends. They painted together at sites along the Seine—Bougival in 1869 and Argenteuil in 1873 and 1874—evolving a new vocabulary for the depiction of light, air, and the out-of-doors. In the early pictures they painted together we see for the first time the juxtaposed strokes of unblended color that became a hallmark of the Impressionist style. With its breathless flutter of brushstrokes, its colored shadows and sense of instantaneity, this small canvas is a superb example of that style.

Seated on a hillside, her white dress dappled with pink and blue in the shade, Renoir's model for this painting was likely Camille Monet, wife of his friend and colleague. The steadiness of her gaze and grace of her pose stand in marked contrast to the toddler (too young to be Monet's son, Jean), who wanders off into the background at right. Madame Monet posed for Renoir on several occasions between 1874 and 1876, generally in informal, familial settings, like this one, that testify to the two artists' friendship.

Oil on canvas
47 x 56.2 cm (18½ x 22⅛ in.)
Bequest of John T. Spaulding, 48.593

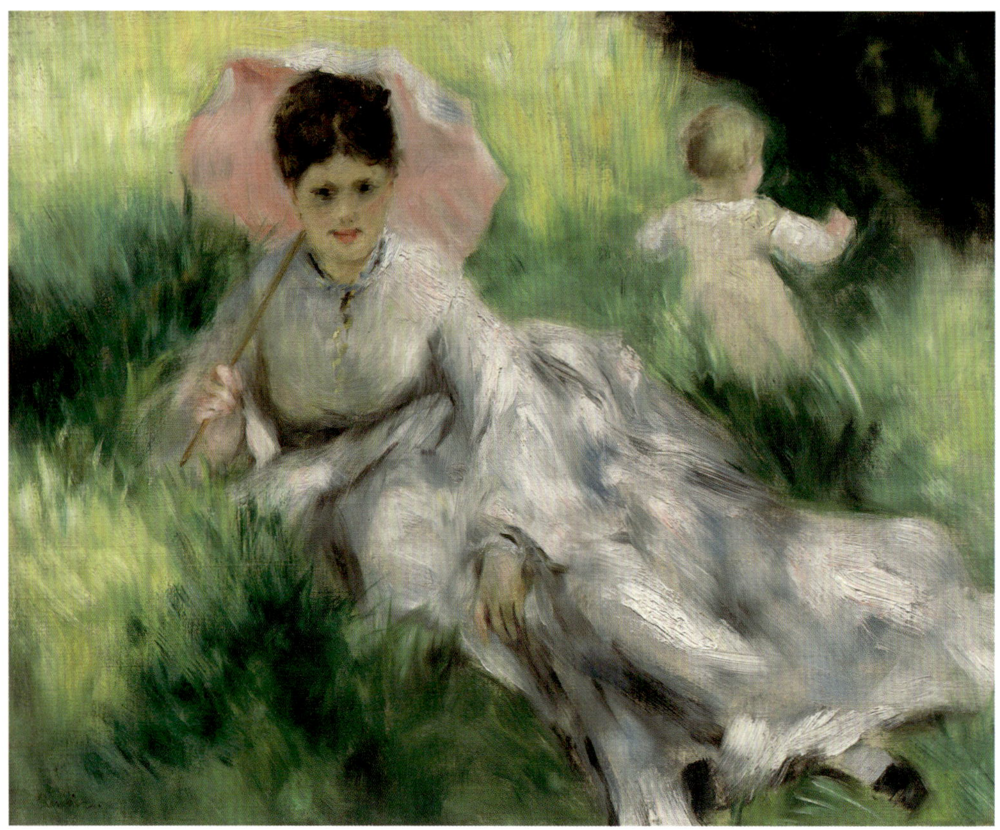

Pierre-Auguste Renoir
French, 1841–1919
Dance at Bougival, 1883

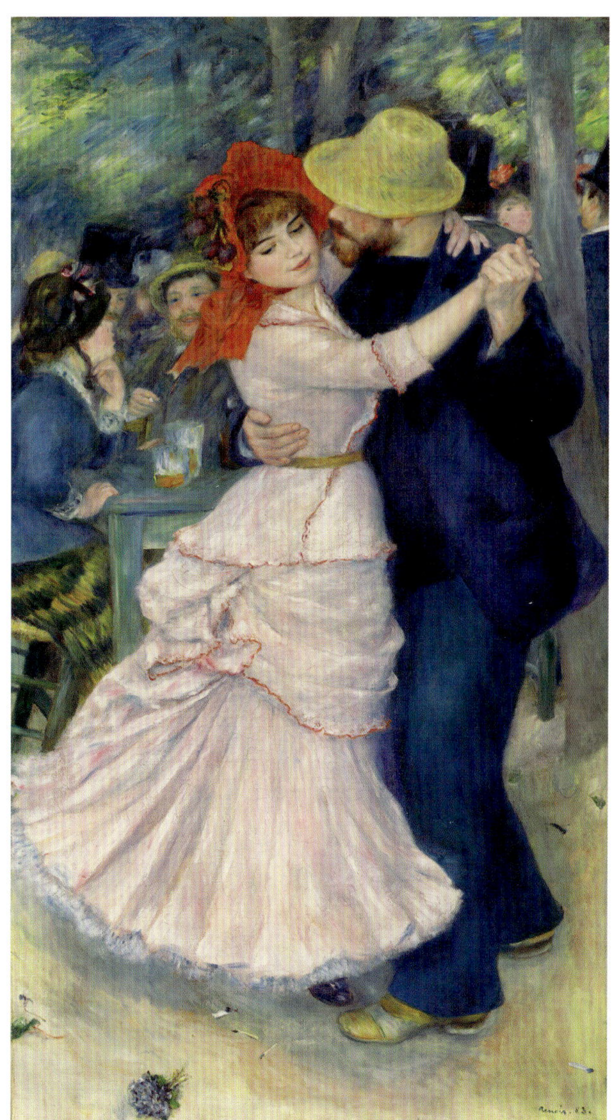

In the 1870s and 1880s city dwellers flocked to Bougival, a Parisian suburb on the Seine, for weekend entertainment. Amid the clink of glasses, the scraping of chairs, the murmur of conversation and laughter, two dancers seem to hear only the tune of a waltz that sweeps them around an outdoor café.

The young woman wears holiday clothes, an airy *toilette de campagne* (country outfit) of the latest style. Her partner's clothes suggest that he is ready for an afternoon's boating. Their costumes are rendered by Renoir, a dressmaker's son, with special care, while the trees behind them—and even their fellow patrons—are reduced to a blur of blue and green, a whirl of broadly applied strokes. Although our dancers are the two most mobile figures in the scene, they also mark its still center. For the couple, Renoir adopted a more solid and deliberate manner—a departure from his high Impressionist style—that sets the dancers apart, inviting us to identify with the rapt intimacy of their embrace. The touch of their gloveless hands and the flush in the girl's cheek suggest an amorous subtext to this suburban idyll.

This picture marked a turning point in its author's career. An 1881 trip to Italy, where Renoir discovered the work of Raphael and other Italian Renaissance masters, had engendered a new desire to recapture, in his own words, "the grandeur and simplicity of the old painters." Renoir began to drift away from the feathery brushstrokes and dappled blue light of Impressionism toward the sculptural solidity and classical spirit that characterize his later work. Suspended between the 1870s and the 1880s, between the young Renoir's enchantment with ephemerality, fashion, and the pleasures of modern life and the mature artist's quest for a more timeless kind of beauty, this most ardent of Renoir's paintings may be his masterpiece.

Oil on canvas
181.9 x 98.1 cm (71 5/8 x 38 5/8 in.)
Picture Fund, 37.375

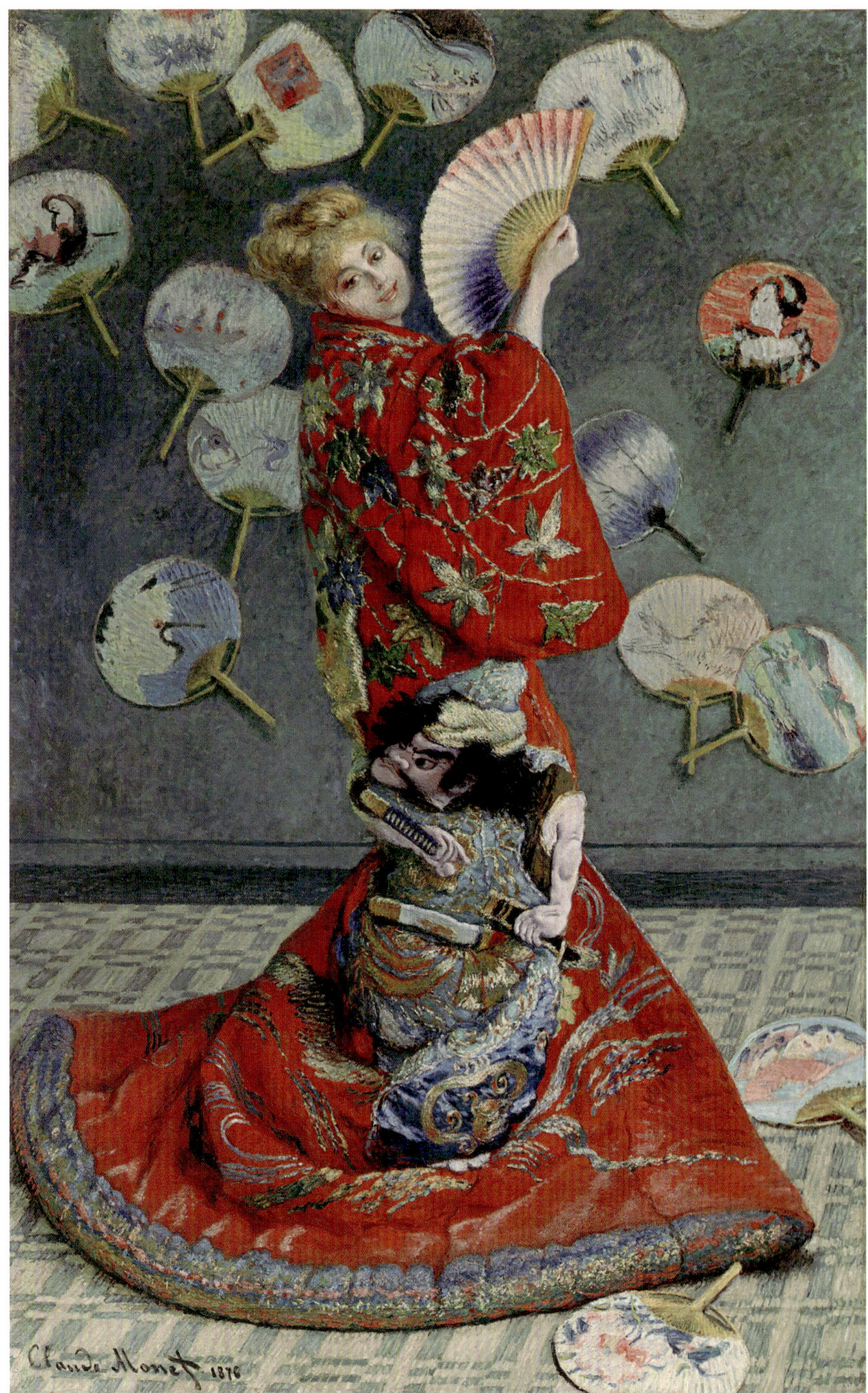
Claude Monet 1876

Claude Monet
French, 1840–1926
La Japonaise (Camille Monet in Japanese Costume), 1876

In a room papered with fans, a young woman poses in Japanese costume. Blonde hair identifies her—despite the painting's title—as a Westerner, and the smiling tilt of her head confers a playful tone to this scene of dress-up. The artist seems to have taken less care with the figure than with the robe itself—thickly embroidered, with golden green leaves spreading across the shoulders and a fierce, mustachioed swordsman crouching above the hem. "The red of the dress," one critic remarked when Monet first showed the picture at the Impressionists' 1876 exhibition, "constitutes the picture's true subject."

It is a painting about color, certainly, but it is also a picture in some way about the fashion for things Japanese that had engulfed Paris by the 1870s. Following the opening of Japan's ports to Western trade in 1854, Japanese textiles, porcelain, and other luxury goods flooded the European market, along with distinctive, brightly colored woodblock prints depicting everyday life in Japan. An early and prolific collector of these prints, Monet conveyed his admiration for them in this painting, but he also betrayed an awareness of the rising French fashion for suggestive pictures of European models in Japanese dress. By the mid-1870s such paintings had become a staple of the Salon, and it is possible that Monet, deeply in debt at the time, chose this subject in hopes of attracting a rich buyer.

His model for the painting was his wife, Camille; Monet at once concealed her identity and emphasized her Frenchness by covering up her naturally dark hair with a blonde wig. The result is both a straightforward image of the quintessential *parisienne* (Parisian woman) in stylish Japanese dress and a sly reflection on the phenomenon of *japonisme* itself. The painting was generally savaged in the press. One critic called it "a Chinese in a red robe with two heads: one of a demimondaine on its shoulders, and another of a monster placed—we dare not say where." The relationship between the languid blonde and the dynamic samurai—his eyes seemingly glued to her posterior—disturbed many early viewers, marking, as it did, a sexually charged encounter between East and West.

Oil on canvas
231.8 x 142.3 cm (91¼ x 56 in.)
1951 Purchase Fund, 56.147

James Jacques Joseph Tissot
French (1836–1902)
Women of Paris: The Circus Lover, 1885

This picture belongs to a series by Tissot celebrating glamorous *parisiennes: La Femme à Paris (Women of Paris)*. He exhibited fifteen canvases from the series in 1885, intending them as the basis for engraved illustrations to a collection of short stories he would commission from Naturalist writers including Guy de Maupassant, Émile Zola, and Charles Yriarte. Though the literary project was never realized, each painting captures the allure and complexity of fashionable life in the city.

This painting plants us in the audience of a circus, but it is no ordinary circus. The crowd is dressed in top hats, frock coats, and bright silks of the latest fashion. Indeed, one acrobat, perched on his trapeze, sports a monocle, the glinting affectation of a society dandy. We are at the Cirque Molier, an amateur performance venue, where men of aristocratic birth and exhibitionistic inclination put on a show for mixed audiences twice a week: once for high society and once for the demimonde (actresses, courtesans, and their companions).

But which day is this? Have the women pictured come to watch their aristocratic friends and family members perform? Or to find new lovers? The ladies' elegant attire could identify them as either aristocrats or courtesans. A spectator in pink looks boldly out at us—in recognition or cold appraisal? The ambiguity of Tissot's painting turns on the perverse democracy of fashion in late nineteenth-century Paris, which led one critic of the painting to remark, "A woman should be judged from her shoes to her hat . . . just as one would measure a fish between its tail and its head."

Oil on canvas
147.3 x 101.6 cm (58 x 40 in.)
Juliana Cheney Edwards Collection, 58.45

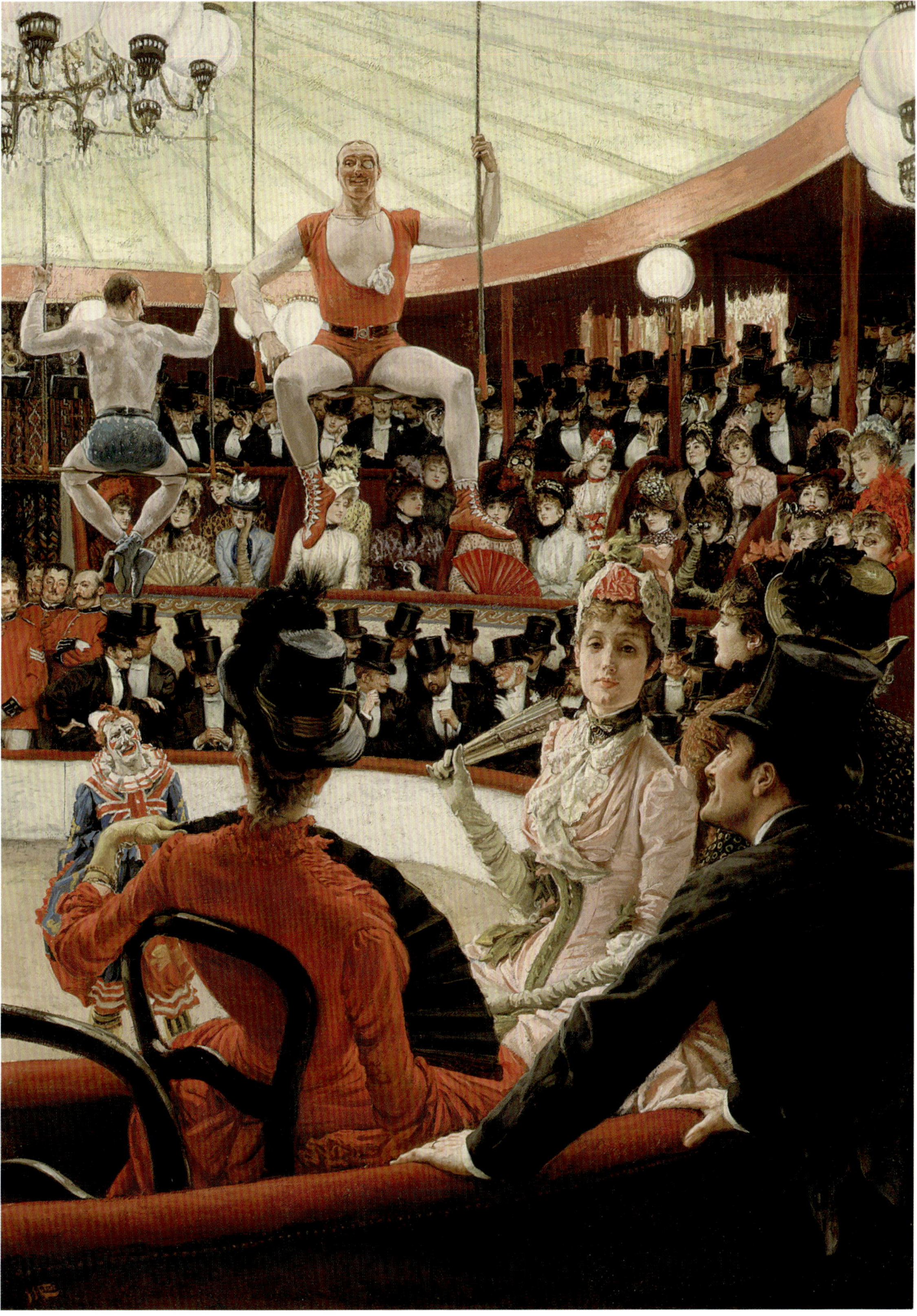

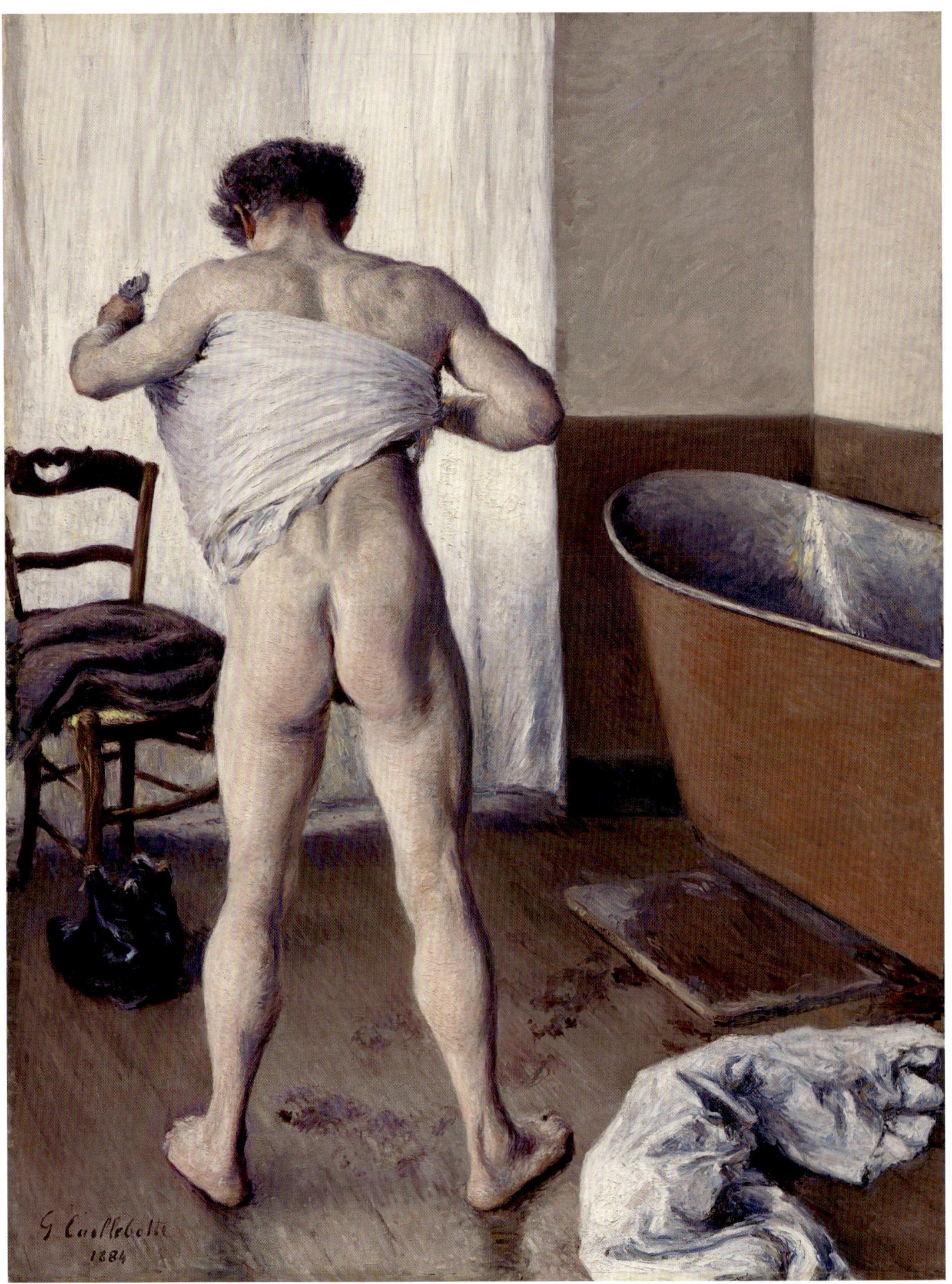
G. Caillebotte
1884

Gustave Caillebotte
French (1848–1894)
Man at His Bath, 1884

An influential member of the Impressionist circle, Caillebotte is best known for his scenes of modern Parisians at home or on the street. Painted at the grand scale of a history picture, this daring composition confronts its viewer with one such scene: a man drying himself after his bath. The tin tub and discarded nightshirt at right, the wet footprints on the parquet, the neatly folded clothing and polished boots make this man less nude in the classical sense than naked: bare, exposed, even—despite his thickly muscled body—somehow vulnerable.

So intimate an image of an unclothed man is rare in Western art of any age and certainly rare in nineteenth-century painting. The closest equivalents may be found in the work of Degas. Caillebotte's personal collection included several pictures by this artist, including two of female bathers in modern interiors. For his own composition, Caillebotte clearly drew inspiration from these works, but this painting's ambitious scale, its lilac-tinged palette, and fluid, dynamic paint application are the artist's own.

Oil on canvas
144.8 x 114.3 cm (57 x 45 in.)
Museum purchase with funds by exchange from an Anonymous gift, Bequest of William A. Coolidge, Juliana Cheney Edwards Collection, and from the Charles H. Bayley Picture and Painting Fund, Edward Jackson Holmes Fund, Fanny P. Mason Fund in memory of Alice Thevin, Arthur Gordon Tompkins Fund, Gift of Mrs. Samuel Parkman Oliver–Eliza R. Oliver Fund, Sophie F. Friedman Fund, Robert M. Rosenberg Family Fund, and funds donated in honor of George T. M. Shackelford, Chair, Art of Europe, and Arthur K. Solomon Curator of Modern Art, 1996–2011, 2011.231

Edgar Degas
French, 1834–1917
***Little Fourteen-Year-Old Dancer*,**
original model 1878–81, cast after 1921

Caught in a moment of repose, perhaps stretching out her upper back and shoulders, and with her eyes nearly closed, the *Little Dancer* was the only sculpture that Degas exhibited. The original wax version of this sculpture, a portrait of a young Belgian dancer named Marie van Goethem, was presented at the 1881 Impressionist exhibition. The wax was tinted to resemble flesh, the dancer wore a hair wig, and she was dressed in pink slippers and bodice in addition to a skirt and ribbon similar to those seen here, all contributing to a realism unusual in sculpture of the time. Degas chose to exhibit the figure in a glass exhibit case resembling those at the Louvre or in a natural history museum. By doing so he controlled people's approach to the sculpture, implying that this was more a museum object than a little girl. The extreme realism of the "little rat," as the youngest dancers were called, shocked and offended many visitors to the exhibition. Some critics recognized the originality of Degas's approach, including Joris-Karl Huysmans, who called it "the only really modern attempt that I know in sculpture." Bronzes taken from the wax model were produced after the artist's death and furnished with skirt and ribbon; the accessories on this version are modern replacements. At least twenty-eight casts are known today.

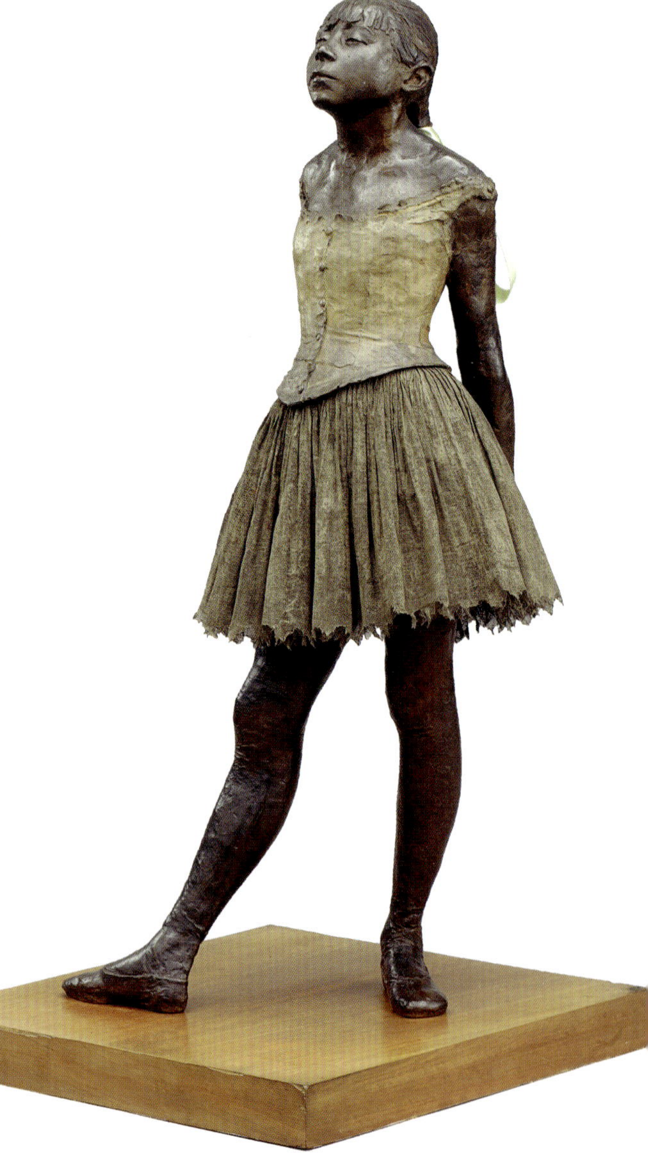

Bronze, gauze and satin
Height including base: 103.7 cm (40⅞ in.)
Frederick Brown Fund and Contributions from William Claflin and William Emerson, 38.1756

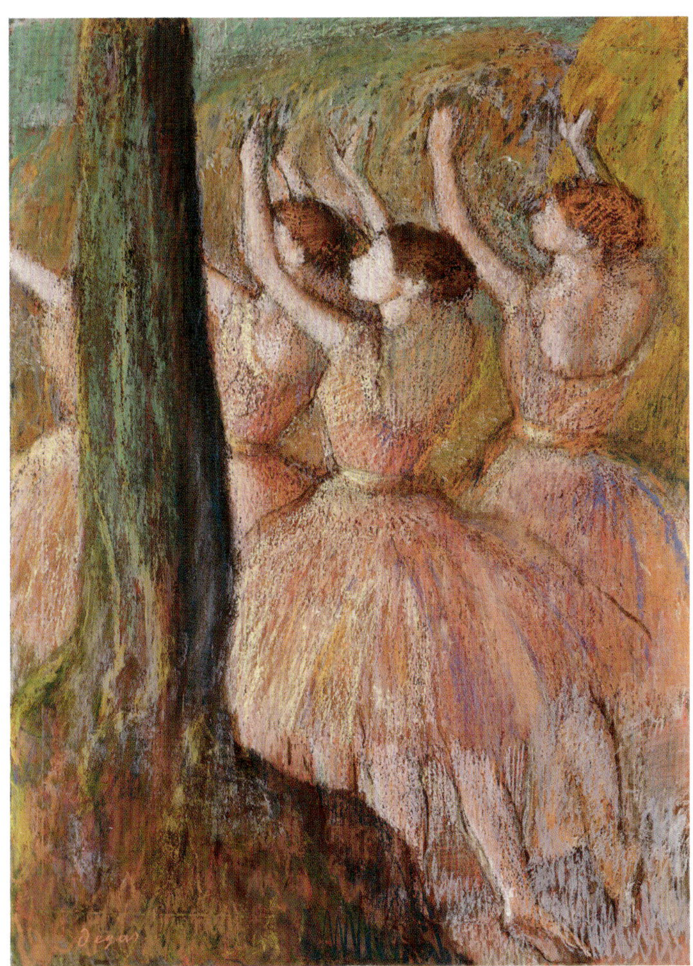

Edgar Degas
French, 1834–1917
Dancers in Rose, about 1900

Degas was the most daring and accomplished pastellist of the nineteenth century. Stumping, wetting, and layering this delicate medium, he created veils and clouds of color deployed to particularly magical effect in his portrayals of the ballet. This late work provides a glimpse from backstage of *corps de ballet* dancers dressed in pink. Powdery pastels evoke the theatrical lighting, melting stiff tulle to a warm glow and bathing the dancers' exposed arms and faces in a kind of artificial moonlight. But the abrupt silhouette of a tree in the foreground disrupts the vision. It is two-dimensional, a piece of scenery, whose very flatness reminds us that the image we see is itself flat, twice fictional: a piece of stagecraft conjured on a piece of paper.

Pastel on paper
84.1 x 58.1 cm (33 1/8 x 22 7/8 in.)
Seth K. Sweetser Fund, 20.164

Claude Monet
French, 1840–1926
Grainstack (Snow Effect), 1891
Oil on canvas
65.4 x 92.4 cm (25¾ x 36⅜ in.)
Gift of Miss Aimée and Miss Rosamond Lamb in memory of Mr. and Mrs. Horatio Appleton Lamb, 1970.253

Grainstack (Sunset), 1891
Oil on canvas
73.3 x 92.7 cm (28⅞ x 36½ in.)
Juliana Cheney Edwards Collection, 25.112

From 1890 to 1891 Monet painted the first of his monumental series, a group of pictures representing wheat stacks in the fields near his home at Giverny under changing conditions of light and weather. Since the Middle Ages, grain had been harvested in early summer and stacked for storage and consumption through the winter. In medieval French manuscript illuminations and architectural decorations portraying the Labors of the Months, June was often represented by the raking of grain into stacks. Monet's series—with its emphasis on the changing seasons and its focus on the humble wheat stack—clearly relates to an older tradition, yet all evidence

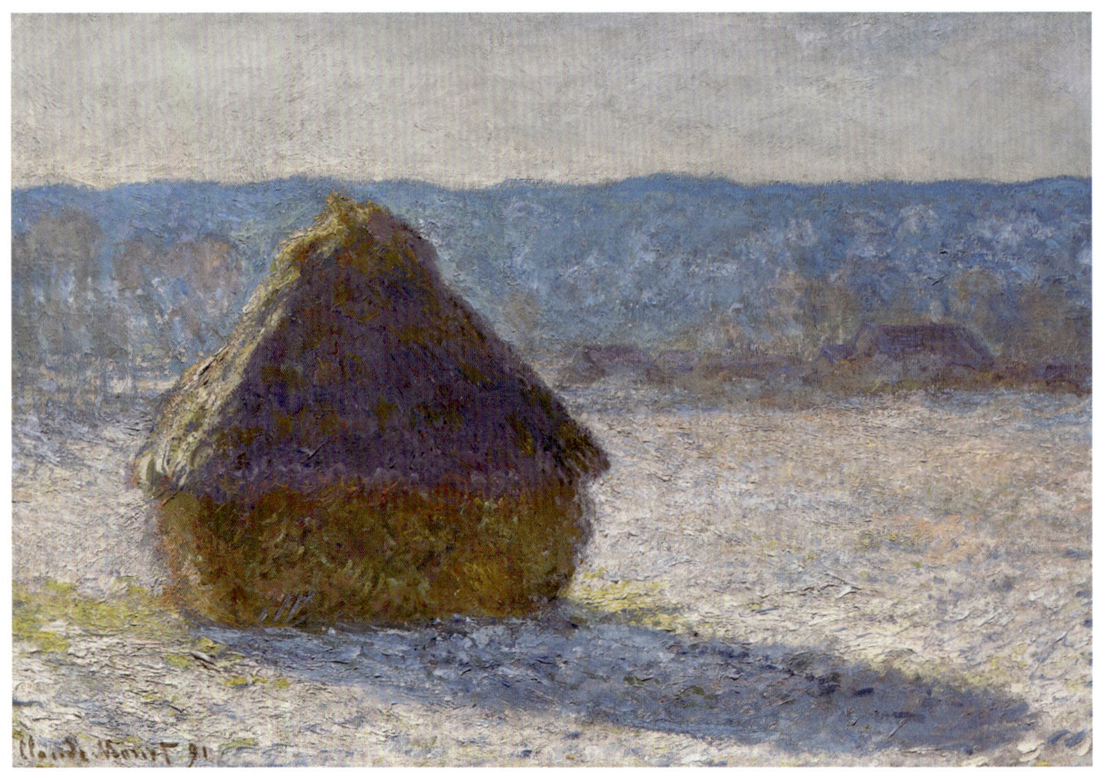

of labor—except, of course, for the artist's own—is absent from these paintings, which focus instead on light, color, and atmosphere. Monet exhibited fifteen pictures from the series at the gallery of his dealer, Paul Durand-Ruel, in May 1891 to critical acclaim and commercial success. Both of these *Grainstacks* figured in the exhibition.

Some scholars have proposed that Monet selected this particular subject to paint over and over because of its cultural resonance. As a common feature of the landscape in rural Normandy, grainstacks stood for the fertility of the soil, the prosperity of the region, even, indeed, for the agricultural basis of French national identity. Monet's interest in these humble, inert forms, however, also reflected the more personal, strictly formal concerns that occupied him in the final decade of the nineteenth century. In the end, these pictures are perhaps less about the objects they portray than about the process of portraying them. With their thickly impasted surfaces and extraordinarily free brushwork, these paintings call attention to their own heroic creation, encouraging us to think of Monet at work, out in the fields all day and all year, brush in hand and eye on nature. They are, in some way, paintings about painting.

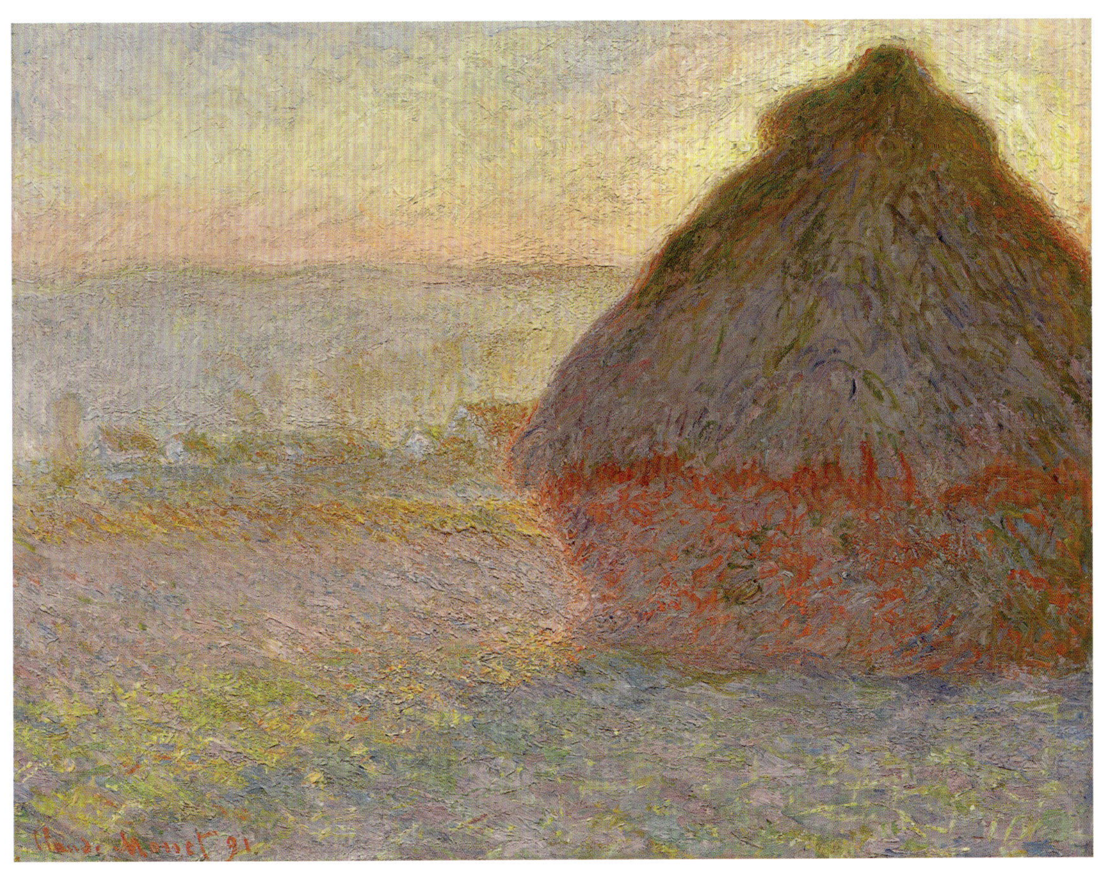

Camille Pissarro

French (born in the Danish West Indies), 1830–1903

Morning Sunlight on the Snow, Éragny-sur-Epte, 1895

A peasant woman trudges through the snow, her back to the viewer, her arms taut with the weight of two buckets. The picture combines Pissarro's sympathy for rural labor with his interest in winter landscapes, to whose infinitely varied shades of white—from pearl pink to ice blue—he returned again and again throughout his career. The extraordinarily lively, three-dimensional painted surface of this picture betrays Pissarro's debt to Monet. This debt was both literal and figurative at the time, since Monet had provided his old friend with a loan that enabled him to relocate in 1884 from the increasingly industrialized Paris suburb of Pontoise to the tiny village of Éragny-sur-Epte, thirty miles to the northwest.

Éragny was to Pissarro what Giverny was to Monet, the place where he spent the last decades of his life painting his immediate surroundings. With eyes increasingly irritated by wind and weather, the aging artist converted the barn on his property into a studio, furnished with a window, through which he could look, working directly from nature but protected from the elements. It was most likely from his barn studio that Pissarro painted these bare trees and this woman in the snow.

Oil on canvas

82.3 x 61.6 cm (32 3/8 x 24 1/4 in.)

The John Pickering Lyman Collection—Gift of Miss Theodora Lyman, 19.1321

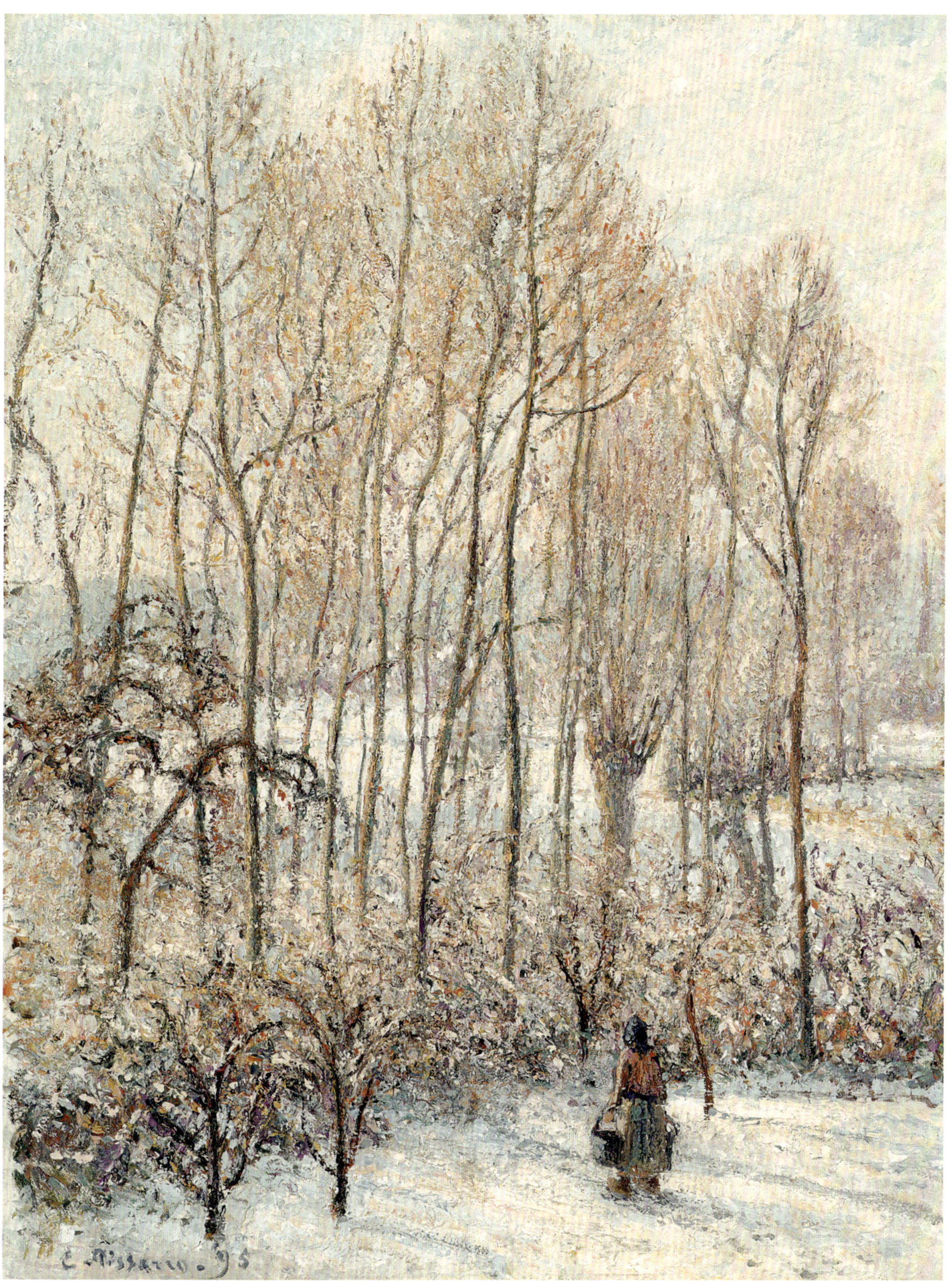

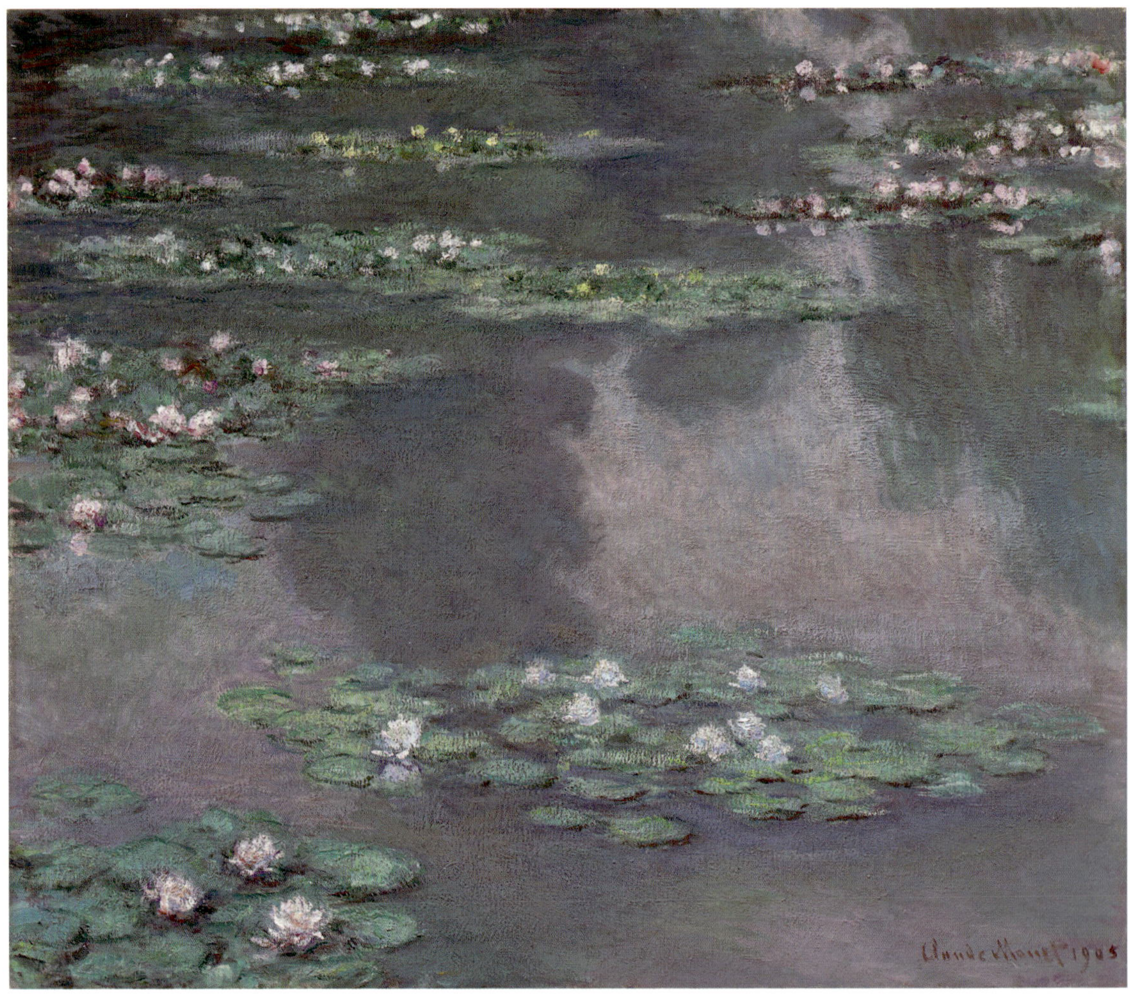

Claude Monet
French, 1840–1926
Water Lilies, 1905
Oil on canvas
89.5 x 100.3 cm (35¼ x 39½ in.)
Gift of Edward Jackson Holmes, 39.804

Water Lilies, 1907
Oil on canvas
96.8 x 98.4 cm (38⅛ x 38¾ in.)
Bequest of Alexander Cochrane, 19.170

In 1883 Monet moved to the village of Giverny, in Normandy; he bought a house there seven years later. After ripping out the vegetable garden to plant flower beds, he bought an additional plot of land across the road, a patch of swamp that would become his celebrated water garden, the focus of his artistic energies through the final decades of his career. This new garden was modeled on those portrayed in the Japanese prints that Monet collected. It featured an arched footbridge, gingko trees, and the famous water lily pond.

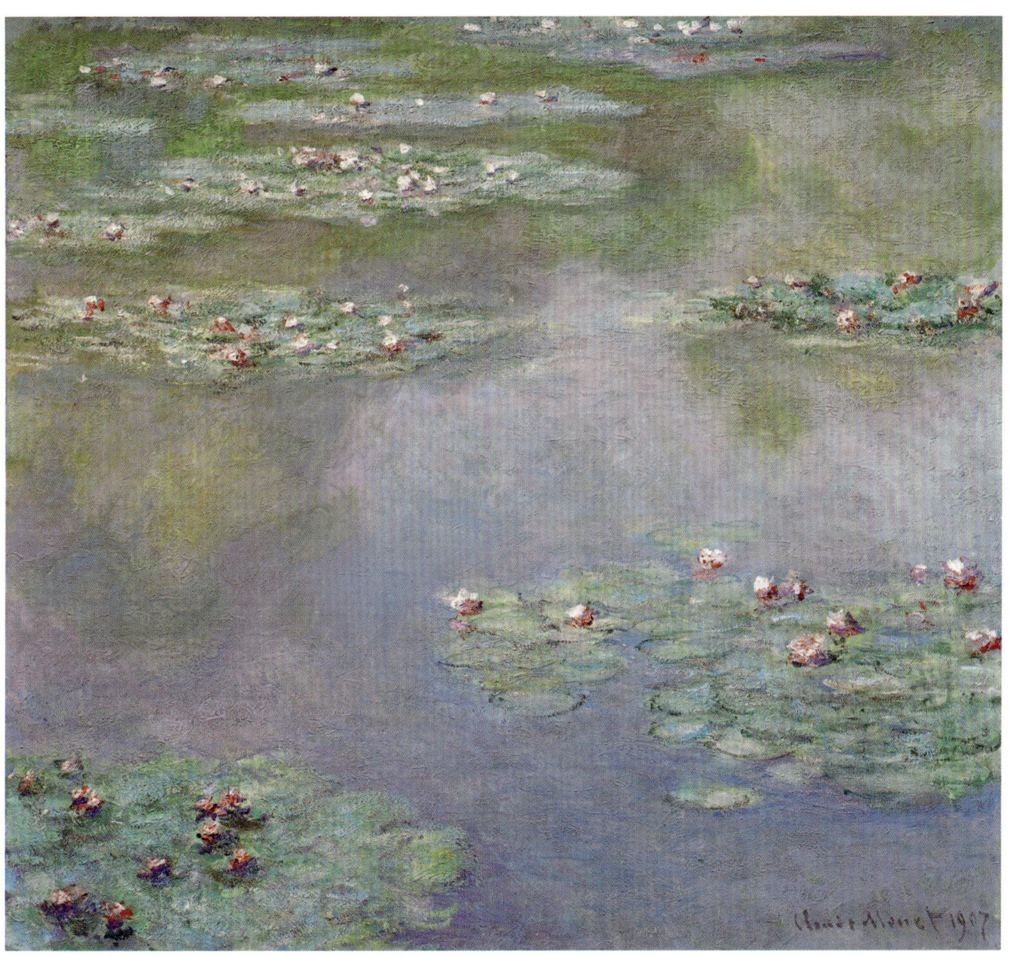

The first views he painted of the garden focused on the bridge and took in trees and reeds along the water's edge, but the artist soon cut his compositions adrift, focusing on the surface of the pond—its floating flowers and endless play of reflections. When Monet exhibited forty-eight pictures from the series at Durand-Ruel's gallery in 1909, one critic effused, "the water invades the entire canvas, becoming the fluid field upon which the mysterious blossoms of the water lilies open out.... His vision increasingly is simplifying itself, limiting itself to the minimum of tangible realities in order to amplify, to magnify ... the impression of the imponderable." Both of these "water landscapes" appeared in the exhibition.

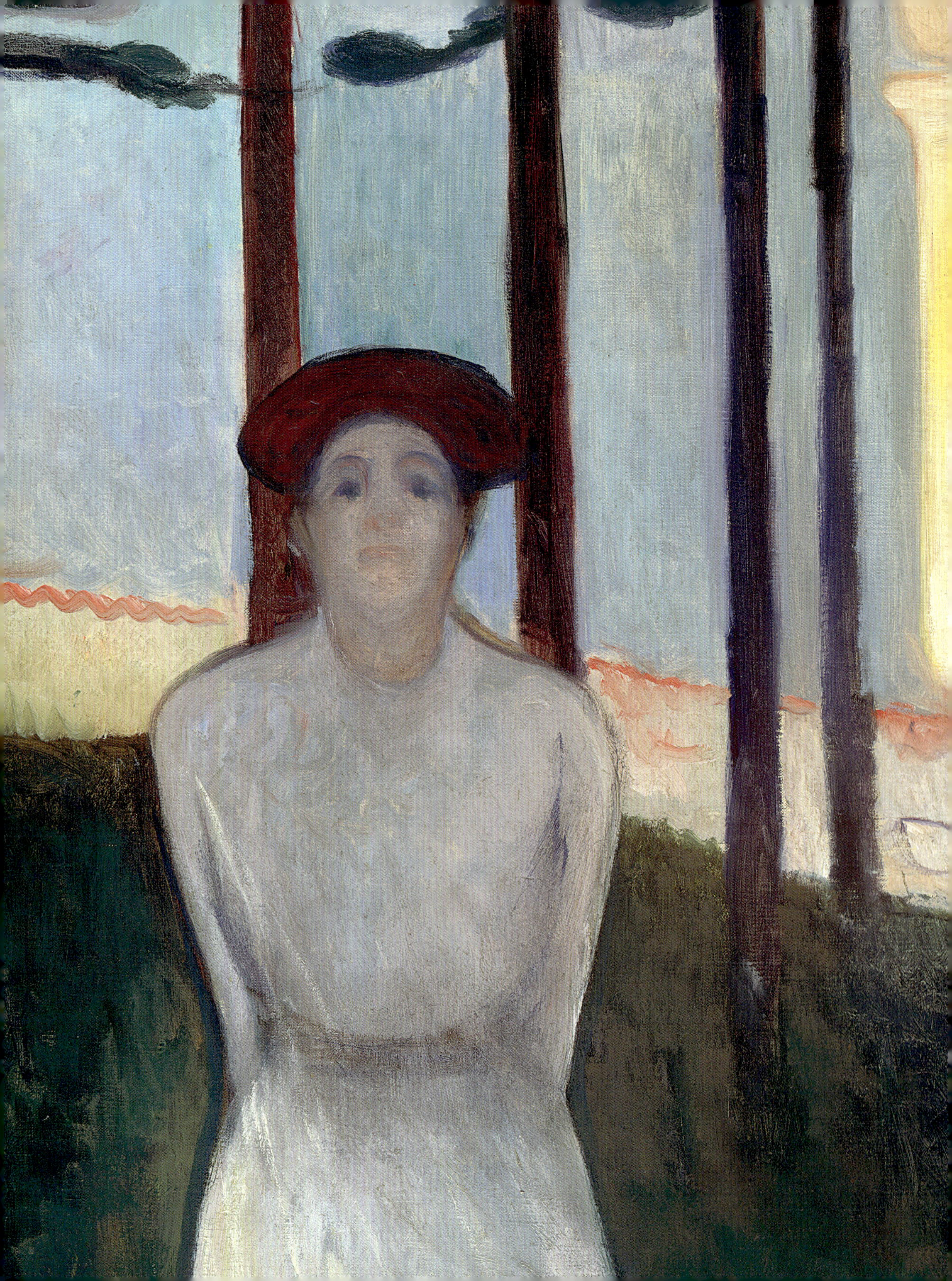

5

BEYOND THE IMPRESSION: post-impressionism, symbolism, and expressionism

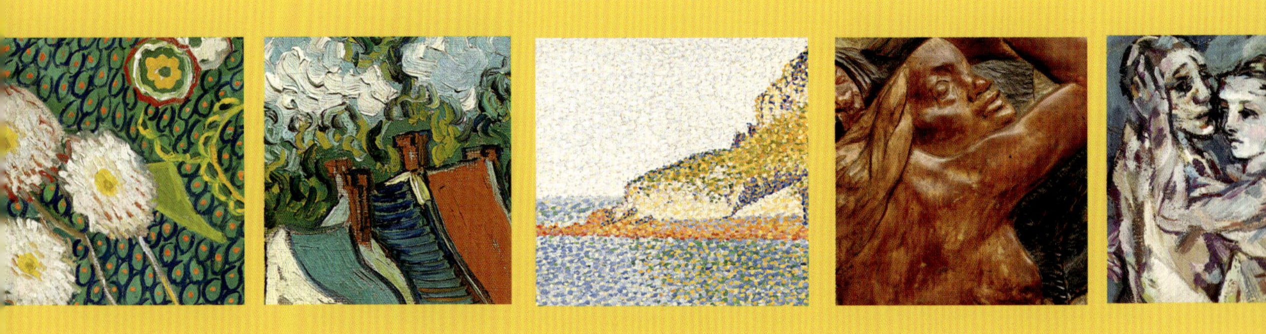

Beyond the Impression: Post-Impressionism, Symbolism, and Expressionism

In 1886 the Impressionists held their eighth and final exhibition. Among the nearly 250 works shown were contributions from the stalwarts Pissarro, Degas, and Morisot, but the exhibition's succès de scandale came from a new generation: that of Paul Gauguin, Georges Seurat, and Paul Signac. These artists took Impressionism as a point of departure, delving deep into the mechanisms of perception and the means of representation. Broadly designated "Post-Impressionism," the resulting styles and approaches varied wildly but shared a feverish, kaleidoscopic intensity. Seurat and Signac covered their canvases with tiny, bright specks of paint, evolving a style they called Divisionism. Gauguin applied glowing, exaggerated color in flat swaths, working first in the Breton countryside and later in the South Seas. Henri de Toulouse-Lautrec captured the bohemian nightlife of Montmartre in the lurid palette of nightmares. Vincent van Gogh turned his brush to new expressive ends, writing from the South of France, "I should not be surprised if the impressionists soon find fault with my way of working. . . . Instead of trying to reproduce exactly what I have before my eyes, I use color more arbitrarily, in order to express myself forcibly."

Though the Divisionists' experiments responded to recent developments in the study of optics, the intense pigments we find in most work by the Post-Impressionist cohort have little to do with the natural world or observed reality. Rather, these artists used their vibrant new palette—in Van Gogh's words—"more arbitrarily," to convey the invisible forces of thought and emotion. In this respect, Post-Impressionism overlapped with Symbolism, a contemporaneous current defined by the critic Albert Aurier in 1892 as "the painting of ideas." Gauguin was both a Post-Impressionist and a Symbolist; his Breton landscapes are invested with spiritual significance. His paintings and wood reliefs from Tahiti evolve a private mythology, conveying meaning through abstract—even abstruse—symbols. Not only color but form, too, held expressive power for the Symbolists. The gracefully contorted figures in Rodin's late sculpture do not so much describe observed movements as evoke emotional states. Symbolism took strongest root in Belgium, Central Europe, and the German-speaking world, where it played a crucial role in the Secessionist movements of the 1890s. Rejecting what they perceived as the shallow materialism of their Academic masters, artists in Munich, Vienna, and Berlin turned inward—to an immaterial realm of dreams and music—in search of truth.

The Berlin Secession, launched in 1898, was led by a group of German Impressionist painters but encompassed a wide variety of styles, most notably Symbolism. Even this progressive, inclusive group, however, proved hostile to the next generation of radicals: the wholesale rejection of the Expressionists'submissions in 1910 divided the jury and helped unravel the whole Secession by 1913. Expressionism arose from an impulse similar to that behind the Post-Impressionist and Symbolist movements. Exaggerated, unnatural color and abstracted forms promised greater expressive potential than narrowly observed reality. But Ernst Ludwig Kirchner, Erich Heckel, and other members of their Expressionist collective, known as Die Brücke (The Bridge), took this principle to a brutal new extreme, emulating the "primitive" forms of non-Western art and shocking contemporary viewers with aggressive, clashing color. Van Gogh and Gauguin furnished crucial inspiration, as did the work of the great French "primitive," Cézanne, a founding member of the Impressionist movement whose mature work had remained virtually unknown until the mid-1890s. All three of these artists—Van Gogh, Gauguin, and Cézanne—became known to German artists thanks to the dealers Paul and Bruno Cassirer, whose gallery served as an avant-garde hub in early twentieth-century Berlin. With Gauguin's canvases arriving in Paris from Tahiti, with African masks flowing into Western capitals from their colonies, and with the work of the recent Post-Impressionist masters circulating throughout Europe, art produced at the turn of the twentieth century reflected the increasingly international character of its market. ***—E.A.B.***

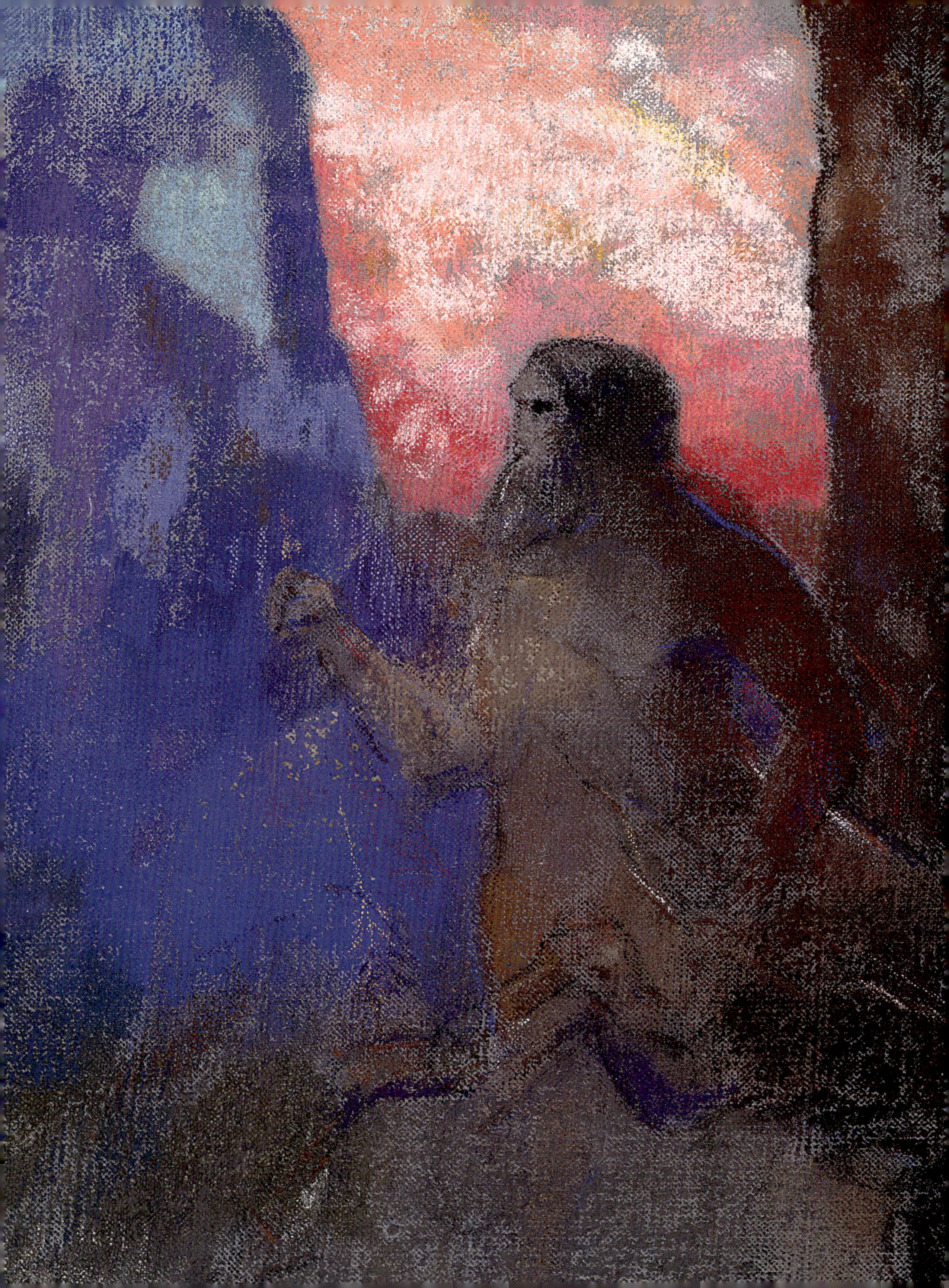

Paul Cézanne
French, 1839–1906
Madame Cézanne in a Red Armchair, about 1877

Cézanne once claimed, "I paint a head as I would a door, as I would anything," but this picture suggests a more complicated relationship with likeness. His wife, Hortense Fiquet, was the artist's most frequent—and perhaps most patient—model, the subject of nearly thirty portraits, of which this example is among the finest. Framed by a vivid, lumpy chair, which the German-language poet Rainer Maria Rilke once described as "the first and final armchair of all painting," Hortense here looks serene. Though modeled with lurid green strokes, her features appear softer and more lovingly rendered than in many of her other portraits.

Drastic variations in paint application enliven the picture. The chair's contours are thick—almost encrusted—while the skirt, a cascade of stripes, is quite thinly painted, revealing underneath a more complicated original concept of folds and creases that Cézanne smoothed out with crisp vertical stripes applied to the surface. The picture can be dated to about 1877, since the distinctive yellow wallpaper places Hortense in an apartment at no. 67 rue de l'Ouest, Paris, where the couple lived at that time.

Cézanne had met Hortense, a nineteen-year-old model, in 1869. She bore him a child three years later, but he kept the existence of this illegitimate family a secret from his father until 1878. On discovering his son's liaison, Cézanne senior cut his allowance, and it was only just before the death of the artist's father in 1886 that the couple finally married. Hence, at the time this portrait was painted, its subject was in fact not yet Madame Cézanne but, rather, Mademoiselle Fiquet.

Oil on canvas
72.4 x 55.9 cm (28½ x 22 in.)
Bequest of Robert Treat Paine, 2nd, 44.776

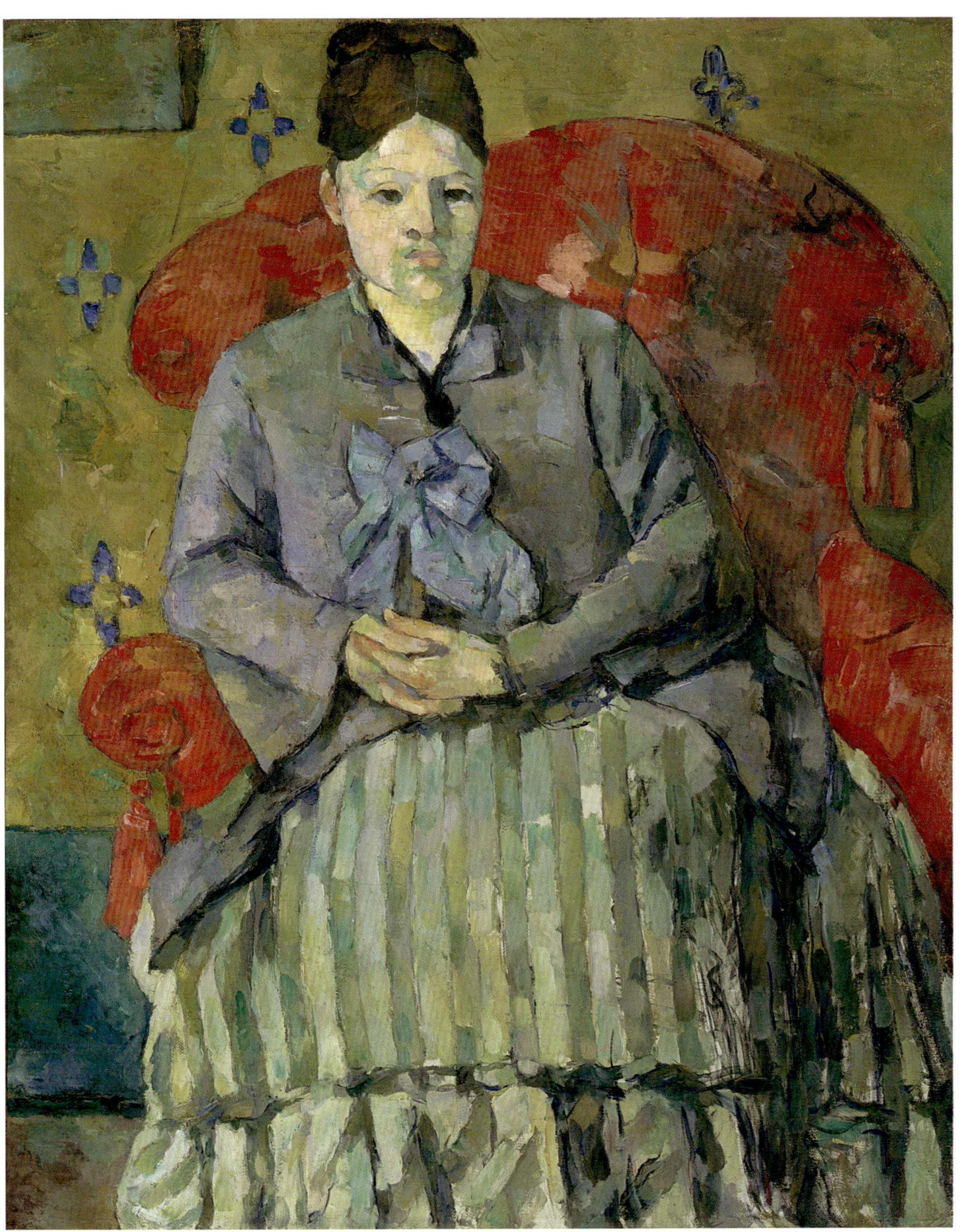

Paul Signac
French, 1863–1935
Port of Saint-Cast, 1890

Signac's friend the critic Félix Fénéon wrote in his first article on the artist, "A single color is limp and flat in comparison with a color resulting from an optical blend; the latter is enlivened by a perpetually shimmering re-composition, elastic, opulent, and shining." It is precisely a sensation of shimmering color that this view of a beach in Brittany produces. The viewer's eye "optically blends" adjacent dots of blue and yellow, orange and green, which coalesce into a vibrating, continuous landscape.

Signac began painting in his late teens, inspired by the example of Monet. But, under the influence of Seurat, whom he met in 1884, Signac's style quickly diverged from the Impressionists' free handling of paint and spontaneous response to nature. Seurat was already pioneering a new technique, composing meticulous pictures from tiny, juxtaposed dots of contrasting color. He called the style Divisionism—it is today more commonly known as Neo-Impressionism or Pointillism (from the French *point*, meaning "dot")—and Signac quickly became one of its most sophisticated practitioners. He befriended scientists and followed contemporary developments in optics, always striving for the effect of "shimmering re-composition."

In addition to his scientific inclinations, Signac felt that visual art should aspire to the condition of music, whose abstract, mathematical purity and proportion he tried to capture in his carefully composed pictures. In the late 1880s he began assigning opus numbers to his paintings—as a composer would to pieces of music—and displaying his work in suites and series. This picture is Opus 209. Signac first exhibited it in 1891 at the avant-garde Salon des XX in Brussels alongside three other ocean views under the joint title *La Mer (The Sea)*.

Oil on canvas
66 x 82.5 cm (26 x 32½ in.)
Gift of William A. Coolidge, 1991.584

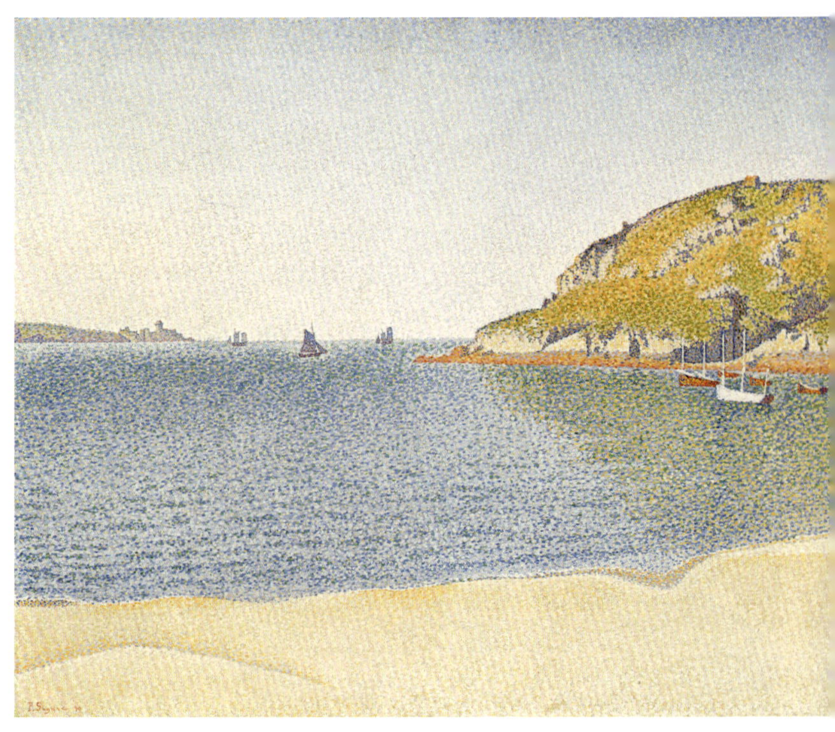

Henri de Toulouse-Lautrec
French, 1864–1901
***At the Café La Mie*, about 1891**

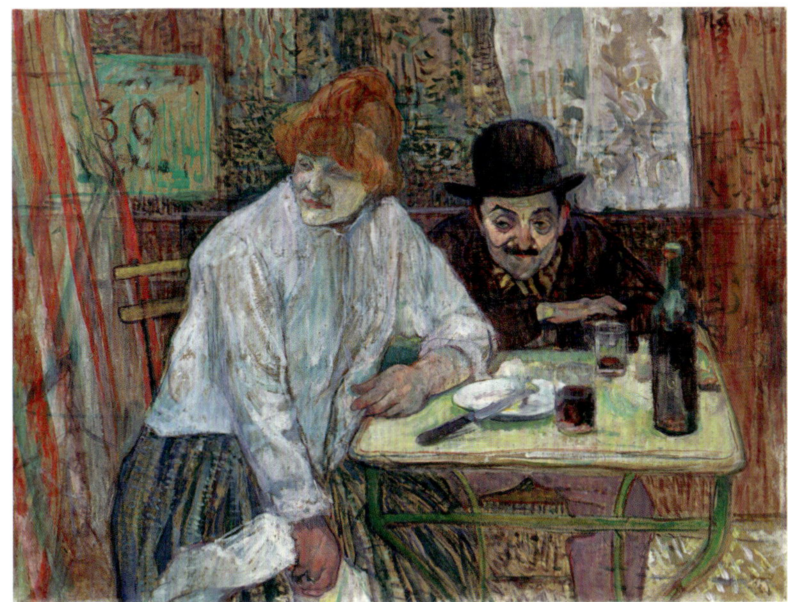

The scene is a café in the working-class neighborhood of Montmartre, the site of a grim, alcoholic repast. A red-headed woman of slatternly appearance—note her rumpled blouse, swollen hands, and vacant look—shares a table with a male companion, his rheumy eyes fixed on a passerby, his hat slightly crooked on his head. The bottle, glasses, and elbows on the table convey an atmosphere of boozy familiarity, and the painting's French title, *À La Mie*, turns on a mildly suggestive pun: *mie*, literally "crumb," was in the late nineteenth century also a slang term for a lower-class woman.

The underclass of prostitutes and performers, indigents and drunks who called Montmartre home provided a source of endless inspiration for Toulouse-Lautrec, an artist of noble birth who nonetheless set up his studio in the rue Tourlaque near the heights of Montmartre in 1884. He quickly became the most celebrated chronicler of the neighborhood's bohemian culture, its cafés, cabarets, and bordellos. Often painted on cardboard with fluid, thinned-out colors, his pictures hover between painting and drawing, absorbing a contingent, improvised quality from their impoverished materials.

This quality, however, should not lead us to mistake his paintings for impressions caught on the fly. His compositions were often rigorously staged. Indeed, this picture is a quite literal interpretation of a photograph—arranged by the artist and taken by his friend Paul Sescau—of a local champagne merchant and his mistress. Contemporary viewers saw the two figures not as portraits but as "types": stand-ins for familiar categories of the urban population, in this case most likely a prostitute and her client. For many observers of the period, such individuals symbolized the decadence and despair of an entire social class. "In their horror," wrote one early critic, "we cannot help but admire them."

Oil paint on millboard mounted on panel
53 x 67.9 cm (20⅞ x 26¾ in.)
S. A. Denio Collection—Sylvanus Adams Denio Fund and General Income, 40.748

Paul Gauguin
French, 1848–1903
Landscape with Two Breton Women, 1889

Between 1886 and 1891 Gauguin escaped from Paris, where he had begun to paint under the influence of the Impressionist circle, to the rural community of Pont-Aven on the coast of Brittany. There, inspired by what he believed to be the local peasants' more authentic, sincere mode of life and belief, he painted everyday scenes invested with symbolic, even religious, significance.

Here two Breton peasants sit in the shade. The right-hand figure seems at first to be praying, but closer inspection reveals that she is in fact eating her lunch—holding a piece of fruit, perhaps, in her left hand and a knife in her right. The painting demonstrates a shift in Gauguin's style away from the brushy, Impressionist manner of his early career toward the broad expanses of color and short, rhythmic strokes that characterize the work of his Cloisonist period.

Other artists followed Gauguin's example, forming a group called the Nabis (from the Hebrew word for sage or prophet), whose principal figures, Ker-Xavier Roussel, Paul Sérusier, Maurice Denis, Pierre Bonnard, and Edouard Vuillard, were joint owners of this painting in the early 1890s. It hung at their various studios in turn, a crucial source of inspiration for their evolving style.

Oil on canvas
72.4 x 91.4 cm (28½ x 36 in.)
Gift of Harry and Mildred Remis and Robert and Ruth Remis, 1976.42

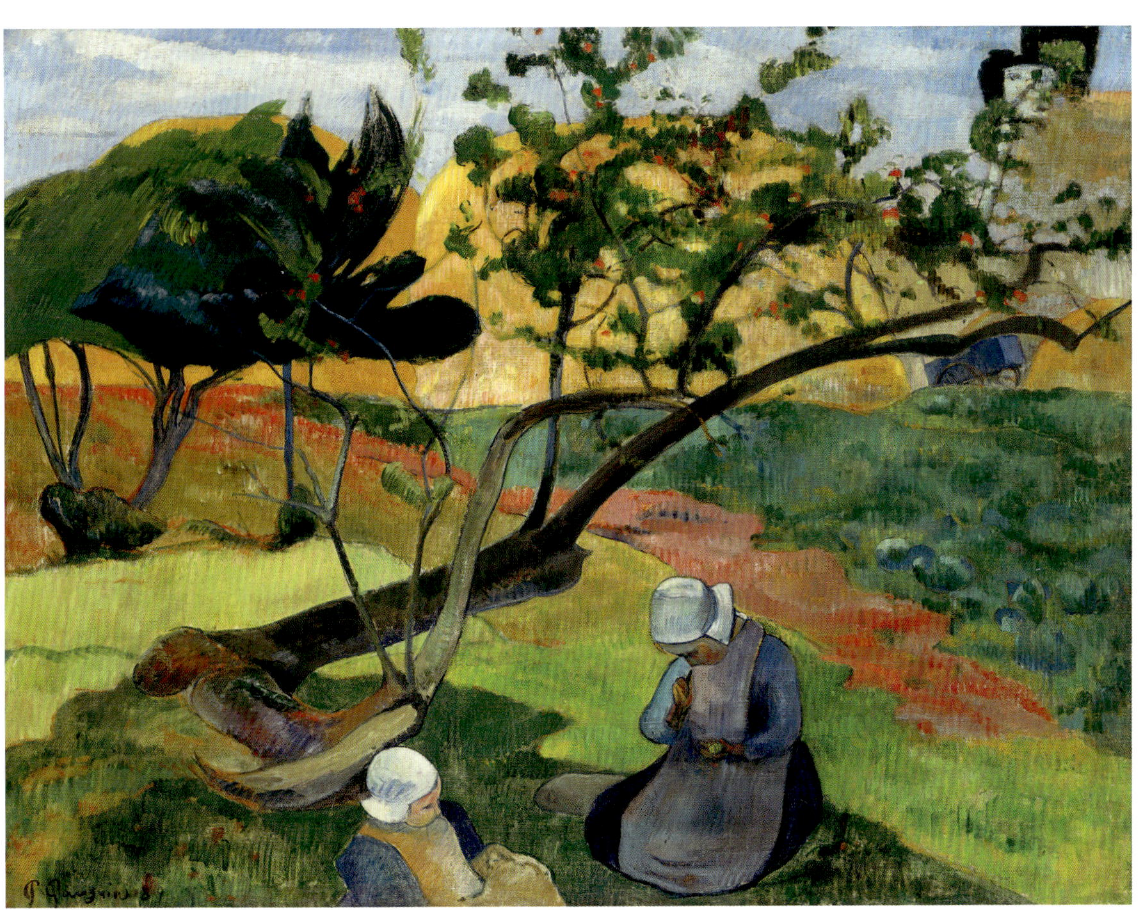

Paul Gauguin

French, 1848–1903

Soyez amoureuses vous serez heureuses (Be in Love and You Will Be Happy), 1889

Painted linden wood

95 x 72 x 6.4 cm (37 3/8 x 28 3/8 x 2 1/2 in.)

Arthur Tracy Cabot Fund, 57.582

La Guerre et La Paix (War and Peace), 1901

Painted tamanu wood

War: 44.4 x 99.5 cm (17 1/2 x 39 1/8 in.)

Peace: 48.3 x 99.7 cm (19 x 39 1/4 in.)

Gift of Laurence K. and Lorna J. Marshall, 63.2764 and 63.2765

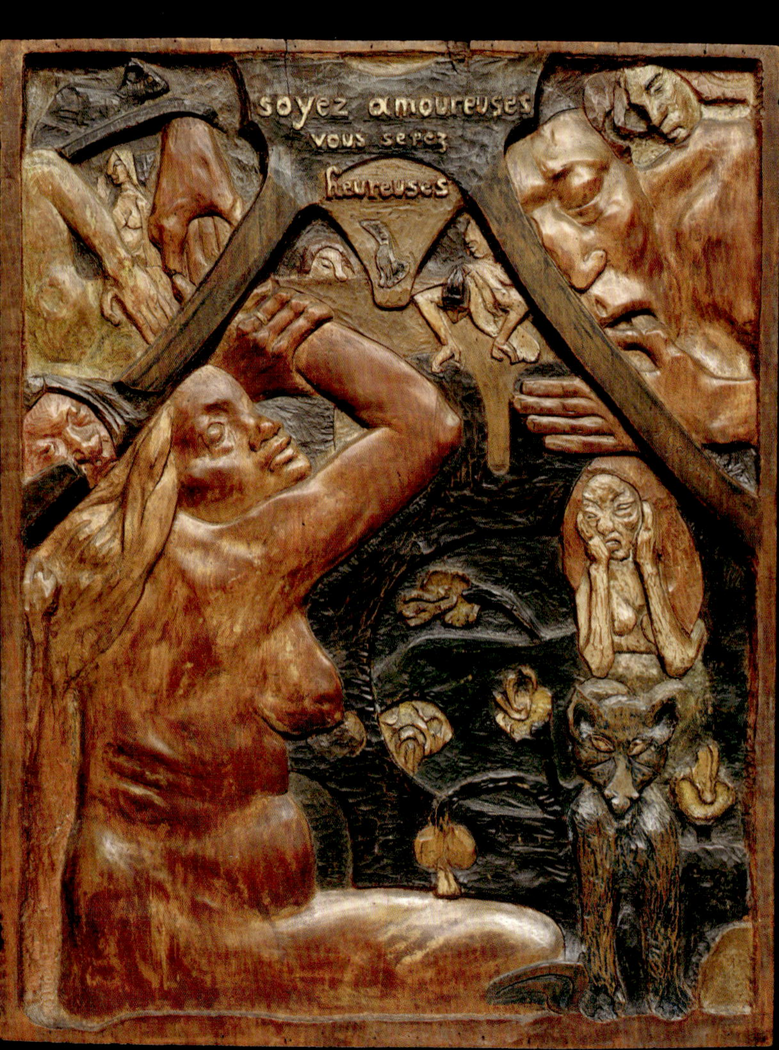

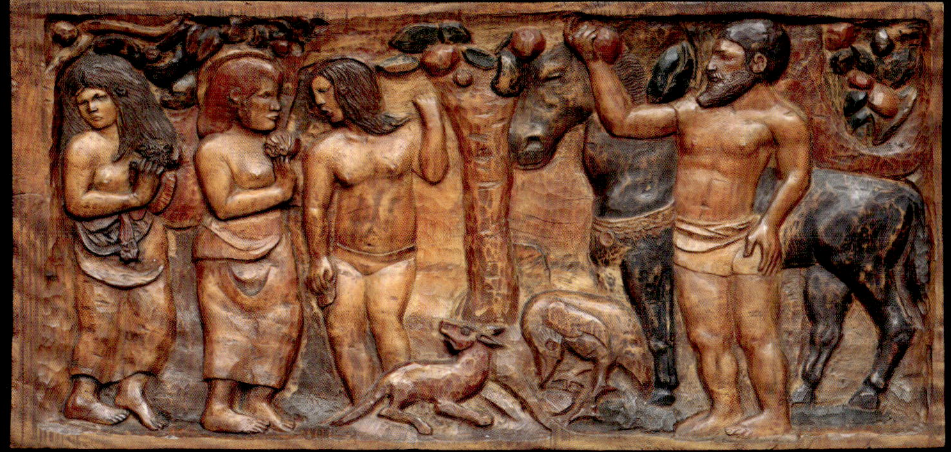

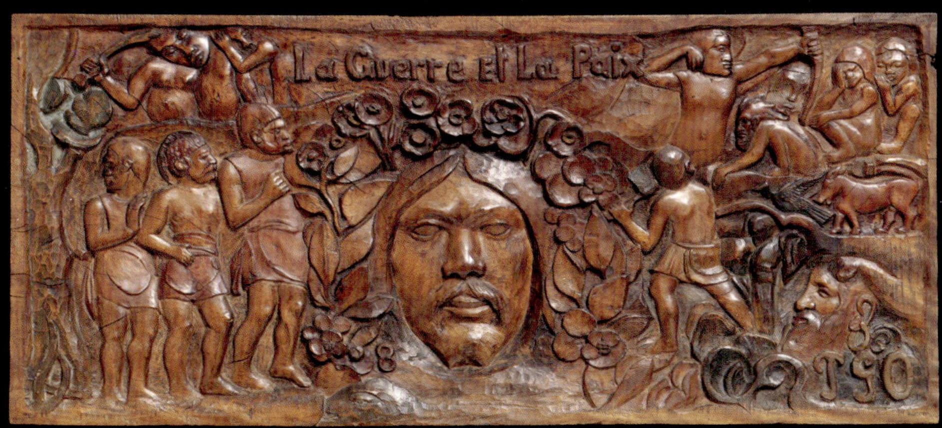

Gauguin described the powerful, haunting relief *Be in Love and You Will Be Happy* of 1889 as "the best and strangest thing I have ever done in sculpture. Gauguin (as monster) seizing the hand of a protesting woman and telling her: Be in love and you will be happy." He recognized that the people represented in the relief, contrary to the exhortation of the title, mostly appeared sad if not tortured. He identified the fox as an "Indian symbol of perversity." The skeletal woman above the fox was based on a Peruvian mummy that Gauguin had seen but the strange, inverted *V* at the top of the composition remains a mystery. The carving of the relief, with smooth planing contrasting with a harsher gouging of the wood, has a raw spontaneity that points to Gauguin's interest in the "primitive," fueled by his childhood memories of Peru, a trip to Martinique, and the African art he saw at the 1889 Universal Exposition in Paris.

Much about *Be in Love* foreshadows the art Gauguin created after he left France for the islands of the South Pacific, including the two panels *War and Peace*. These were carved in a local wood in 1901 while Gauguin was in Tahiti but made for a patron back in Paris. Meant to be shown one above the other, the harmonious garden setting of peace grows out of the lower panel with warriors, an archer, and a central all-seeing, mysterious masklike head crowned with flowers.

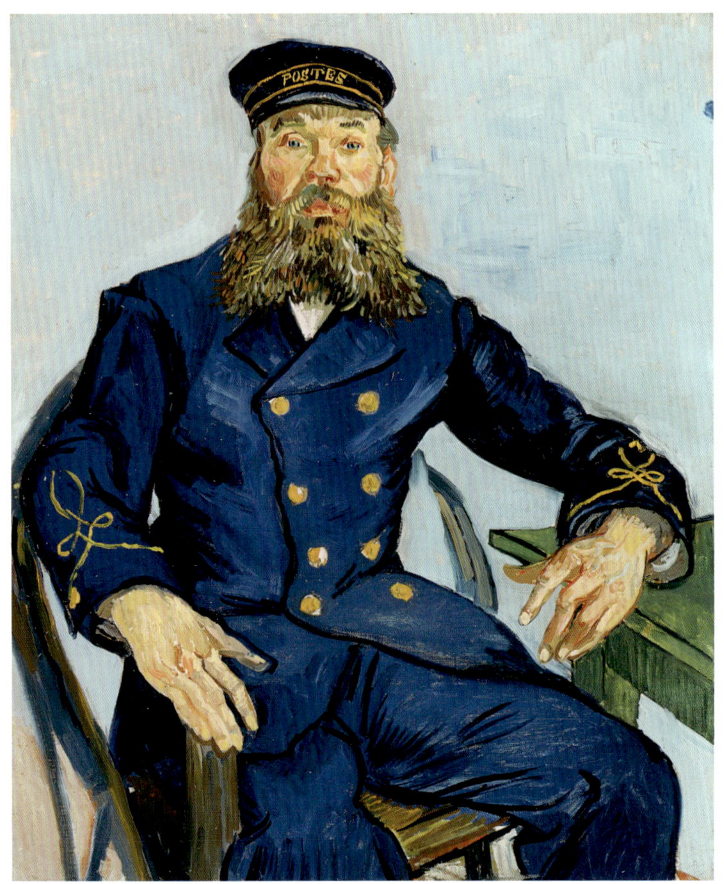

Vincent van Gogh
Dutch (worked in France), 1853–1890
Postman Joseph Roulin, 1888
Oil on canvas
81.3 x 65.4 cm (32 x 25¾ in.)
Gift of Robert Treat Paine, 2nd, 35.1982

Lullaby: Madame Roulin Rocking a Cradle (La Berceuse), 1889
Oil on canvas
92.7 x 72.7 cm (36½ x 28⅝ in.)
Bequest of John T. Spaulding, 48.548

These portraits belong to the two most celebrated series Van Gogh painted. One is the first of six versions; the other may be the last of five. Together they demonstrate the evolution of their author's approach to portraiture, which he described as "the thing that enables me to cultivate what's best and most serious in me."

Van Gogh arrived in Arles in February 1888, relinquishing the artistic life of Montmartre in Paris for a more quiet existence in small-town Provence. Among the closest friends and favorite models he found in this new home was a postal worker, Joseph Roulin, with whom he liked to drink at the train station café and with whose fiery left-wing politics he sympathized. This is the first of six pictures Van Gogh made of Roulin between July 1888 and April 1889. While painting it, the artist wrote to his brother, "I am now at work with another model, a postman in a blue uniform trimmed with gold, a big bearded face, very like Socrates. . . . A more interesting man than many people." In this frank likeness the ordinariness of Roulin's features, his standard-issue uniform and rough worker's hands in no way diminish the intelligence of his gaze and nobility of his bearing. The flush in Roulin's cheeks may reflect a new father's pride; Van Gogh's letters reveal that the postman's wife, Augustine, gave birth to a child during the period when her husband was posing for this portrait.

In December 1888 the artist embarked on the first painting in his series representing Mme Roulin rocking the very same child, by then four months old. Pictured at half-length against a vivid background of green and pink wallpaper, she holds in her hand a cord attached to the unseen cradle. An inscription at lower right, "La Berceuse" (she who rocks), identifies her as a woman rocking her child but points to a broader allegorical meaning as well: a *berceuse* in French is also a lullaby. Van Gogh suffered a nervous breakdown on Christmas Eve 1888 but returned to his interrupted painting in January 1889, regarding it as a soothing project and quickly turning out four further variations on the theme. Our picture has been variously identified as the first, middle, and final painting in the series, but recent technical research indicates that it is most likely the last—the furthest in spirit from a straight portrait, the closest to what Van Gogh called a "lullaby sung with color."

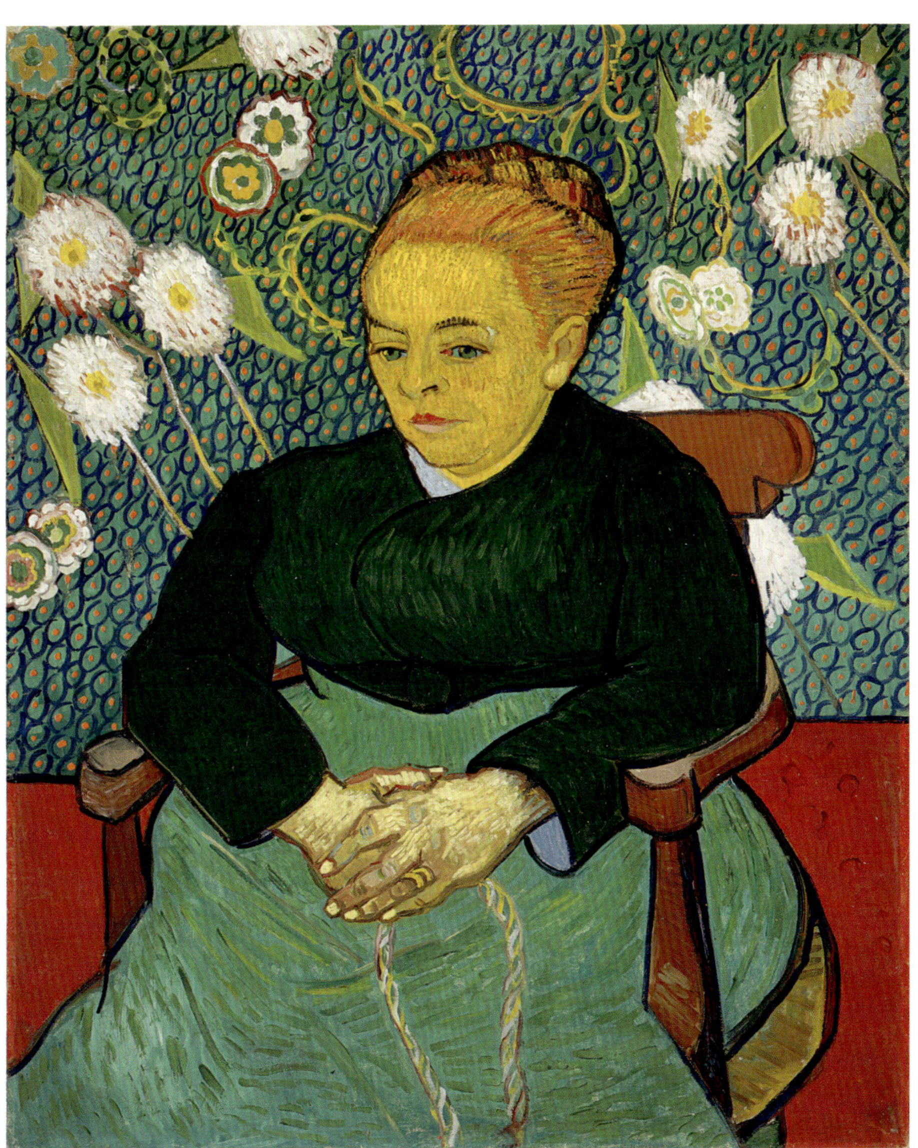

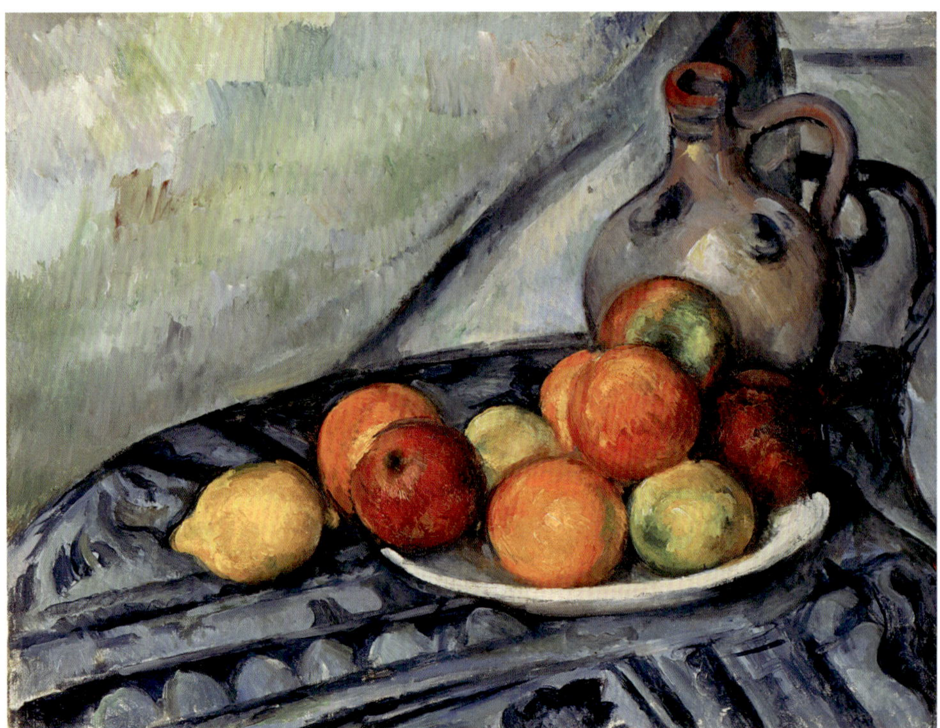

Paul Cézanne
French, 1839–1906
Fruit and a Jug on a Table, about 1890–94

Cézanne's deceptively simple still lifes of fruit on sloping tabletops are among his most iconic paintings, each one an exploration of space, form, and the painter's means of representing them. This intimate composition responds to many of the same concerns—and indeed contains many of the same objects—as his larger-scale still lifes. The blue patterned tablecloth and Provençal jug are familiar actors in Cézanne's domestic dramas, though of course glowing fruits—lemons, apples, and oranges or peaches—remain the star attraction.

The little scene unfolds in a richly ambiguous space. At right, the background chair and foreground table edge are peculiarly elided, and the relationships of the gray curtain to that same chair and to the sloping tabletop are unresolved: How much space are we to imagine lies between these objects, which seem to collide and overlap? The motionlessness of the piled fruit seems quite implausible, given the table's rakish angle.

A famously slow worker, Cézanne once explained his attraction to fruit in practical terms: "As to flowers, I have given them up. They wilt immediately. Fruits are more reliable. They like having their portraits done." The artist, in fact, once admonished his dealer, Ambroise Vollard, to "sit still as an apple," when posing for his portrait.

Oil on canvas
32.4 x 40.6 cm (12¾ x 16 in.)
Bequest of John T. Spaulding, 48.524

Vincent van Gogh
Dutch (worked in France), 1853–1890
Houses at Auvers, 1890

In May 1890, after his release from the hospital at Saint-Rémy-de-Provence, Van Gogh left the South of France for Auvers, a small town twenty miles from Paris. There, under the watchful eye of Paul Gachet—a physician and art collector who had promised the painter's brother to look after him—Van Gogh produced some of his finest pictures in a final blaze of inspiration before his suicide in July. *Houses at Auvers* shows the village landscape in early summer, with a bright sky overhead and blue shadows on the road.

Residents of Auvers, Van Gogh remarked, had by this time begun replacing their old-fashioned thatch roofs with modern tile; we sense the artist's affection for the obsolescent material—and, by extension, for a vanishing way of life—in his treatment of the thatch, rendered with precise parallel strokes. This rich texture complements that of the clouds, painted in such thick impasto that the surface becomes a kind of bas-relief sculpture.

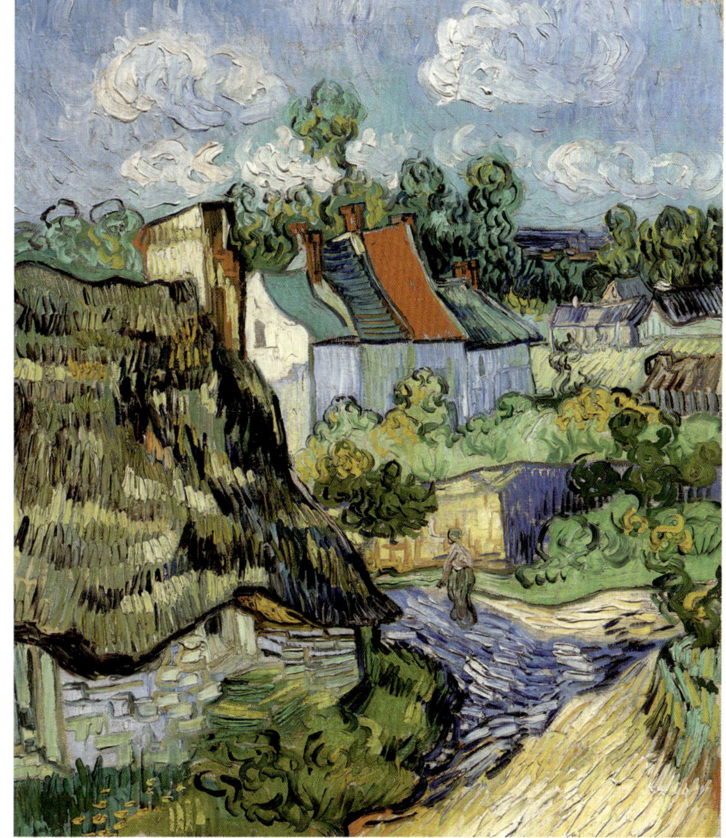

Oil on canvas
75.6 x 61.9 cm (29 3/4 x 24 3/8 in.)
Bequest of John T. Spaulding, 48.549

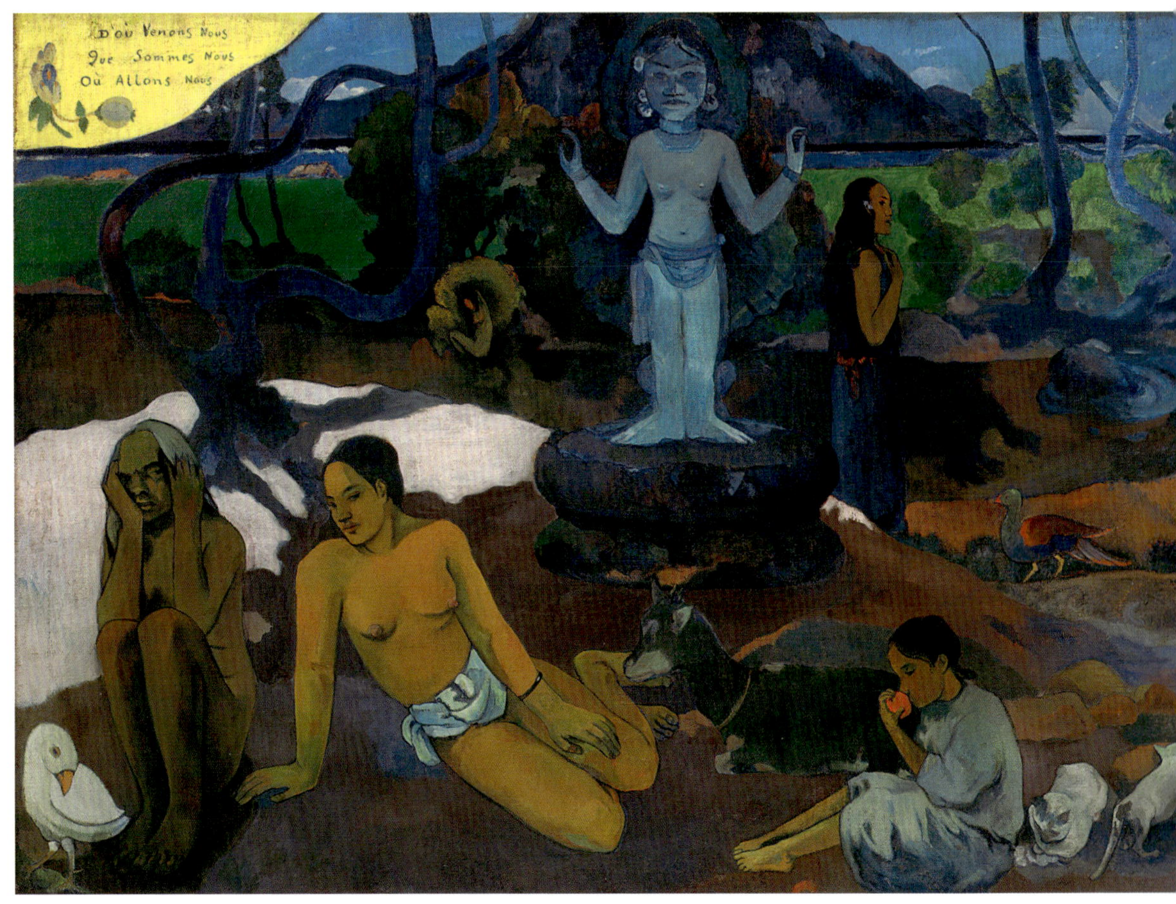

Paul Gauguin
French, 1848–1903
Where Do We Come From? What Are We? Where Are We Going? 1897–98

Gauguin left France behind forever in 1895, settling in Tahiti, in the South Pacific, where he had hoped to discover an earthly paradise unsullied by European civilization. Instead he confronted the effects of French colonization and endured his own mental and physical decline. Painted at the nadir of these disappointments, *Where Do We Come From? What Are We? Where Are We Going?* was intended as a pictorial last will and testament. Gauguin completed the picture in a fever of activity in January 1898 and immediately set out for the mountains, where he planned to take his life. In a letter he wrote after this suicide attempt to Daniel de Monfreid, his friend, fellow artist, and the first owner of this painting, Gauguin explained, "Before I died I wished to paint a large canvas that I had in mind. . . . I believe that . . . I shall never do anything better, or even like it. Before death I put into it all my energy . . . and my vision was so clear that all haste of execution vanishes, and life surges up."

In the crucible of his despair, Gauguin had forged an imaginary world: a lush landscape peopled with Tahitian models and animated by an invented, hybrid mythology. He explained to Monfreid that the

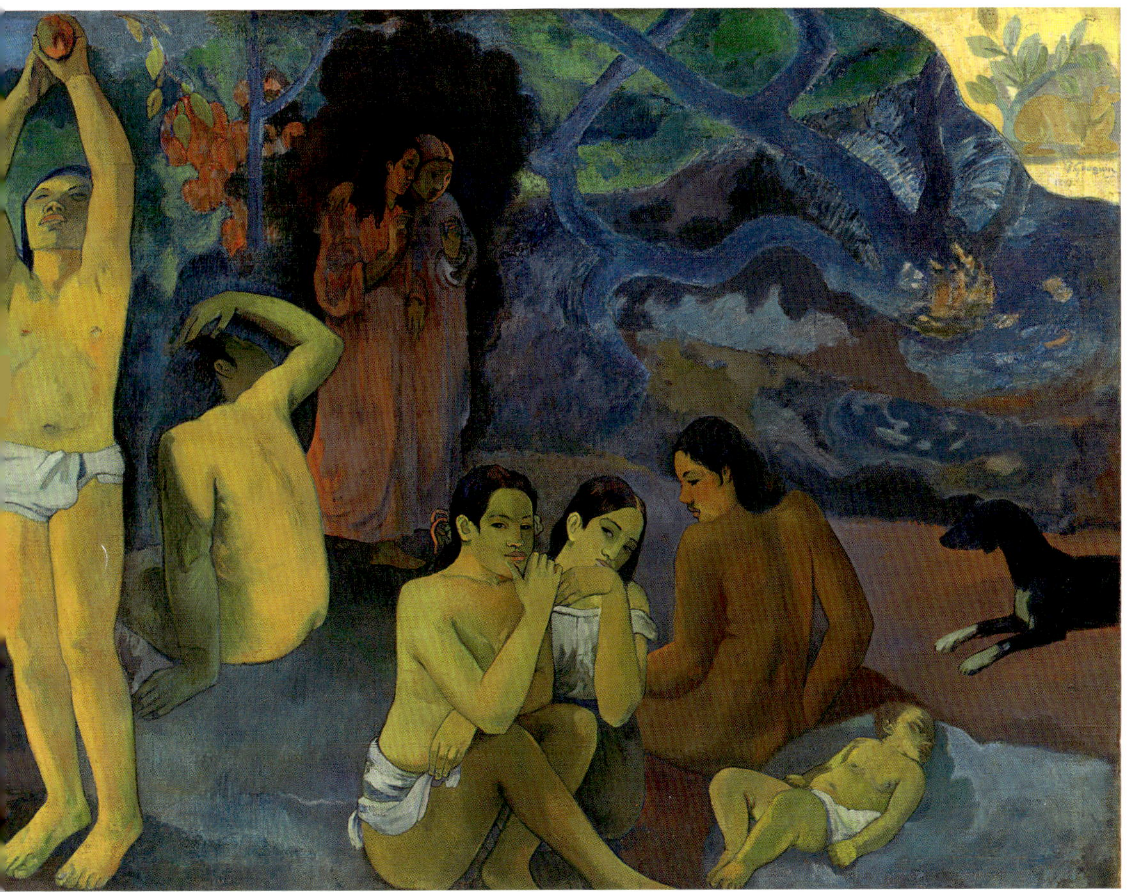

composition was meant to be read from right to left, addressing the three titular questions—inscribed, in French, in the upper left-hand corner. Hence the infant asleep on a rock at right evokes innocence and origins: Where do we come from? The central figure—whose pose suggests Adam in the garden of Eden, plucking fruit from the tree of knowledge of good and evil—indicates self-knowledge, maturity, and man's fall from grace: What are we? The crouching figure at left gestures to age, sorrow, the approach of death: Where are we going?

But the painting spins a web of allusion and symbol far more delicate and complex than this or any straightforward account can satisfy. Despite Gauguin's declared intention to escape from European culture, classical tradition edges in everywhere. With its glowing nudes, arranged frieze-like against the landscape, the painting draws on a range of sources from ancient Greek sculpture to the Renaissance paintings of Sandro Botticelli. Yet, by filtering these through other references—Maori artifacts, Buddhist sculpture, even a Peruvian mummy—the picture also estranges the classical tradition, injecting it with new poetry and life.

Oil on canvas
Image: 139.1 x 374.6 cm (54¾ x 147½ in.)
Framed: 171.5 x 406.4 x 8.9 cm (67½ x 160 x 3½ in.)
Tompkins Collection—Arthur Gordon Tompkins Fund, 36.270

Charlotte Besnard
French, 1855–1930
Ceres or ***Persephone***, 1895

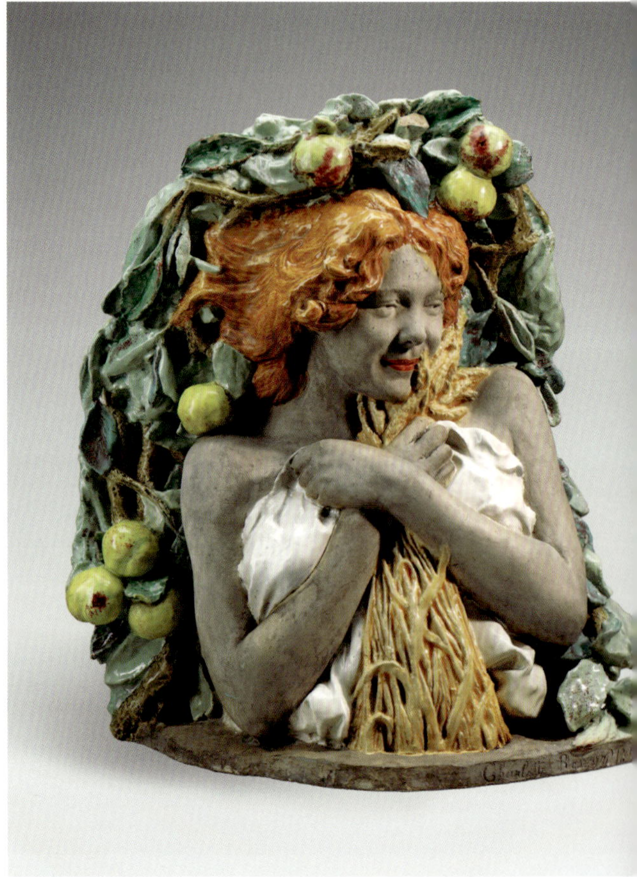

This image of an agricultural deity cannot be securely identified as either Ceres or her daughter Persephone. Shown as a half-length figure, she seems to emerge from the earth, clutching to her chest stalks of wheat along with a swath of white drapery. Branches of trees ripe with fruit create a niche-like background behind her, and as they arch over her head, they become like a crown or garland. Her rich curls of red hair are caught up in the branches as she turns to her left and smiles. The sculpture is made of stoneware; the flesh is coated with slip, and the hair, lips, drapery, branches, fruit, and wheat are fired in colored glazes. The ceramic techniques are traditional, yet the extensive use of color was shocking for a sculpture in the 1890s. Even today such exuberant color in sculpture challenges expectations that works like this one, representing an ancient Roman goddess of fertility, might be better served by marble or some other monochrome stone. Evoking ancient practices of coloring sculpture and recalling Renaissance glazed terracottas, this figure has a febrile character that is most clearly expressed in her bright red, shiny lips.

Besnard was the daughter of a sculptor and the wife of a painter. She showed a painted plaster version of this sculpture at the Salon of 1892, where it seems to have confounded some of its viewers. This version was made in 1895 in stoneware, a material appreciated at the time as a humble yet highly expressive medium for art pottery. It was glazed by a master ceramist at the Sèvres porcelain manufactory.

Painted and glazed stoneware
74 x 64 x 40 cm (29 1/8 x 25 1/4 x 15 3/4 in.)
In memory of John F. Paramino, Boston Sculptor, 1998.401

Sarah Bernhardt
French, 1844–1923
Fantastic Inkwell (Self-Portrait as a Sphinx), 1880

An internationally renowned actress, Bernhardt was also a painter and a sculptor. This complex self-portrait plays on notions of the mutability of her personality, her inner life, and her professions. Photographs of the artist confirm that the face is a close likeness, but the head is set on a fantastic hybrid creature, with the wings of a bat, the body of a griffin, and the tail of a fish. The creature wears masks of Tragedy and Comedy on its shoulders like epaulettes. The container for the ink is guarded by a horned skull, mimicking the deep, foreboding gaze of the sitter and conveying darkness and evil lurking within. This image of the artist as a sphinx becomes a metaphor for Bernhardt's ability to transform herself, both onstage and off.

The self-portrait plays on Symbolist ideas about the complex nature of creativity and femininity. This chimera has its roots in fantastic hybrids found in Renaissance bronze sculpture as well as in the charged images of sphinxes by such contemporary painters as Redon and Gustave Moreau. The inkwell further transcends its utilitarian function through its realization in precious bronze, a metal alloy transformed by heat and cooling, the medium itself partaking of the notion of metamorphosis.

Bronze
Overall (without base): 31.8 x 34.9 x 31.8 cm (12½ x 13¾ x 12½ in.)
Helen and Alice Colburn Fund, 1973.551

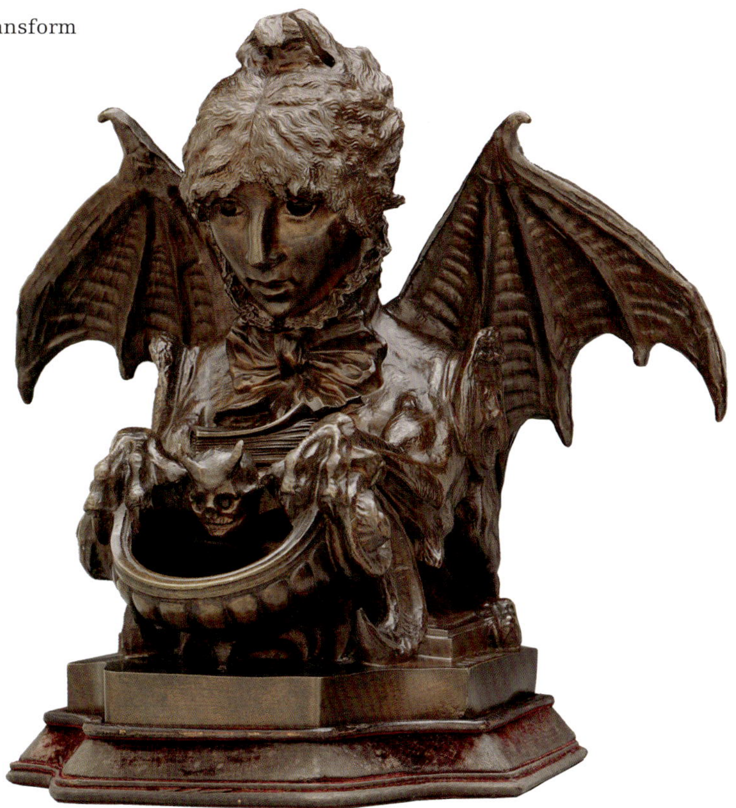

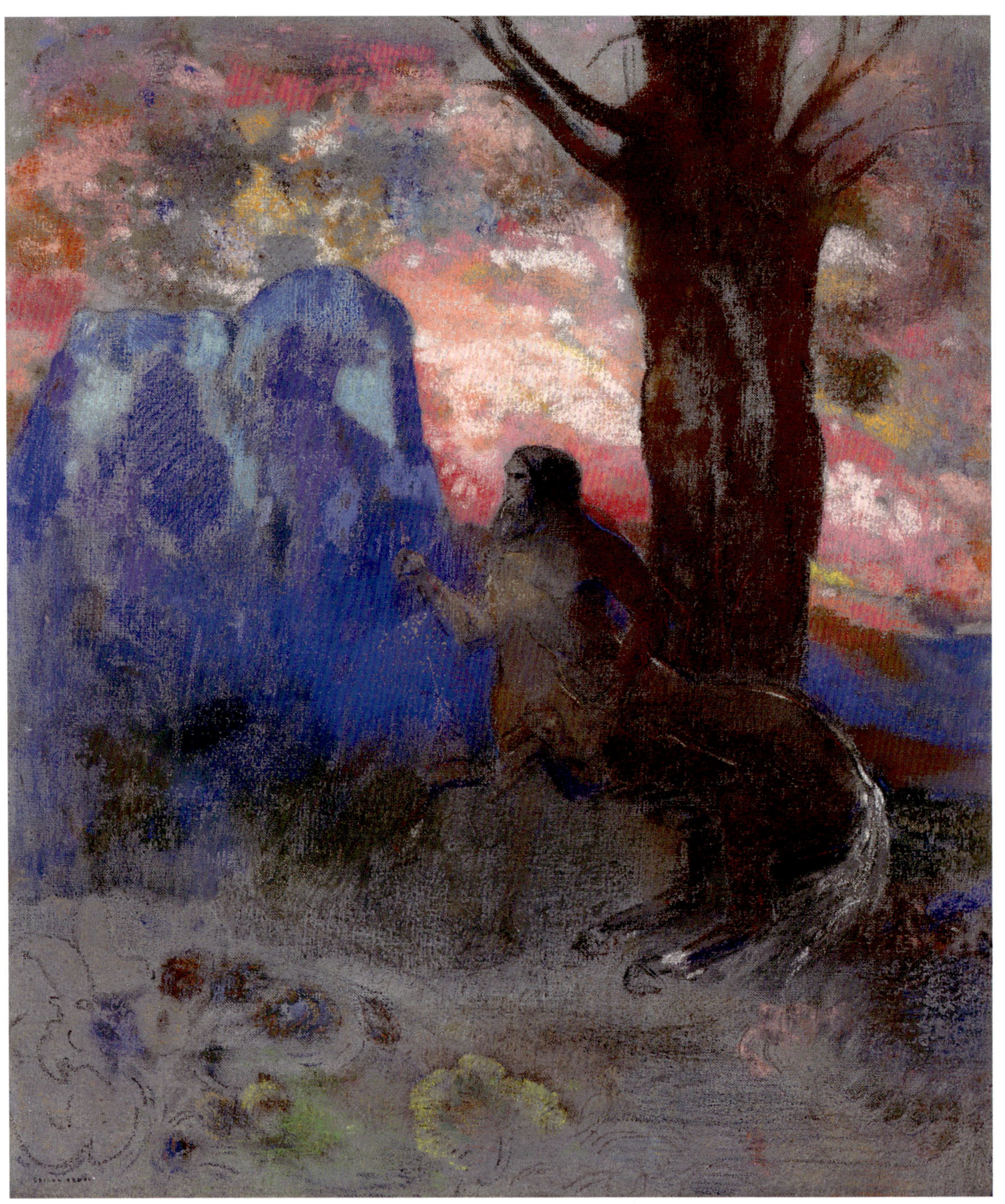

Odilon Redon
French, 1840–1916
Centaur, 1895–1900

Against a flushed and glimmering sky, Redon's picture unfolds an ecstatic landscape: blue rocks, a lone tree, and an arabesque of undergrowth, barely traced out in the left foreground. From this landscape emerges the silhouetted Centaur, half-man, half-horse, wielding his gossamer-fine bow and arrow. The story of this misbegotten creature appears in the *Odes* of the Classical Greek poet Pindar. Seeing the Lapith king Ixion lusting after Hera, queen of the gods, Zeus, her husband, sends Ixion a cloud in Hera's guise as punishment:

> The man in his ignorance chased a sweet counterfeit and lay with a cloud, for its form was like the supreme celestial goddess. . . . She bore to him, without the blessing of the Graces, a monstrous offspring—there was never a mother or a son like this—honored neither by men nor by the laws of the gods. She raised him and named him Centaurus.

The elusive medium of pastel—all dust, color, and light—seems perfectly suited to body forth this cloud-born creature. Swift-footed and skilled in archery, the Centaur remains an outcast, both a prodigy and a monster. Whether Redon himself, an artist of prodigious—and occasionally monstrous—imagination, identified with the Centaur, is a matter of speculation. His iconographic repertoire was intensely personal and often gnomic in its signification. The ultimate Symbolist, Redon produced many images, like this one, whose meaning is not fixed but determinedly indeterminate.

Pastel on canvas
73 x 60.3 cm (28¾ x 23¾ in.)
Gift of Laurence K. Marshall, 64.2206

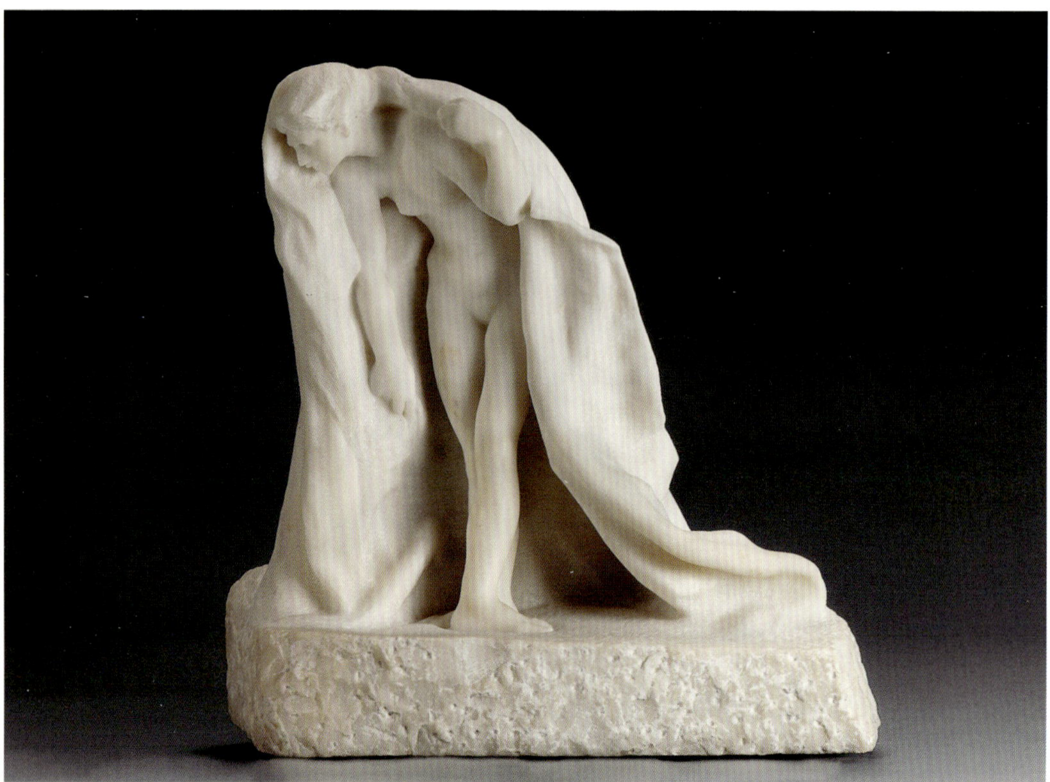

Auguste Rodin
French, 1840–1917
Psyche, 1898–99

Psyche was the beloved of Cupid, ancient god of love. Here, Rodin captures an intimate moment in their complicated love story, when Psyche furtively sought a glimpse of her mysterious lover as he slept. As told by the ancient Roman poet Apuleius, Cupid's mother, Venus, was envious of Psyche's beauty and ordered Cupid to marry Psyche off to a horrid beast. Instead, Cupid fell in love with her and married her himself, but to maintain her safety and his secret, he pretended to be the awful creature, visiting her only in the darkest night and ordering her never to look at him. Psyche could not resist, and while Cupid slept, she held an oil lamp out to see his face. A drop of oil fell, waking him, and he was forced to flee. Ultimately love prevailed and Cupid and Psyche were reunited, but here Rodin presents the most intimate and silent moment in the story. He shows only Psyche, draped with a cloth, her long hair falling loose as she arches forward to look at her lover. Drapery and hair create a foil for her delicate body, enhancing the sense of secrecy and evoking the shadows of night. Rodin left the block rough and seemingly unfinished at the base; he thus contrasts the hard reality of the stone with marble's capacity to emulate soft skin, warm flesh, and flowing hair through carefully controlled variations in polish. Though Rodin employed marble carvers to produce his statues, he closely supervised their production and often applied the finishing touches.

Marble
73.7 x 68.6 x 38.1 cm (29 x 27 x 15 in.)
Anonymous gift in memory of Ward Thoron (1867–1938) and Louisa Chapin Hooper Thoron (1874–1975), 1975.738

Auguste Rodin
French, 1840–1917
Eternal Springtime, modeled about 1881, cast about 1916–17

Rodin's lovers express bliss through their dynamic, precarious postures. The woman's open, arching, kneeling pose conveys complete abandon to passion as she is literally swept up into their kiss. The man's left leg crosses into the embrace, and his left arm extends its reach beyond her, as if to encompass the space around them. That Rodin's naturalistic figures embody emotional states like passion is due in great part to his drawing practices. Instead of placing models in static poses, as in academic drawing classes, the sculptor observed and drew them as they walked around the studio, trying to capture natural movements and postures. Like many of Rodin's individual sculptures, this composition developed out of his work on a major commission for a pair of bronze doors, based on Dante's poem *Inferno*, known as *The Gates of Hell*. Rodin often reused or reworked figures, postures, and gestures to explore fully their expressive possibilities. This group was never used on the *Gates* but was nevertheless repeated in many versions on different scales. The male figure here sports wings, making this one of the casts alluding to the love story of Cupid and Psyche. This cast is distinguished by two small but important details: a head was added to the back of the work, as if emerging from the rocky landscape; and an inscription dedicates it to Rodin's young cousin Henriette Coltat. She visited him late in his life and was with him when he died.

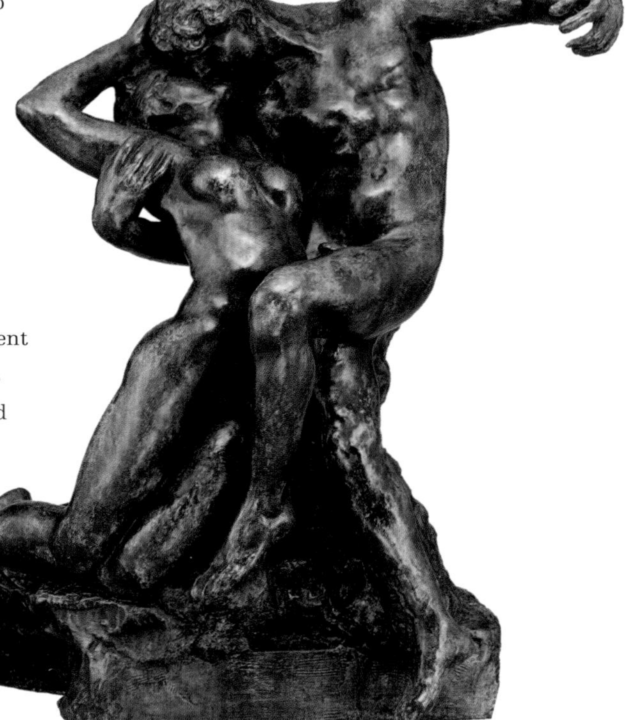

Bronze
H. 62.9 cm (24 3/4 in.)
Bequest of William A. Coolidge, 1993.50

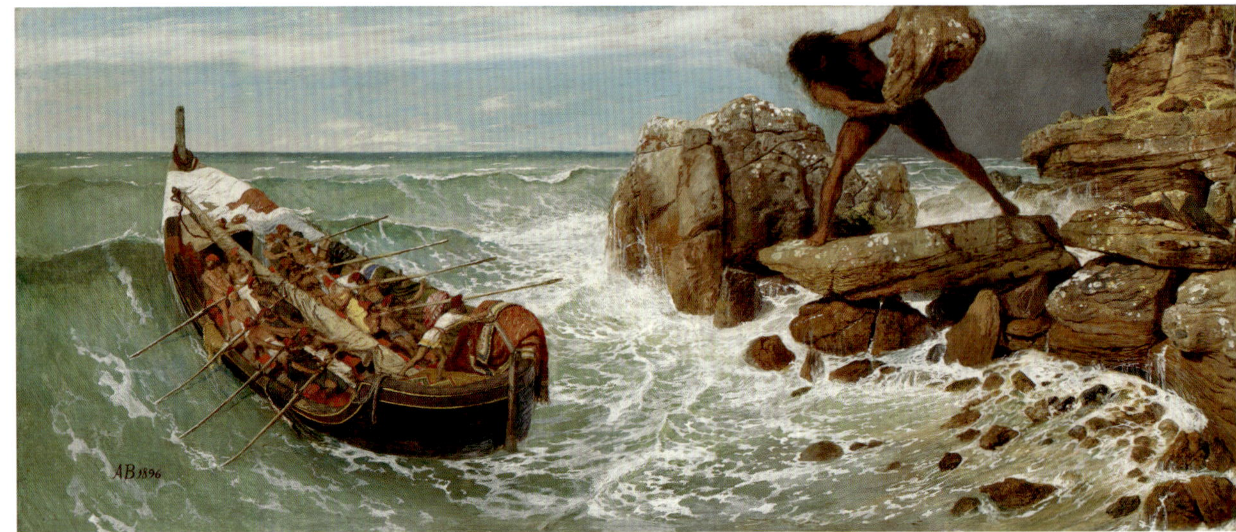

Arnold Böcklin
Swiss, 1827–1901
Odysseus and Polyphemus, 1896

A proto-Symbolist painter championed by the avant-garde generation of the fin de siècle, Böcklin was, for a brief moment, among the most celebrated artists in the world. Unlike his Academic colleagues who treated ancient mythology with reverence and solemnity, Böcklin often played up strange, grotesque, and even ridiculous elements of these stories, conjuring a pre-Classical world governed by violence and lust.

In this work, he portrayed an episode from the *Odyssey* of Homer. Odysseus, the Greek hero returning from the Trojan War to his home in Ithaca, escapes with his men from the island of the Cyclops, a race of ill-tempered, one-eyed giants. Polyphemus, one of these monsters, pursues the Greeks to their ship, but Odysseus has blinded him with a hot poker, and so it is with a gesture of impotent rage that Polyphemus heaves his boulder after the ship, while Odysseus stands in its stern, hurling taunts back to shore. The picture seems calculated to inspire both fear and laughter: awe at the crashing waves and jagged rocks; cruel amusement at the stumbling giant.

Originally trained as a landscape painter, Böcklin used an innovative variety of techniques and materials to create scenic effects. Here he layered oil- and water-based paints to convey the textures of rough rock and seething foam.

Oil and tempera on panel
66 x 150 cm (26 x 59 in.)
Museum purchase with funds by exchange from the Gift of Laurence K. and Lorna J. Marshall, 2012.626

Arnold Böcklin
Swiss, 1827–1901
Head of Medusa, about 1894

Medusa was a mythological snake-haired creature whose gaze could turn men to stone. The Greek hero Perseus avoided this fate by holding up his highly polished shield in which he could see Medusa's reflection. Protected in this way, he beheaded her. The image of the head of Medusa was believed to ward off evil, from ancient times onward. This rare example of a sculpture by the painter Böcklin presents Medusa with staring eyes, open mouth, and a wreath of snakes around her head. Böcklin drew on a variety of sources, including a circular painting by the Italian Baroque painter Caravaggio that shows Medusa's head just after decapitation, still dripping blood. Caravaggio thus represented the reflection of the Medusa in Perseus's shield, rendered powerless, but the monster's direct gaze at the viewer was still frightening. Böcklin's setting of the three-dimensional head projecting from the center of the convex shield pushes the face forcibly into the viewer's space, denying the notion that this is a reflective shield. The physical reality is intensified by Böcklin's expressive use of color. Medusa's skin has a greenish pallor, her lips are a blackish red, and her eyes, hair, and the snakes' heads are painted in a blood red highlighted with iridescent bronze. Her staring eyes hypnotically draw the viewer's gaze, transforming a protective image into a femme fatale.

Painted plaster and papier mâché
H. 61 cm (24 in.)
Bequest of the Estate of Mr. C. Adrian Rübel, 1978.514

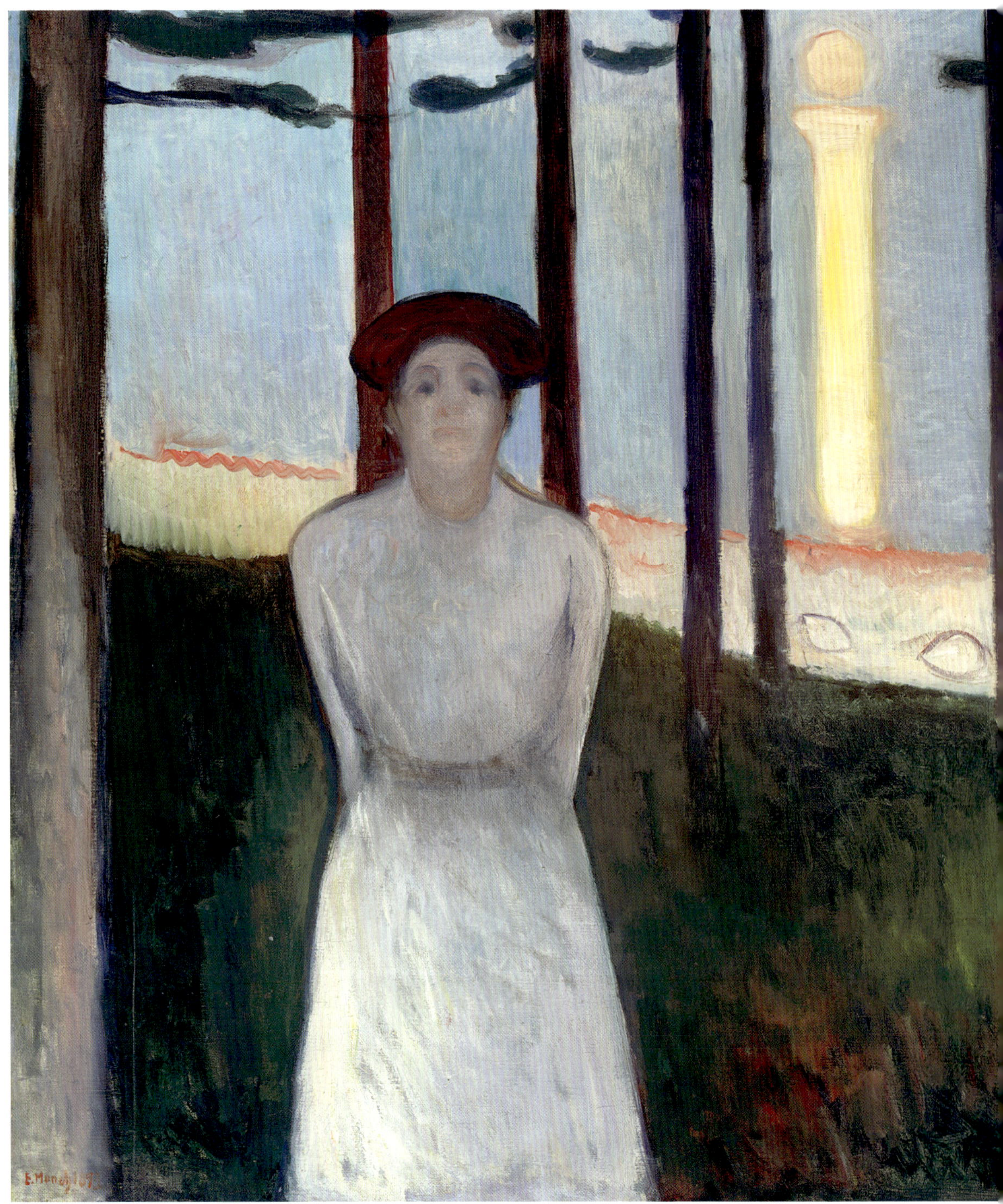

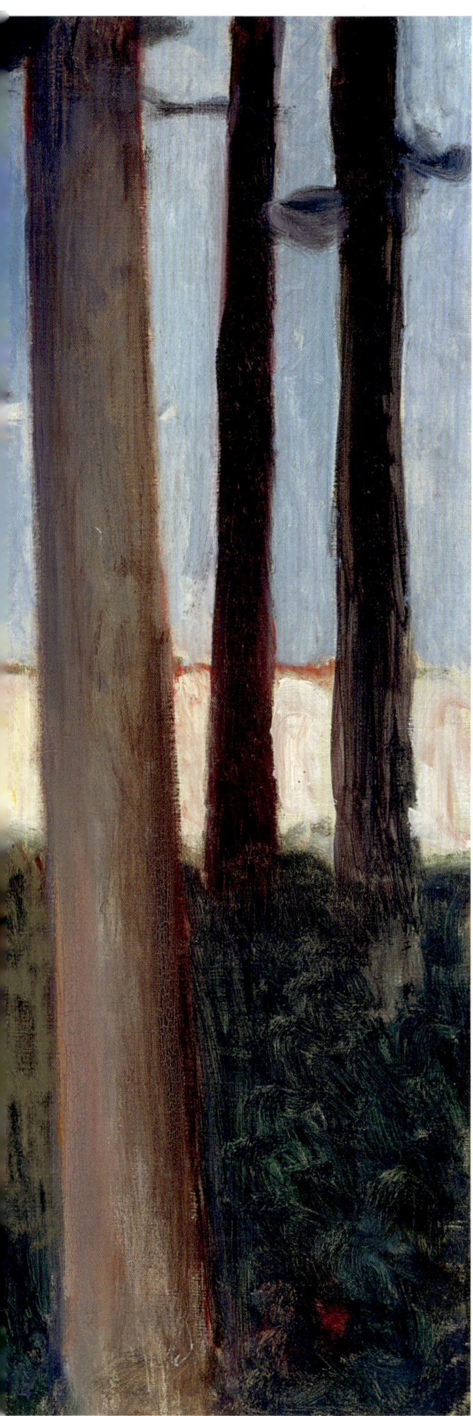

Edvard Munch

Norwegian, 1863–1944

Summer Night's Dream (The Voice), 1893

In a moonlit wood by the sea, a woman in white turns to face us. Her eyes are wide, her expression difficult to read. Behind her, the moon rises, casting its reflection almost to the shore. The atmosphere is charged with desire and foreboding. Bright water and dark fir trees indicate a Scandinavian setting; it is midsummer in the land of white nights. As in many of his works, Munch here simplified and exaggerated forms, using emphatic contrasts of light and dark to open up new expressive possibilities.

The picture was inspired by its author's recollection of an unhappy love affair with Emily "Milly" Thaulow, the wife of his cousin. Munch had first wooed her in the Borre Forest, a picturesque spot just north of Åsgårdstrand, the seaside resort where he went in summer to escape from city life. Intended to evoke the dawning of a doomed love, the picture strikes the same tone as Munch's written address to Milly in his journal: "Stand on the knoll, and there I can look into your eyes. . . . How pale you look in the moonlight, and how dark your eyes are—They are so large that they cover half the sky."

Munch originally exhibited the picture in Berlin in 1893 as the first of six paintings jointly titled *Study for a Series Called Love*. The other works in this series, which traced the arc of a love affair, from passion to anxiety, doubt, and disillusionment, were *The Kiss*, *Love and Pain*, *Madonna Face*, *Jealousy*, and *Despair*. The last of these, *Despair*, is today known as *The Scream* and remains Munch's most famous composition. It originally formed a grim bookend to *The Voice*'s evocation of love's beginning.

Oil on canvas

87.9 x 108 cm (34 5/8 x 42 1/2 in.)

Ernest Wadsworth Longfellow Fund, 59.301

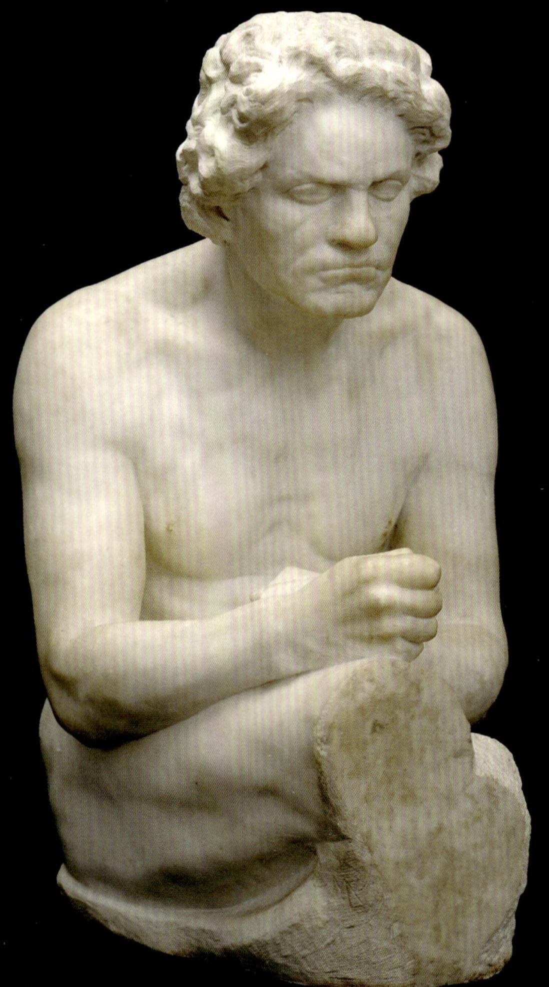

Max Klinger
German, 1857–1920
Beethoven, after 1902

Klinger trained as a painter and a printmaker, but he also worked as a sculptor. In the 1880s he was inspired by a vision of a monument to Beethoven and spent nearly two decades planning his sculpture and collecting various materials for it. His original monument to Beethoven, with the figure made in a combination of white marble and colored stone for the drapery, and the throne in bronze ornamented with ivory and precious stones, became the centerpiece of the fourteenth annual exhibition at Vienna's Secession House in 1902. The Beethoven pavilion, a primary example of *Gesamtkunstwerk*—the joining together of all the arts to create a complete sensory and aesthetic experience—included Klinger's monument along with Gustav Klimt's painted Beethoven frieze. At the inauguration, Gustav Mahler conducted portions of Beethoven's Ninth Symphony. This smaller version was commissioned from Klinger by the steel tycoon and art patron Karl Wittgenstein for his music room.

The over-life-size image of the composer is pared down to the marble core of the larger monument, without the colored drapery or the embellished throne. The figure leans forward, his legs crossing, his arms held closely to his body, hands held one behind the other, with fists clenched. The tightly bound pose seems about to burst with contained energy. The piece is a fragment, cut off at the thighs where the colored stone drapery begins on the original figure, bringing the viewer into much more direct interaction with the image of the composer. Klinger was inspired by the physical and psychological naturalism of Rodin's sculpture, as well as by his marble-carving techniques, which contrast various levels of finish and polish.

Marble
101.6 cm high (40 x 21 x 27 ⅛ in.)
Gift of Paul Wittgenstein, 52.204

Oskar Kokoschka
Austrian, 1886–1980
Two Nudes (Lovers), 1913

Two life-size nudes, wrapped in an anxious embrace, seem to circle each other against a background of blue-green vegetation. We are in Eden, perhaps, but not quite paradise. The dancers' eyes do not meet; their troubled expressions suggest an estrangement that belies their caresses. Kokoschka exhibited the painting as *Adam and Eve* and *Dancers, Green Version*, but it is in fact a double portrait of the artist himself with Alma Mahler, the woman who changed his life and his art.

Alma (née Schindler) was a brilliant figure in turn-of-the-century Viennese society. A talented composer in her own right, she had married Gustav Mahler, the famous opera director and composer, at age twenty-two. Widowed nine years later, she met Kokoschka at a dinner party in 1911 and became his lover the following spring. The affair was passionate and stormy, a transformative experience for them both. It lasted until 1915, when Alma, tormented by the painter's jealousy, married Walter Gropius, the great modernist architect and founder of the Bauhaus.

Kokoschka's mature style, characterized by the slashing strokes and thickly applied paint that give this picture its rushing urgency, grew from his relationship with Alma. Like other avant-garde artists in Vienna—particularly Gustav Klimt and Egon Schiele—Kokoschka was drawn to emerging theories of psychoanalysis and the unconscious mind. As a portraitist, he had an uncanny ability to capture his sitters' inner lives. Here, portraying himself and his beloved, he evoked the longing and loneliness at the heart of their passion.

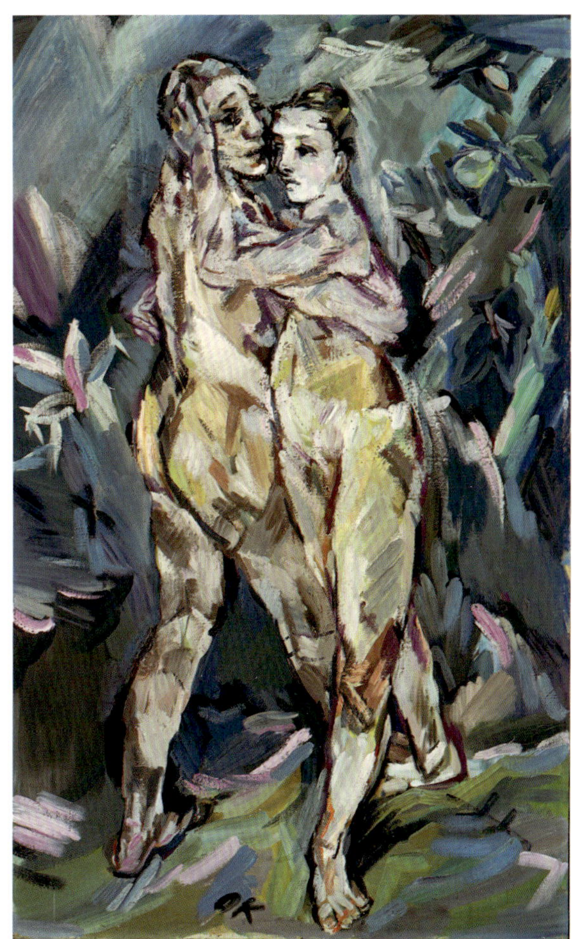

Oil on canvas
163.2 x 97.5 cm (64¼ x 38⅜ in.)
Bequest of Sarah Reed Platt, 1973.196

Oskar Kokoschka
Austrian, 1886–1980
Self-Portrait as a Warrior, 1909

Kokoschka made his first foray into the Expressionist style with this portrait bust, one of only a few works by him in sculpture. His features are distorted with suffering, his skin in places seems peeled back to reveal nerves and raw flesh. The skin is painted in a buff tone mixed with black, suggesting decay. Garish colors pick out features in a completely unnatural way, as in the bright orange left eyelid. The neck seems twisted almost to the breaking point, with the clavicle displaced to the right and painted red. Kokoschka called his self-portrait *The Warrior* and with it he took up artistic arms against the graceful, linear forms of the reigning Art Nouveau style.

When it was first displayed in Vienna in 1909, the bust was ridiculed by most who saw it. The artist wrote in his autobiography that the gallery in which it was displayed was called a "chamber of horrors" and that the bust was defaced by people putting bits of chocolate in its mouth. Even the technique was raw and brutally expressive, as Kokoschka modeled the bust in clay, applied paint directly to the unfired, rough surface, and set it on a simple wooden base, giving it the immediacy of a work still in progress.

Unfired clay painted with tempera
36.5 x 31.5 x 19.5 cm (14 3/8 x 12 3/8 x 7 5/8 in.)
John H. and Ernestine A. Payne Fund, 60.958

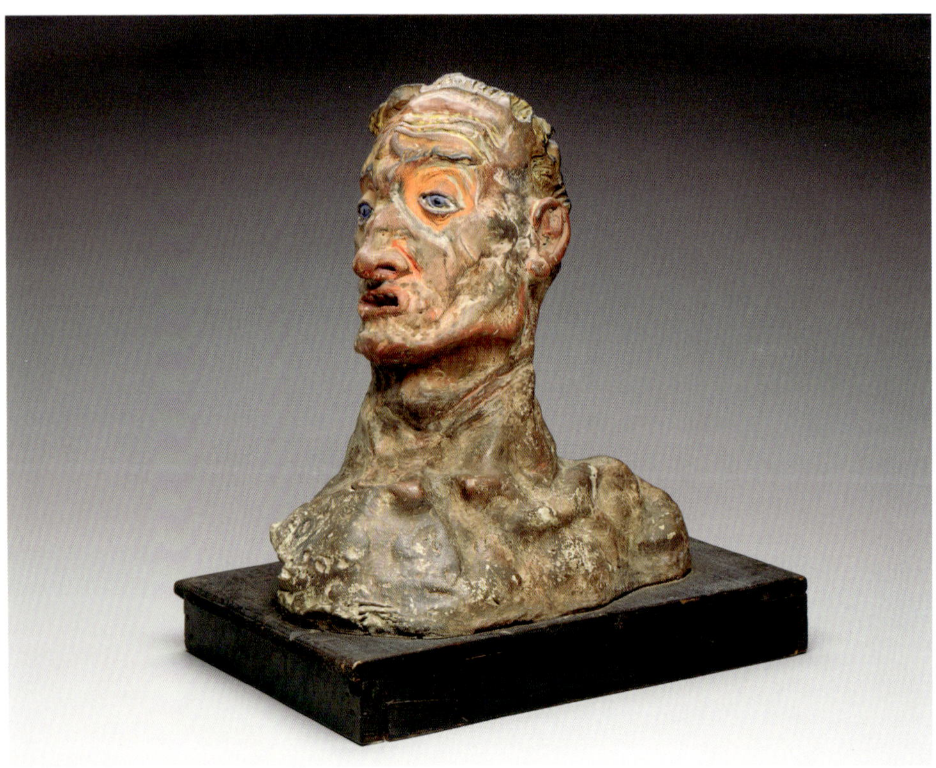

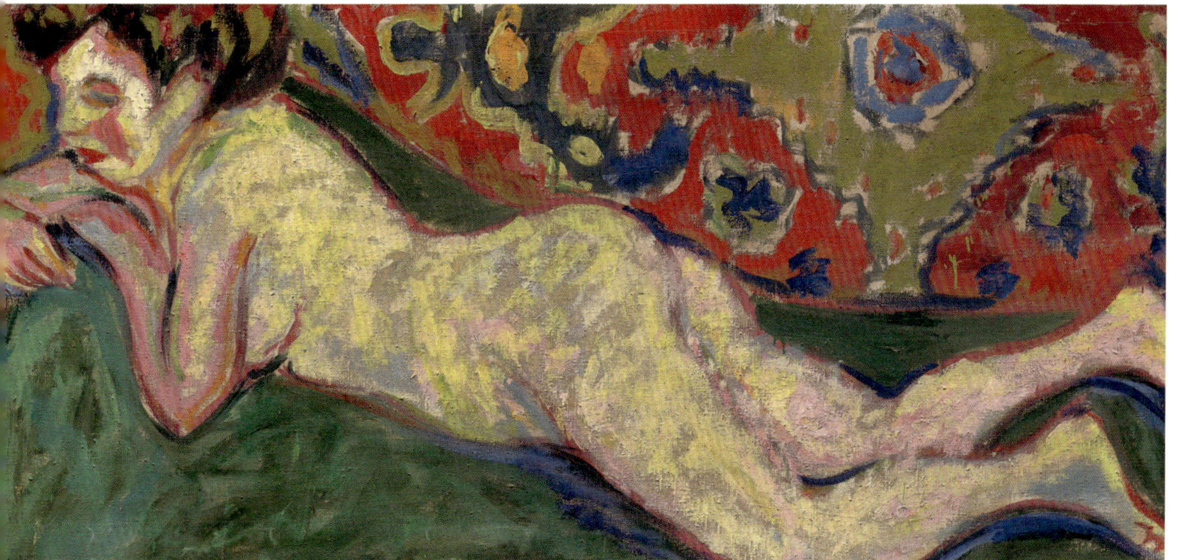

Ernst Ludwig Kirchner
German, 1880–1938
Reclining Nude, 1909

Kirchner was one of the four founders of Die Brücke (The Bridge), an artists' collective that initiated the German Expressionist movement in 1905. Kirchner and his cohort were architecture students in Dresden; they had received no formal training in painting but drew inspiration from recent exhibitions of avant-garde art from outside Germany that had introduced them to the work of Van Gogh, Gauguin, and Munch. Van Gogh's vigorous touch, Gauguin's bold use of color, and Munch's expressive distortions of form came together in this new style: rough, loud, and modern.

Reclining Nude, likely painted in January 1909, reflects this threefold influence. Against the saturated greens and reds of the background, the figure stands out, thinly painted in acidic pink and yellow. Yet the bold, horizontal composition and paper-doll flatness of the nude reveal yet another influence on the artist: Henri Matisse, an exhibition of whose work opened at the Cassirer gallery in Berlin shortly before Kirchner, by then living in the German capital, set to work on this canvas. From Matisse, Kirchner absorbed a more hedonistic approach to his subject matter and materials, luxuriating in the range of color and texture at his disposal. Like Matisse, Kirchner and his fellow members of Die Brücke were increasingly drawn to forms found outside European art. The Turkish carpet that provides the foil to our nude is among the first non-Western objects to appear in his work.

Oil on canvas
74 x 151.5 cm (29 1/8 x 59 5/8 in.)
Tompkins Collection—Arthur Gordon Tompkins Fund, 57.2

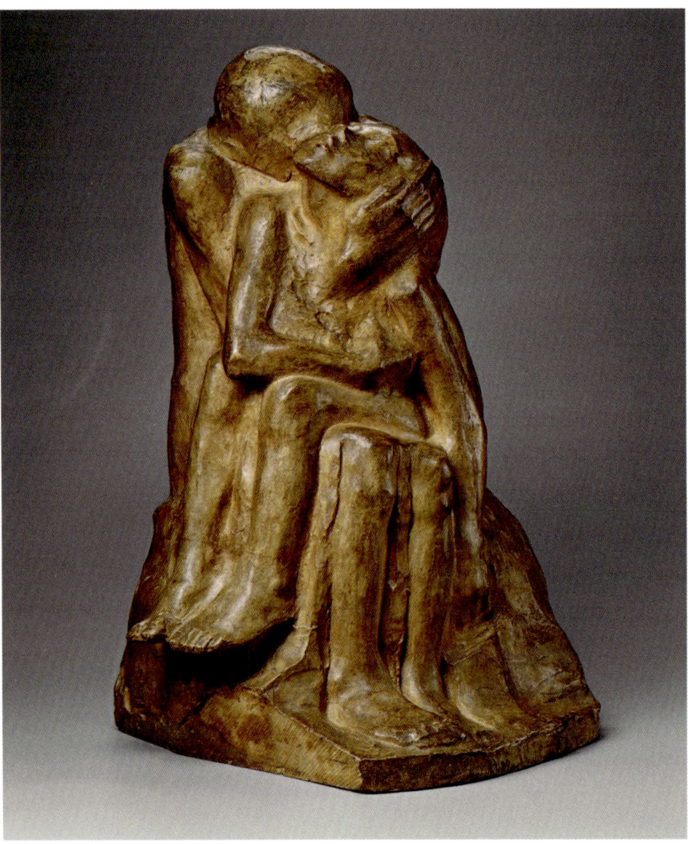

Käthe Kollwitz
German, 1867–1945
The Lovers, 1913

There has been confusion about the subject of this sculpture, which represents a smaller figure on the lap of a larger one. Its composition refers directly to a medieval and Renaissance type of religious sculpture known as the *Pietà*, which shows the body of the dead Christ on the lap of his grieving mother, and Kollwitz's sculpture has sometimes been identified as a *Pietà* image. The limp, hanging left arm of the smaller figure is a motif used since antiquity to indicate death, and was later often used in images of the dead Christ. However, the group represents a pair of lovers, their heads brought together in a kiss, the left arm of the woman hanging limp as she abandons herself to the moment. This ambivalence of subject, which seems to combine love, passion, and grief, is typical of Kollwitz's subject matter throughout her life. Her prints, sculptures, and writings express a deep empathy for these powerful human emotions. Kollwitz uses the sculptural medium to further the emotional power of her group. Modeled as if they were to be carved from a single block of stone, her figures seem to merge one into the other. The sculpture was cast in white plaster, but its surface has discolored, resulting in a buff tone that suggests clay or warm sandstone. Her own life was touched by sorrow from an early age, from the death of her younger brother in childhood through the tragedies of two world wars, including the loss of a son a year after this sculpture was made, and this sadness pervades her work.

Plaster
74.3 x 45.7 x 48.3 cm (29¼ x 18 x 19 in.)
Gift of Mr. and Mrs. Hyman W. Swetzoff in memory of Mr. and Mrs. Solomon Swetzoff, 58.390

Henri Gaudier-Brzeska
French, 1891–1915
The Wrestlers, 1914

Gaudier showed precocious talent for drawing. He turned to sculpture before he was twenty, expressing intense admiration for the work of Rodin. He moved to England in 1911, appended the name of his companion Sophie Brzeska to his own, and began exploring new directions in his art. He was inspired by a broad notion of the "primitive" that he sought out, for example, at the British Museum—where, as he described in a letter to Sophie, he took "particular notice of all the primitive statues, negro, yellow, red, and white races, Gothic and Greek." When the poet Ezra Pound first met Gaudier-Brzeska in London in 1913, he described him as like "a well-made wolf or some soft-moving, bright-eyed wild thing." The artist quickly absorbed influences from many sources. He encountered the sculptor Constantin Brancusi and saw his work at an exhibition in 1913, and responded immediately to Brancusi's smoothly finished, simplified volumes. He experimented with the pared-down, linear style we see in this plaster relief of two figures wrestling. These sinuous, seemingly weightless creatures also illustrate the excitement Gaudier felt at wrestling matches: "I went to see the wrestlers—God! I have seldom seen anything so lovely. . . . They fought with amazing vivacity and spirit, turning in the air, falling back on their heads, and in a flash were up again on the other side, utterly incomprehensible."

Pound was the founder of the Vorticist movement, which sought to overthrow staid British art and life through explosive energy, even wildness. He became a supporter of and friend to Gaudier-Brzeska, helping find commissions for the impoverished artist and providing him with the block of stone from which to carve his portrait. Pound also wrote a biography and tribute to the young sculptor, who was killed in action in 1915 in World War I at the age of twenty-three.

Plaster
71.8 x 92.1 cm (28¼ x 36¼ x 2 in.)
Otis Norcross Fund, 65.1683.1

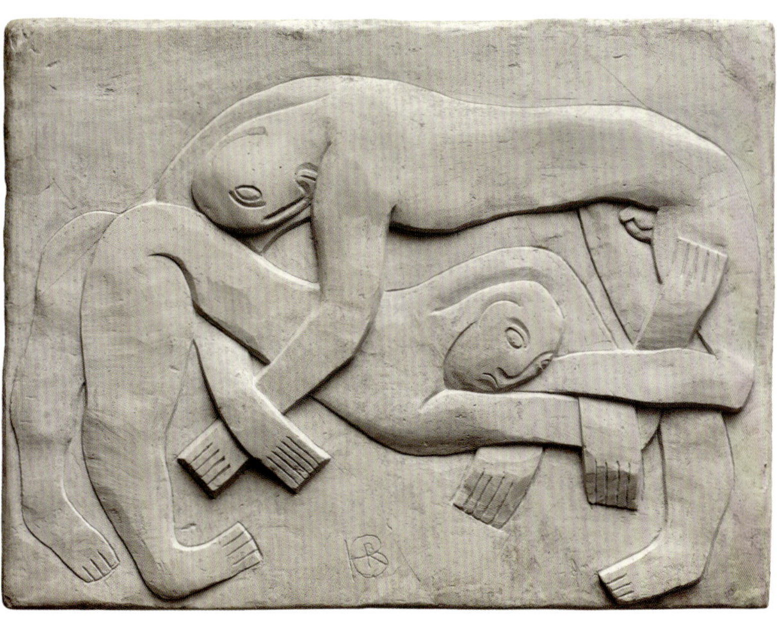

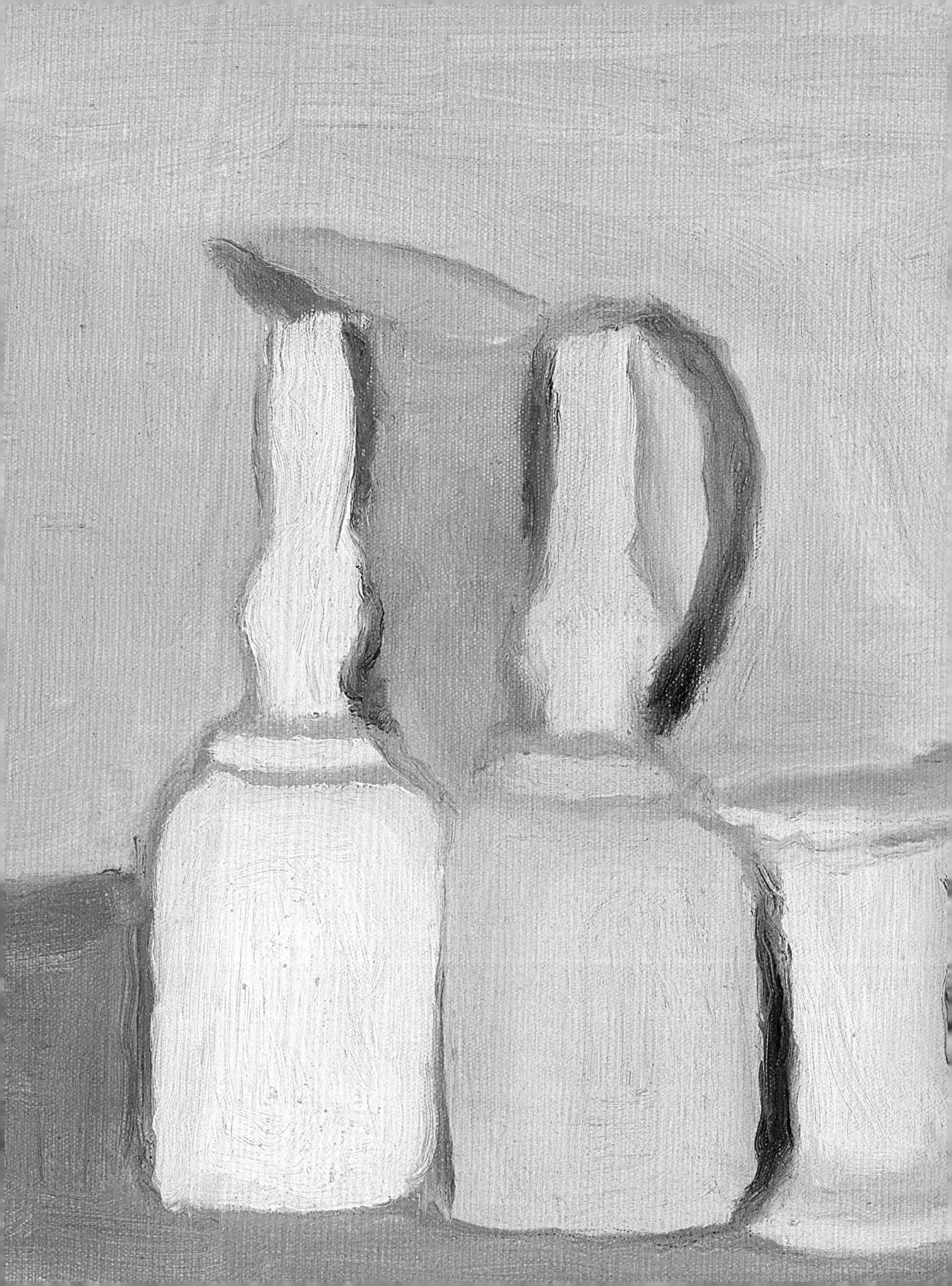

6 INTO THE TWENTIETH CENTURY: abstraction and beyond

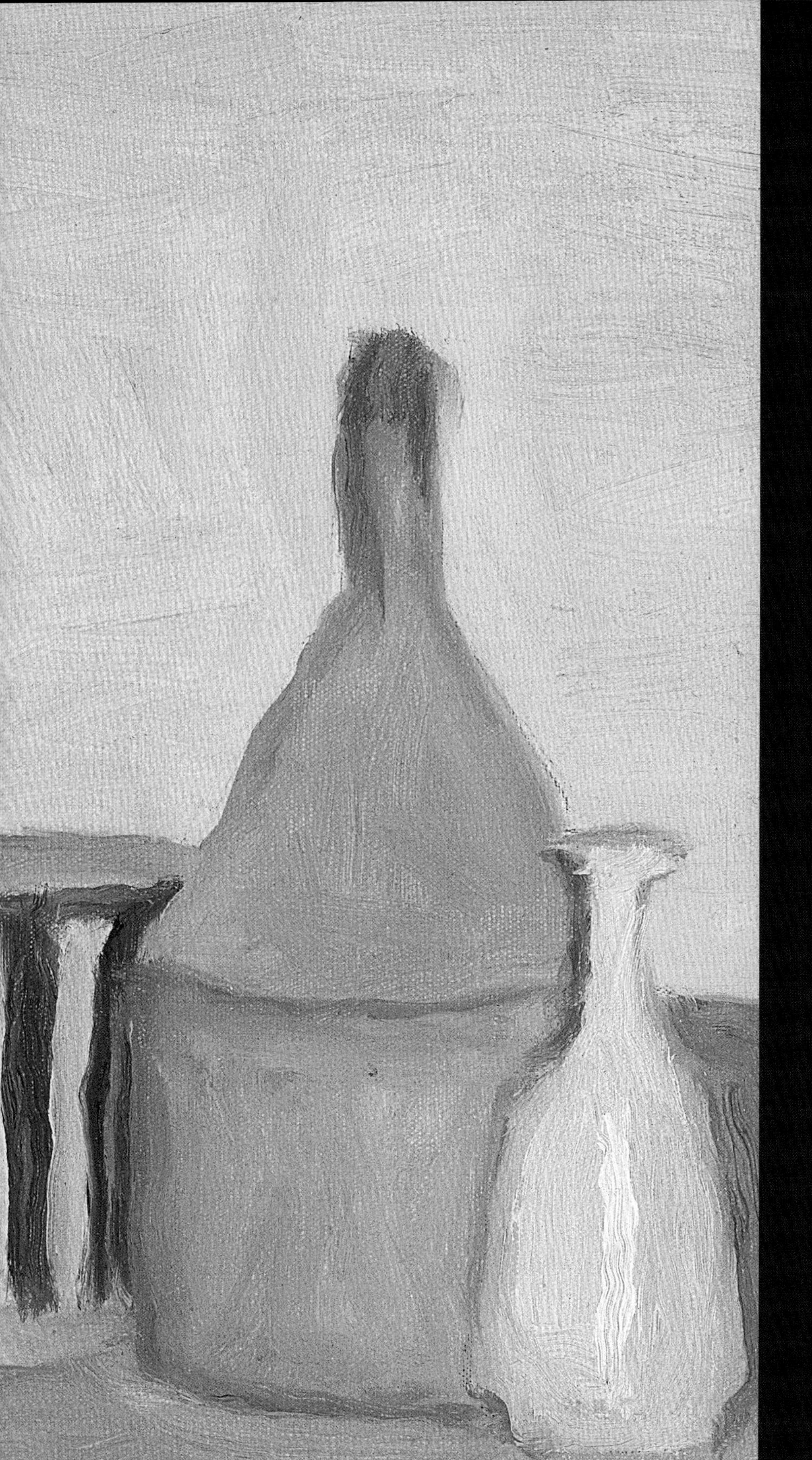

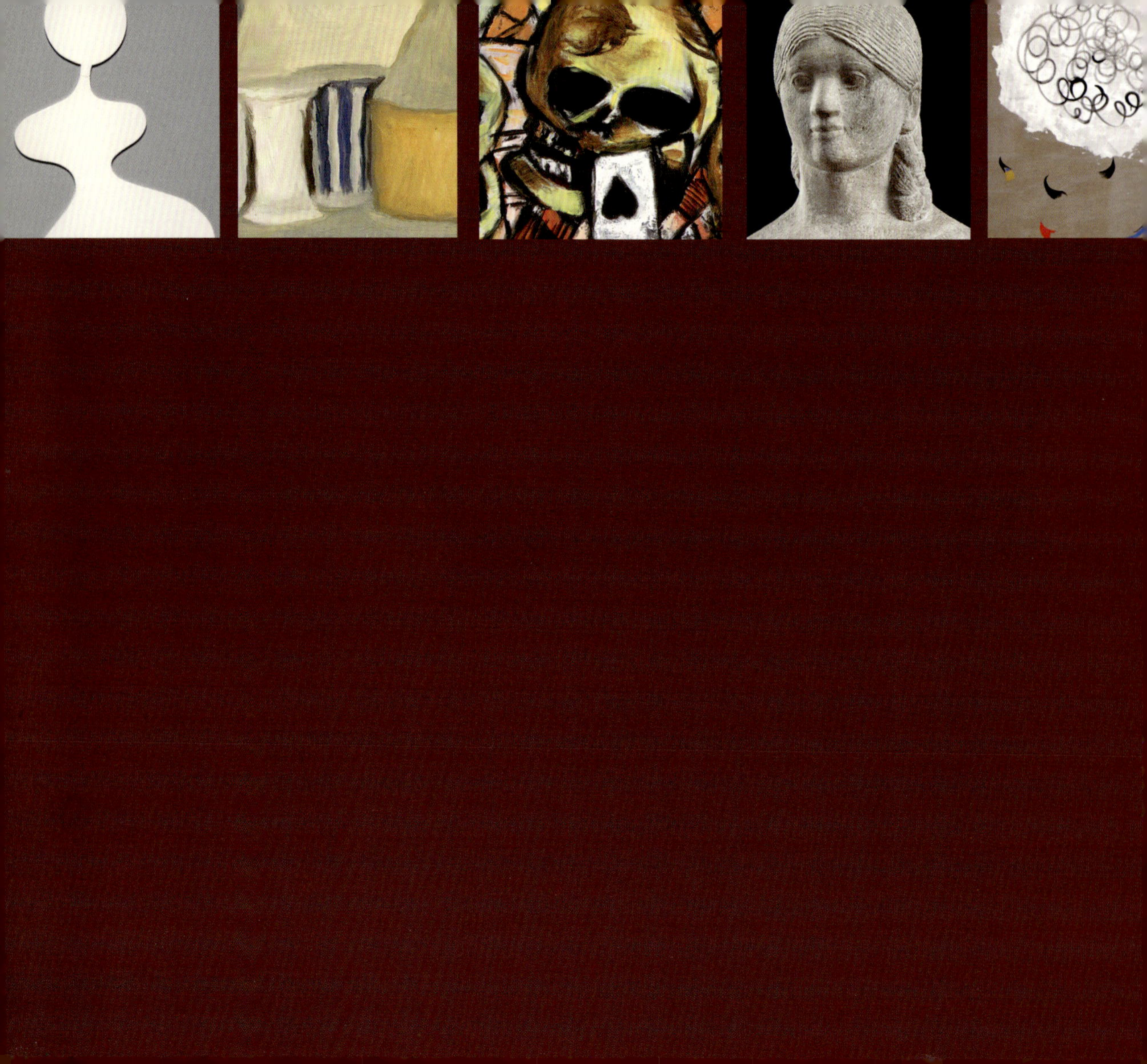

Into the Twentieth Century: Abstraction and Beyond

The history of European art in the early twentieth century is one of provocation and reaction, of aesthetic and intellectual boundaries tested and political forces unleashed. To what extent could progressive art exist in the "real" world, and to what extent should it fashion a world apart, obeying its own imperatives and independent of observed reality? Experimenting with a broad range of styles and approaches, European artists in this period tested the relationship between meaning and form, representation and abstraction, life and art. The resulting works concentrate our attention as never before on the means of their making. We see the bronze before we see the body, the paint before the picture.

The third annual Salon d'Automnc, in October 1905, marks the first chapter in this story. Comprising more than sixteen hundred paintings, sculptures, works on paper, and decorative art objects, the exhibition's most memorable contributions came from a group of young painters—Henri Matisse, Maurice de Vlaminck, André Derain, and their colleagues—whose wild palettes and willful naïveté quickly earned them the nickname "Fauves" (wild beasts). The Fauves set out to overturn all the conventions of Western picture making—from perspective to modeling to anatomy—in an approach today known as "de-skilling."

The great master of this antitechnique, however, was Pablo Picasso, a Spanish artist twelve years Matisse's junior, who used a systematic study of African sculpture in Parisian anthropological collections to unlearn the Academic training he had received as a teenager in Madrid. Goaded by his artistic collaborator, Georges Braque, and encouraged by the progressive dealer Henry Kahnweiler (himself an avid collector of African masks), Picasso explored the distinction between representation and imitation from about 1907 to 1917, using a range of approaches that would become collectively knows as Cubism. In Cubism, geometric shapes (curves, lines, squares, wedges) take on representational significance only in context (becoming eyes, breasts, bottles, guitars); the relationship between the individual sign and the individual object signified is no longer mimetic.

Cubism was a scandal. When examples of the style appeared in the 1912 Salon d'Automne, the French house of representatives almost withdrew state funding from the exhibition. Why should the government subsidize art most viewers found incomprehensible? This violent reaction to modernist provocation had a profound effect in the aftermath of the First World War. The late 1910s and the 1920s saw such former provocateurs as Matisse and Picasso return to classical tradition, obeying a broader cultural imperative known as the *rappel à l'ordre* (call to order).

Innovation in this period found alternative channels; the Bauhaus, for example, a progressive school of art and design founded in Germany in 1919, offered artists and architects an intellectual community and suggested new means of integrating modernist principles into everyday life. The Bauhaus helped propagate and popularize the principles of De Stijl, a Dutch art and design movement pioneered by Piet Mondrian and Theo van Doesburg. In 1925 the Bauhaus Press published Mondrian's *Neo-Plasticism in Pictorial Art*, a manifesto, written in 1920, in which the artist set forth his tenets for "pure painting." Though Cubism had relinquished mimesis, it had remained moored to the real world by the thread of representation; Mondrian's Neo-Plasticism cut that thread, floating off into pure abstraction.

At the same moment, in Paris, the Surrealist movement, too, was pursuing an alternative to the representation of reality: in this case, the world of the unconscious mind, of dreams, madness, and automatism. The movement's spiritual father was André Breton, a poet and the author of the 1924 *Manifesto of Surrealism*. The artists in his orbit, including Joan Miró and Hans Arp, created formless forms, inchoate and suggestive, neither straightforwardly representational nor purely abstract. The Surrealists conducted these playful explorations in the shadow of fascism. The heated artistic manifestos of the period—of Neo-Plasticism, Dadaism, Surrealism, Futurism—presaged the increasingly polarized, volatile political climate of 1930s Europe. Courting abstraction, absurdity, even abjection, many avant-garde artists seemed to pose a threat to totalitarian regimes and their triumphal agendas for culture. Hitler, Mussolini, and Franco made canny use of culture, favoring heroic figuration in the visual arts, an amped-up Neo-Neoclassicism. In Berlin, the propaganda ministry of the Third Reich closed down the modern wing of the National Gallery in 1936. The following summer, a notorious exhibition of "degenerate art" opened in Munich, launching a systematic campaign of confiscations and imprisonments; Gerhard Marcks and Max Beckmann were among the artists designated "degenerate." As German forces conquered Europe, the sale of objects seized from private and public collections helped finance the war effort, in the most systematic campaign of looting in recorded history.

After the war, what was next? How to make art after Auschwitz and the atom bomb? Many artists plunged further into abstraction, attempting to create work wholly independent of politics, paintings and sculptures that they hoped could never be deployed to propagandistic ends. Others confronted political realities with striking bluntness. Picasso's late, wrenching *Rape of the Sabine Women* is an outcry against atomic warfare framed in the visual vocabulary of the eighteenth-century master Jacques-Louis David, a return to the revolutionary roots of modern art. ***—E.A.B.***

Henri Matisse

French, 1869–1954

Carmelina, 1903

In the autumn of 1932, a distinguished patron of the Museum, seeing this newly acquired picture on the wall, left an irate message for the curator of European paintings: "Will you tell Phillip that if he does not take *that painted woman* off exhibition I shall never bring my wife or my sister-in-law into the paintings galleries ever again." The "painted woman" in question was Carmela Caira, known as Carmelina, who had already posed for the American artist James McNeill Whistler and for Rodin's *Kiss* when Matisse hired her to sit for this early work in 1903. That the resulting likeness could produce so strong a reaction nearly thirty years after it was painted is a testament to Matisse's budding powers as a provocateur.

In the harsh, raking light of his studio on the quai Saint-Michel, the model's contours take on a rough, planar quality that suggests the young artist's admiration for Cézanne. Though her pose is emphatically frontal, Carmelina's steady gaze does not quite meet ours, which is aligned instead with that of the painter, looking out at us from a mirror propped against the rear wall of the studio. This reflection at once adds a dimension of spatial complexity to the composition and, with its splash of red, asserts the artist's role as artificer of the scene. Both the studio itself and the encounter between artist and model, introduced in this work, would become central concerns for Matisse's later production, through his radical Fauve period and subsequent classicism.

Oil on canvas

81.3 x 59 cm (32 x 23¼ in.)

Tompkins Collection—Arthur Gordon Tompkins Fund, RES.32.14

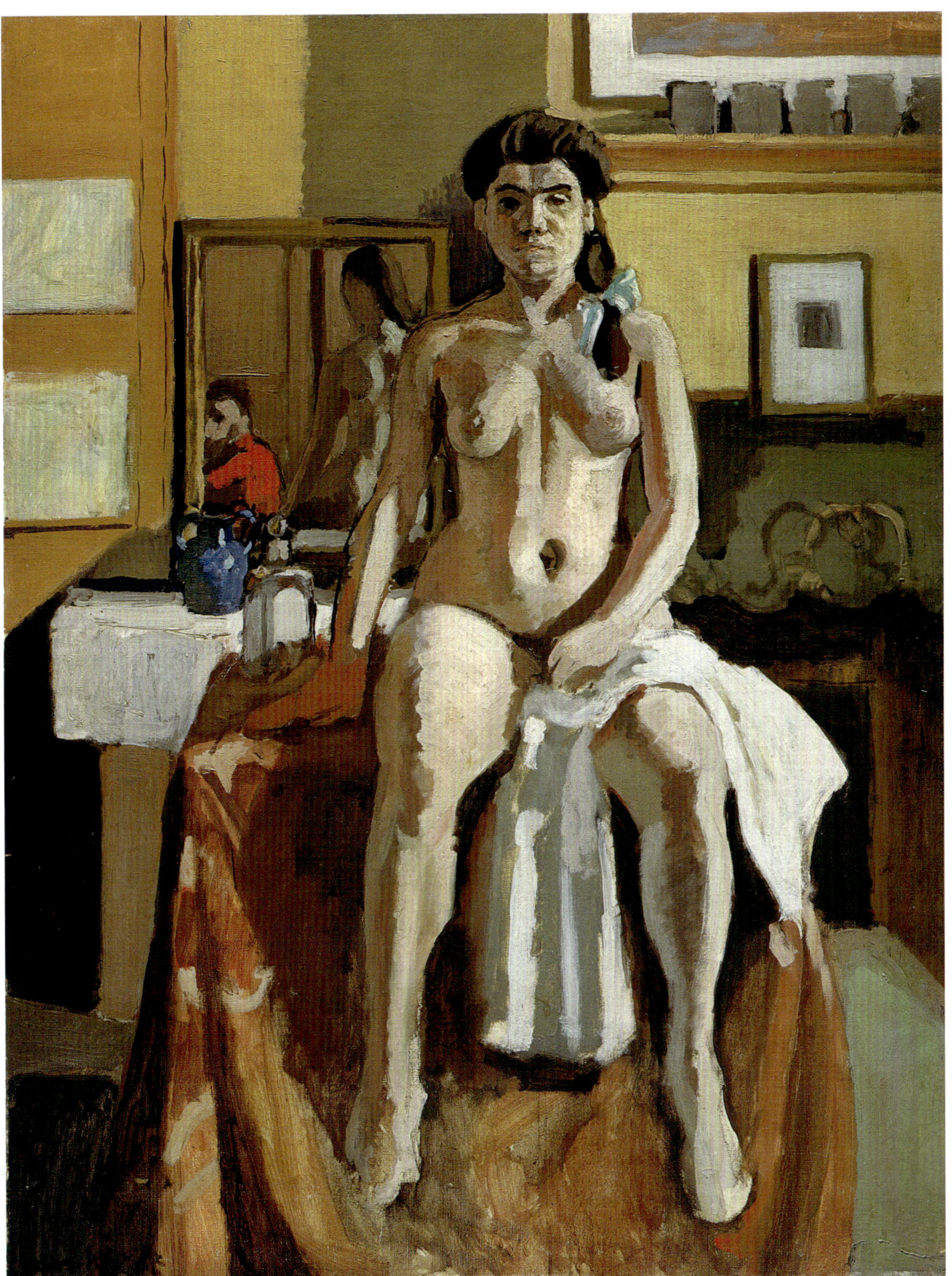

Pablo Picasso
Spanish (worked in France), 1881–1973
Fernande Olivier, 1905–6

Picasso's dramatic shifts of style have often been mapped onto the series of love affairs that inspired him throughout his career. The first of his great lovers and muses was Fernande Olivier, whom the artist met in Montmartre in 1904. She moved into his communal studio—the so-called *bateau-lavoir* (laundry boat)—the following year, sharing its cramped living quarters with Picasso and his colleagues André Salmon and Kees van Dongen. "La belle Fernande," as his friends called her, was Picasso's bohemian muse, the model who presided over his evolution from the starved, elongated style of his early Blue Period to the more classical, monumental forms of his Rose Period and early Cubist work.

Fernande's almond-shaped eyes, sensuous mouth, and sturdy neck are recognizable in many works Picasso produced between 1904 and 1910, but this portrait seems to be among his most faithful likenesses. The picture hovers somewhere between a painting and a drawing. Using oils thinned almost to the consistency of ink, the artist worked out the contours of his sitter's face—her high cheekbones and arching brows—with a meticulous network of hatch marks, a reminder of his recent experiments with etching. Fernande's body and clothing, by contrast, are barely indicated with a series of loose, open lines. This wide variation of finish may reflect Picasso's growing interest in the Neoclassical artist Jean-Auguste-Dominique Ingres, whose pencil portraits of a century earlier display a similar pattern of attention.

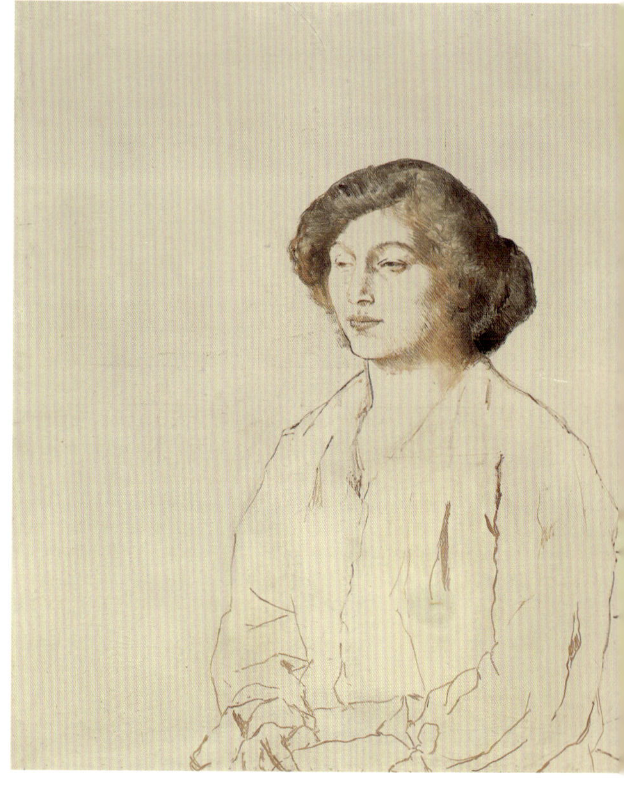

Oil on canvas
100 x 81 cm (39 3/8 x 31 7/8 in.)
Arthur K. Solomon Collection, 2004.446

Pablo Picasso
Spanish (worked in France), 1881–1973
Head of a Woman, 1909

This portrait of his mistress and muse Fernande Olivier was Picasso's first Cubist sculpture. The challenge of applying the ideas of Cubism to a three-dimensional object means that *Head of a Woman* is less abstracted and less fragmented than Cubist works on paper or canvas. It maintains the basic volumetric structure of the head as well as the general disposition of the features. Within that structure, Picasso breaks up the planes of the face and hair, accentuating projecting edges and creating deep and sharply cut shadows. The visual effect depends strongly on the way light is caught and reflected from those edges and absorbed into the deep crevices, and the way it moves over the textured surfaces of the fragmented forms. Tension is created between the Cubist faceting of planes and the natural form of the head. The head tilts downward, the eyes are deeply shadowed, and the lips tightly pursed, conveying a sense of melancholy and pensiveness, as the individuality of the sitter asserts itself.

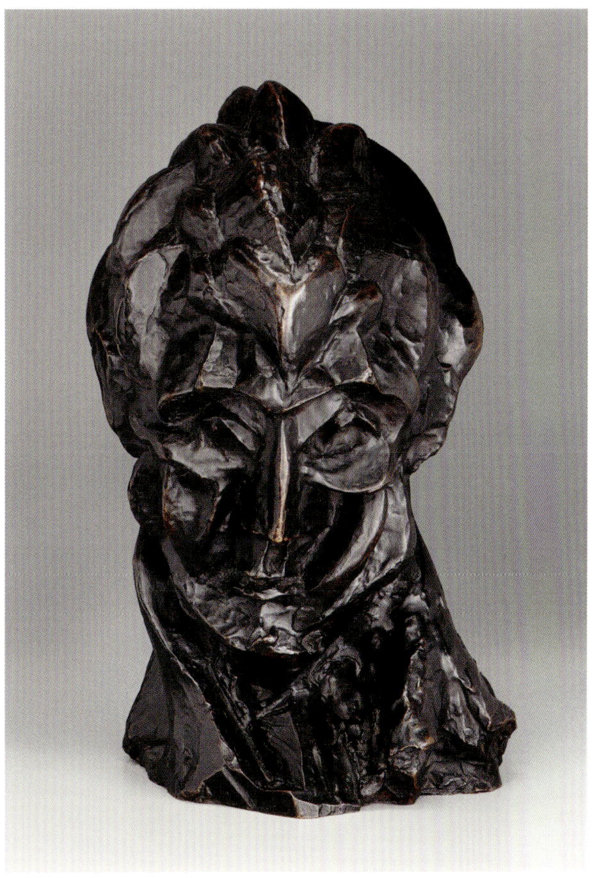

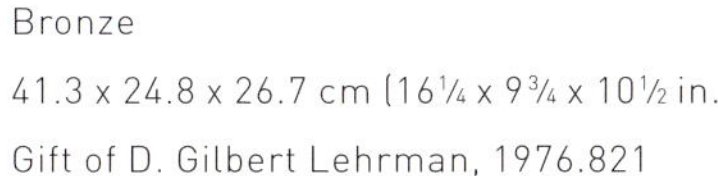
Bronze
41.3 x 24.8 x 26.7 cm (16¼ x 9¾ x 10½ in.)
Gift of D. Gilbert Lehrman, 1976.821

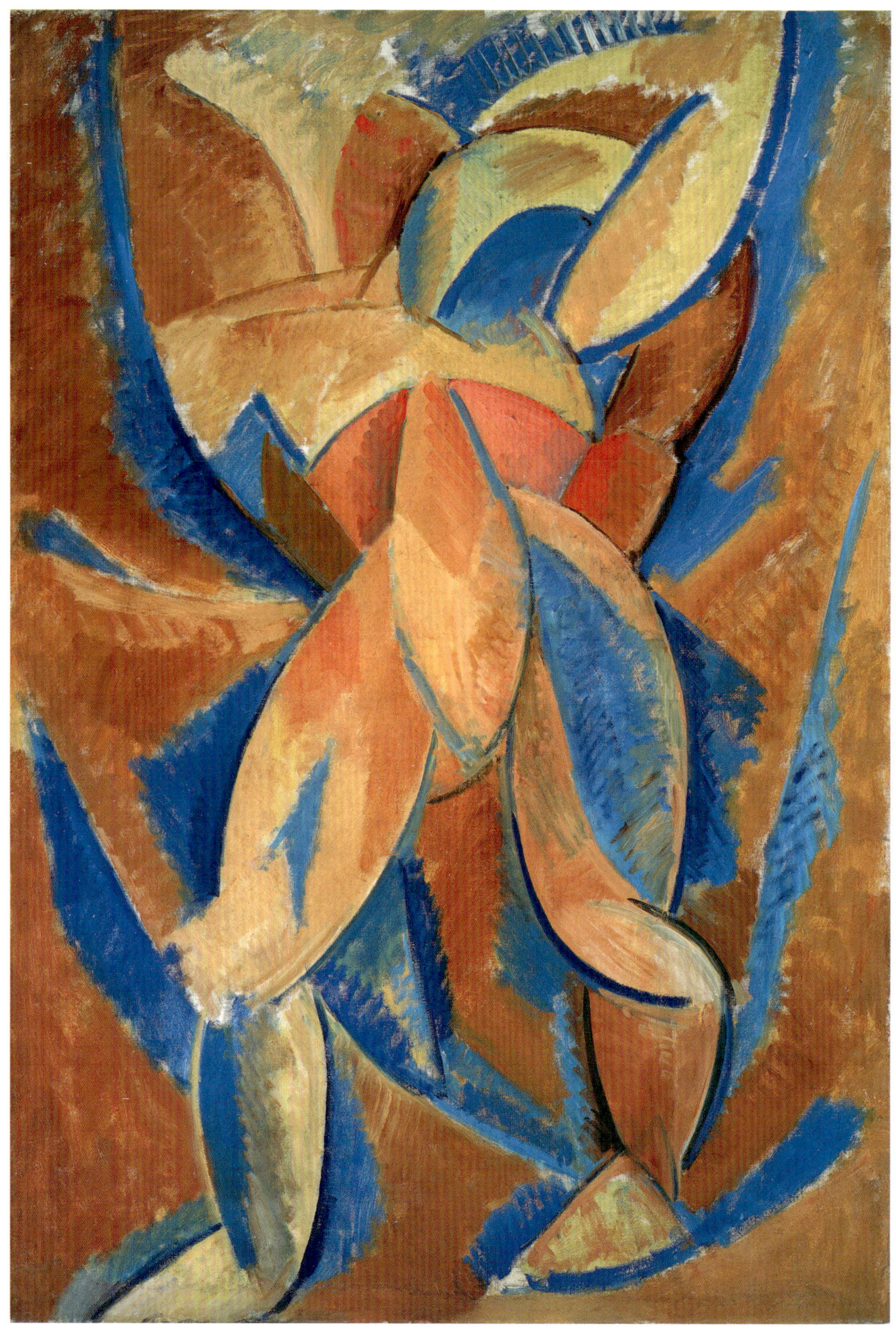

Pablo Picasso

Spanish (worked in France), 1881–1973

Standing Figure, 1908

With its bold dissection of the human figure into a series of arbitrary, interlocking forms, this picture demonstrates why Picasso was the most influential European artist of the twentieth century. The painter here set out to treat the nude, that most classical of all subjects, but the resulting image systematically dismantles classical tradition and its means of portraying figure, ground, and space.

Strokes of blue—contour and shading—carve up the body into its constituent forms: muscular, faceted thighs; a lozenge for the abdomen; angular, downward-pointing breasts. These features are borrowed from the West African wood sculptures Picasso so admired in the collections of his Parisian friends and patrons. Like Gauguin before him, Picasso turned to non-Western art in an effort to disrupt and renew European tradition.

An equally powerful influence at this moment was the work of Cézanne, whose posthumous retrospective the young artist had seen at the Salon d'Automne in 1907, and whose presence is felt in the short, chiseling strokes of blue throughout this picture. While some of these articulate the forms of the nude, others disengage her from her inchoate surroundings, though figure and ground remain strangely entangled, creating an effect of simultaneous flatness and relief. Cézanne's own explorations of surface and space are here pushed to a new extreme: analysis unmoored from mimesis.

Oil on canvas

150.2 x 100.3 cm (59⅛ x 39½ in.)

Juliana Cheney Edwards Collection, 58.976

Pierre-Auguste Renoir
French, 1841–1919
Small Victorious Venus, 1913

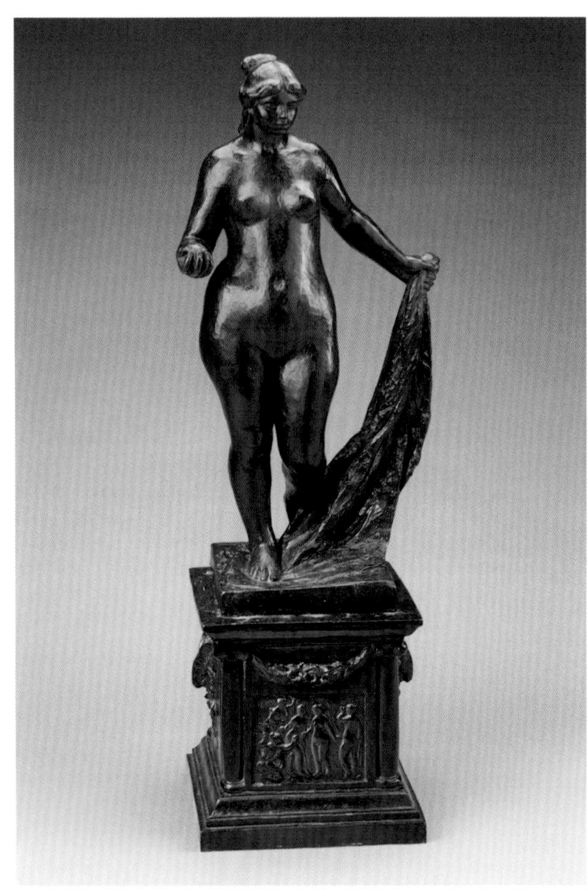

The ancient goddess of love and beauty holds an apple in her right hand, the prize awarded to her as winner at the Judgment of Paris, the contest among three goddesses that helped spark the Trojan War. A relief on the base of the statue presents this event. The subject matter and standing nude figure hark back to classical antiquity and ancient art; they also mark a distinct path followed by Renoir later in his life, away from the spontaneous outdoor approach of his Impressionist beginnings and toward a greater focus on the idealized figure of the female nude. In old age, Renoir was nearly completely crippled with rheumatoid arthritis and could only paint with his brushes tied to his hands, yet he was drawn to the idea of creating sculpture. He turned to the dealer Ambrose Vollard, saying "I am looking for a pair of hands." Vollard first suggested the sculptor Maillol, whose smooth, classicizing female figures were close to Renoir's vision for his sculpture, but Maillol was too busy producing his own work. He, in turn, suggested Richard Guino, a young Spanish artist. Guino acted as Renoir's hands, working under his direct instructions or following his drawings, allowing Renoir's sculptural vision to come to life while bringing his own skills to the process.

Bronze
Modeled by Richard Guino, Spanish, 1890–1973
Cast by C. Valsuani, Paris
85.1 x 22.9 x 22.9 cm (33½ x 9 x 9 in.)
William Francis Warden Fund, 56.259

Pierre-Auguste Renoir
French, 1841–1919
Model for a clock case, 1915

When Renoir took up sculpture late in his life, he explored a range of themes and styles. He once said, "I am of the eighteenth century," and his paintings were often inspired by Rococo masters such as Jean-Honoré Fragonard. This plaster model for a clock case epitomizes this aspect of Renoir's art. A popular form of sculptural and allegorical decoration in the eighteenth century, the clock case appears in Renoir's work only in this one instance and is very rare and pointedly nostalgic in the early twentieth century. An allegory of time passing, it represents the life cycle, with nude figures celebrating the triumphant baby who sits in the clouds atop the globe and holding a flaming torch, while the female figure offers a bunch of flowers. The open circle in the center of the composition would hold the clock in the final bronze. The case as a whole was modeled by Richard Guino, the young sculptor who helped Renoir make his sculptures a reality. The energy and vigorous youth of the figures are a poignant contrast to Renoir's old age, given that he needed another artist to execute his sculptural ideas, his own hands crippled with arthritis.

Plaster
Modeled by Richard Guino, Spanish, 1890–1973
83.8 x 61 x 32.5 cm (33 x 24 x 12¾ in.)
Gift of Mr. A. M. Sonnabend, 61.954

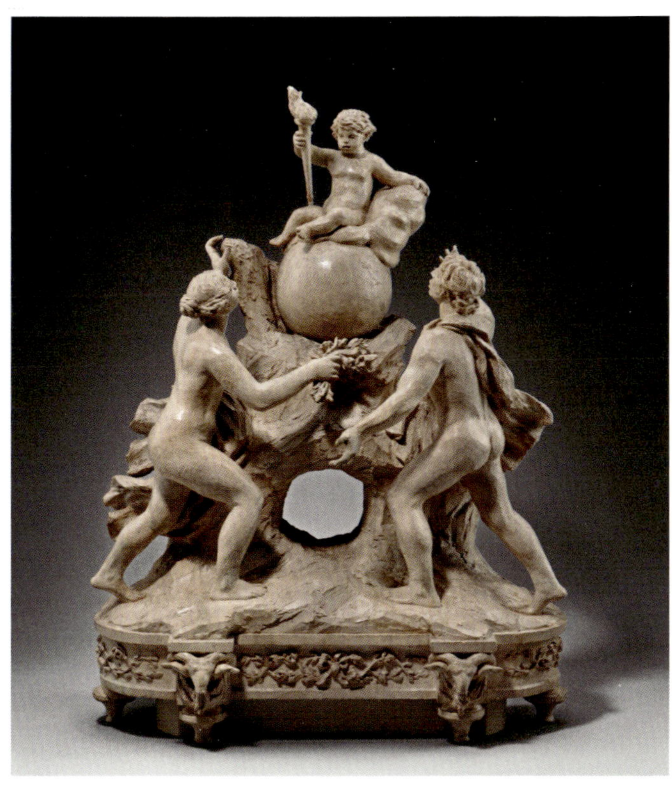

Henri Matisse
French, 1869–1954
Reclining Nude III, 1929

Matisse is best known as a painter and a brilliant colorist, yet he also made sculpture in monochrome reflective bronze. *Reclining Nude III* shows the artist treating one of the most traditional subjects for sculpture, the female nude. Though small in scale, it is monumental in conception. The basic pose of a female figure lying on her back, with her right arm bent to support her head, can be traced back to ancient sculptures of sleeping figures and was popular in Renaissance art as well. Matisse explored it in large-scale sculpture as well as in painting. In this small bronze, Matisse used an innovative approach to the theme by presenting the body without a base so that the limbs, the twisting torso and hips, and the head are set free in space. The bronze rests easily, as a body would rest on a flat surface.

The artist said, "I took up sculpture because what interested me in painting was a clarification of my ideas. [I] worked in clay to have a rest from painting, where I had done all I could for the time being. . . it was done for the purposes of organization, to put order into my feelings and find a style to suit me." While Matisse seems to have used sculpture primarily to fuel his work as a painter, the results have their own sculptural integrity. The form is pared down to the essentials, the figure is softened and generalized, the head without distinct features. The modeling of the malleable clay is still evident on the surface of the finished bronze, giving it a sense of intimacy and tactility.

Bronze
Length: 47.6 cm (18¾ in.)
Gift of Fiske Warren and Edward Perry Warren, by exchange, 53.949

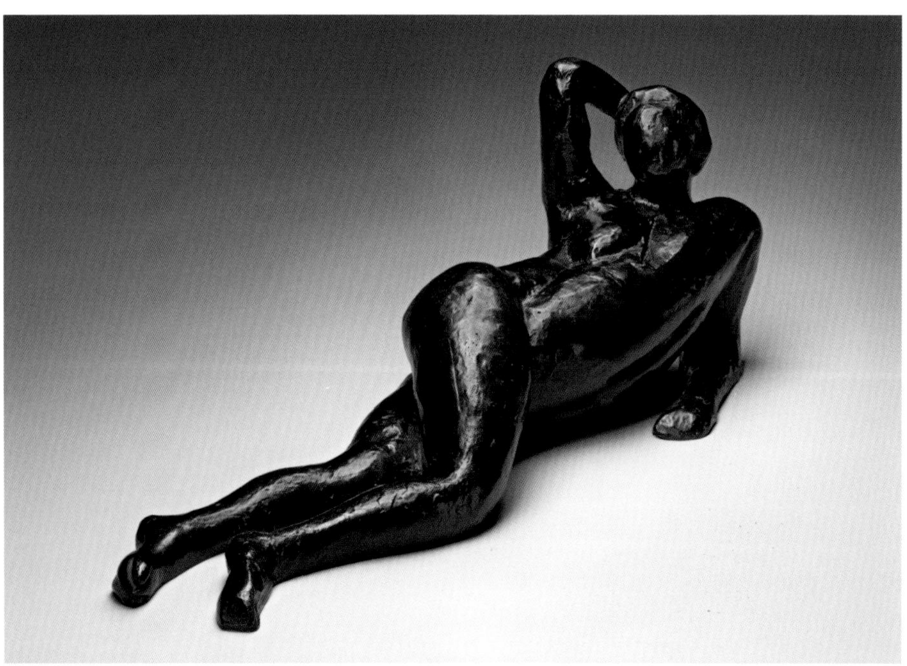

Aristide Maillol
French, 1861–1944
Torso of Summer, about 1910–11

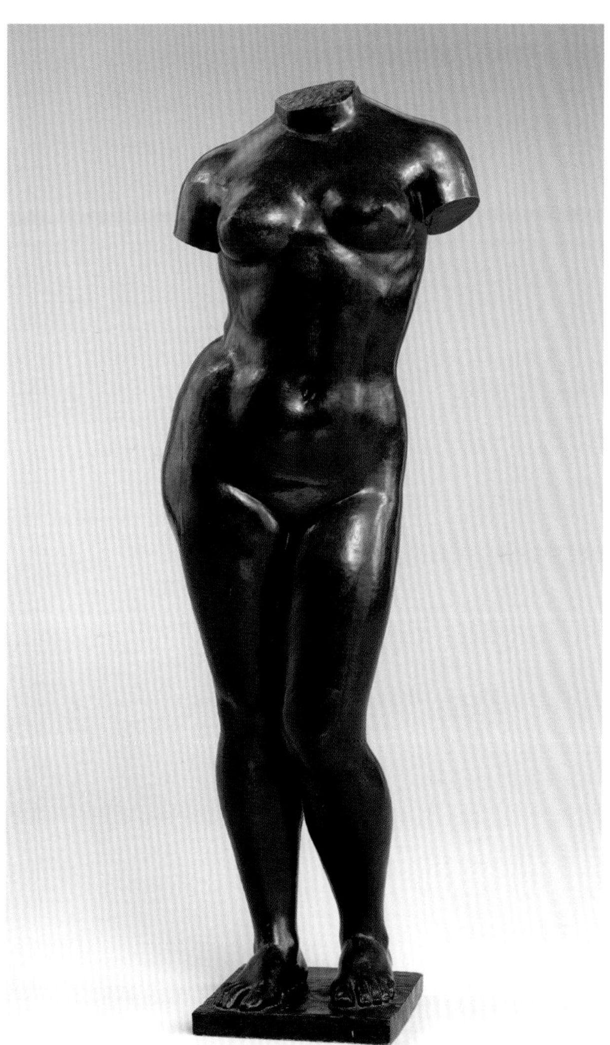

Maillol's primary subject as a sculptor was the female nude. Sitting, reclining, or standing, like this figure, the female body became for him an idealized form through which to express ideas of nature, beauty, and eternity. Maillol was the principal sculptor exploring a modern classicism in the early twentieth century, in an artistic environment that rejected classical principles in favor of energy, change, and the unrelenting pursuit of the new. He simplified, generalized, and fragmented the female body, creating a calm vision in the midst of a chaotic world. For artists pursuing this path, classicism presented a purity and severity of style and meaning that could also be considered "primitive" in spirit.

This figure was developed as an allegory of Summer, part of a group of the Four Seasons. It conveys the lush warmth of summer through the full, muscular body of a woman. The life-size figure is shown with head and arms truncated as if it were a fragment of ancient statuary. By eliminating the head and arms, Maillol also removes the particular, communicative aspects of facial expression and gesture, allowing the body to stand free as a volumetric form in space.

Bronze
Cast by Alexis Rudier Fondeur, French (Paris)
142.2 x 45.7 x 33 cm (56 x 18 x 13 in.)
Gift of Mr. and Mrs. John J. Wilson, 1986.1022

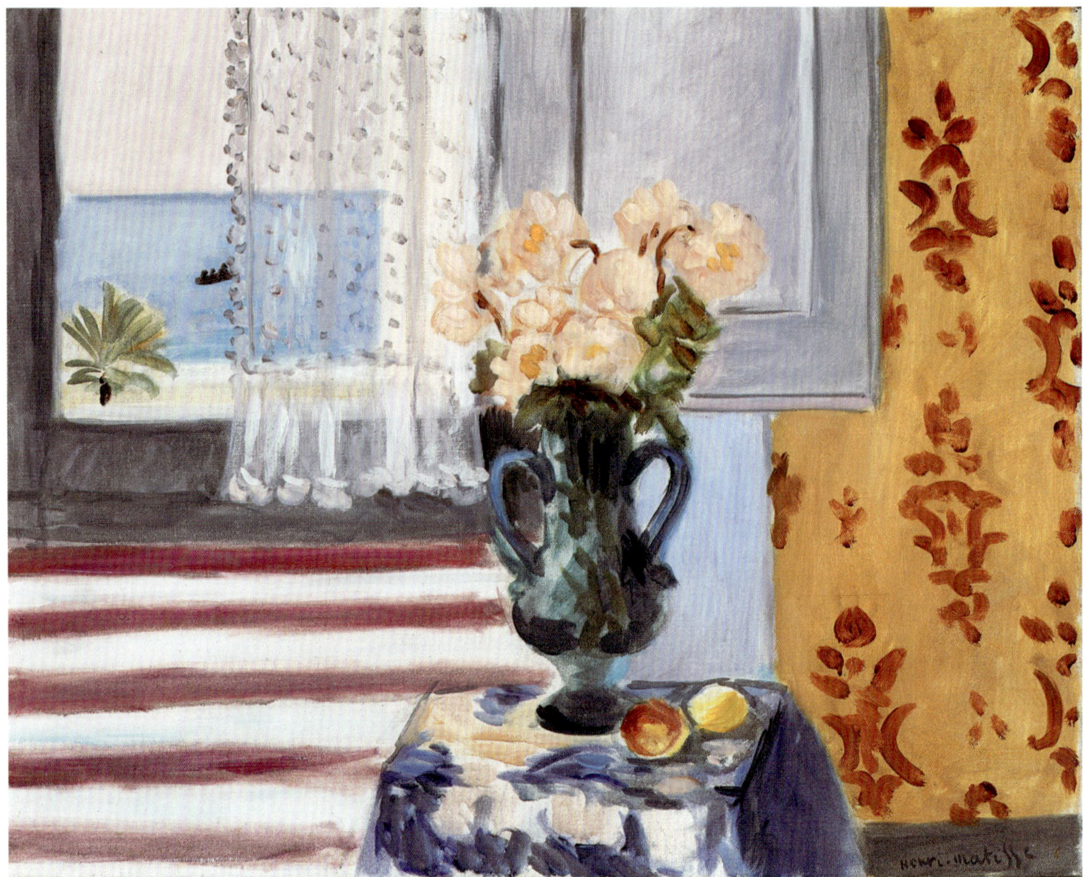

Henri Matisse
French, 1869–1954
Vase of Flowers, 1924

In 1916 Matisse began spending considerable periods of time on the French Riviera, far from the tumult and privations of wartime Paris. From 1921 onward, he worked for six months of almost every year in Nice, painting in a series of rented apartments and hotel rooms overlooking the Mediterranean. This still life, staged in his third-floor studio on the place Charles-Félix, exemplifies the lyrical sensuality of the artist's so-called Nice period.

Brightly patterned textiles and wallpaper overlap in a series of flat, geometric fields, smoothing the space of the room into a single continuous patchwork parallel to the picture plane. The open window gives onto a view of the sea, its surface as still and unruffled as the motionless curtain. Many of Matisse's Nice pictures feature recumbent models, "odalisques," dressed—or undressed—in vaguely North African fashion. In this composition, though, the green glass vase, with its graceful curves and cloud of soft, pink petals, takes the place of the reclining nude: the feminine form at the heart of the painting.

Oil on canvas
60.6 x 73.7 cm (23⅞ x 29 in.)
Bequest of John T. Spaulding, 48.577

Piet Mondrian
Dutch, 1872–1944
Composition with Blue, Yellow, and Red, 1927

Mondrian took the ideal of abstraction further than the Cubists ever imagined. While Picasso's pictures in the first decades of the twentieth century explore the vexed relationship between fictive space and flat support, Mondrian insisted that painting should free itself from representation altogether, relinquishing any claim to the illusion of three-dimensionality. Only, he wrote, by narrowing its focus to its own "plastic means"—line and color—could painting achieve "purity," that is, freedom from representation.

Mondrian called his new theory of painting "Neo-Plasticism" and devoted considerable time through the 1910s and 1920s to elaborating its doctrine, principally in the pages of the journal *De Stijl (The Style)*, which Mondrian and his friend Theo van Doesburg founded in 1917. *Composition with Blue, Yellow, and Red* exemplifies the Neo-Plasticist ideal of "pure painting": the only pigments used are white, black, gray, and the three primary colors; the only forms present are vertical and horizontal lines, squares, and rectangles. These establish a grid of flat color and line as two-dimensional as the canvas on which it is painted.

Oil on canvas
40 x 50.5 cm (15¾ x 19⅞ in.)
Gift of Maria and Conrad Janis in memory of Sidney and Harriet Janis, with gratitude to Arne Glimcher, 2009.5042

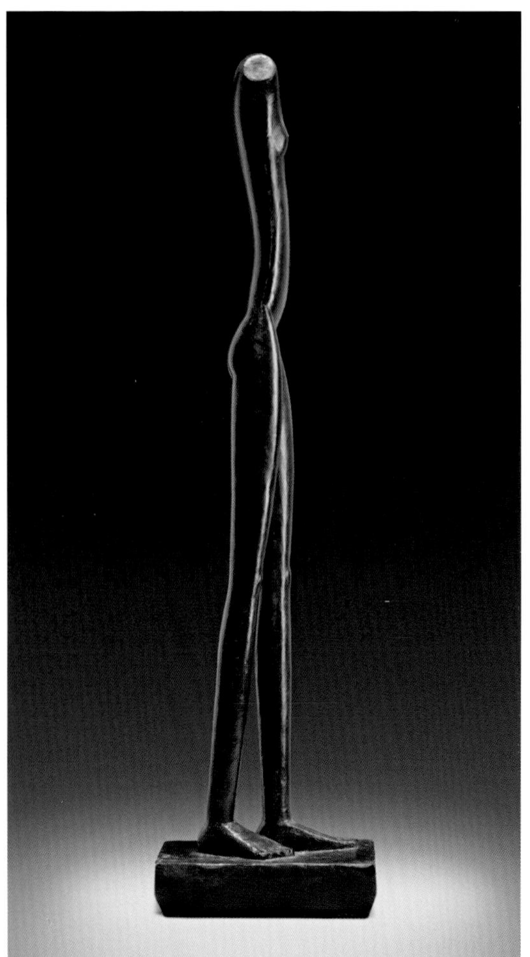

Alberto Giacometti
Swiss, 1901–1966
Walking Woman, modeled 1933–34, cast 1955
Cast by: Fiorini's Foundry, London

The abstract form, slender and elongated contours, and stylized walking pose of this bronze reflect Giacometti's interest in African art as well as his fascination with ancient Egyptian sculpture, which stemmed from a trip to Rome where he saw the Vatican collections. Giacometti pares the body down to its essentials. The elimination of head and arms creates a unified, contained shape. The cavity below the breasts suggests the anatomy of the sternum, but in its abstraction creates mystery. The extreme elongation of legs and torso recalls the smooth geometric shapes of the Romanian sculptor Constantin Brancusi, an important early influence for Giacometti.

This elegant walking figure was made in a period Giacometti later described as one that alternated between the extremes of roundness and calm, which we see here, and the sharpness and violence explored elsewhere. It was one of Giacometti's earliest explorations of the walking figure, a central theme in his later sculptures, which became increasingly attenuated, seemingly weightless, and loosely modeled, creating a sense of energized movement in space. The artist produced this sculpture in plaster and gave his permission for its later production in bronze. The polished, evenly patinated surface enhances the sublime smoothness of the form.

Bronze
151 x 11.2 x 38.1 cm (59½ x 4⅜ x 15 in.)
Major Henry Lee Higginson and William Francis Warden Funds, 64.520

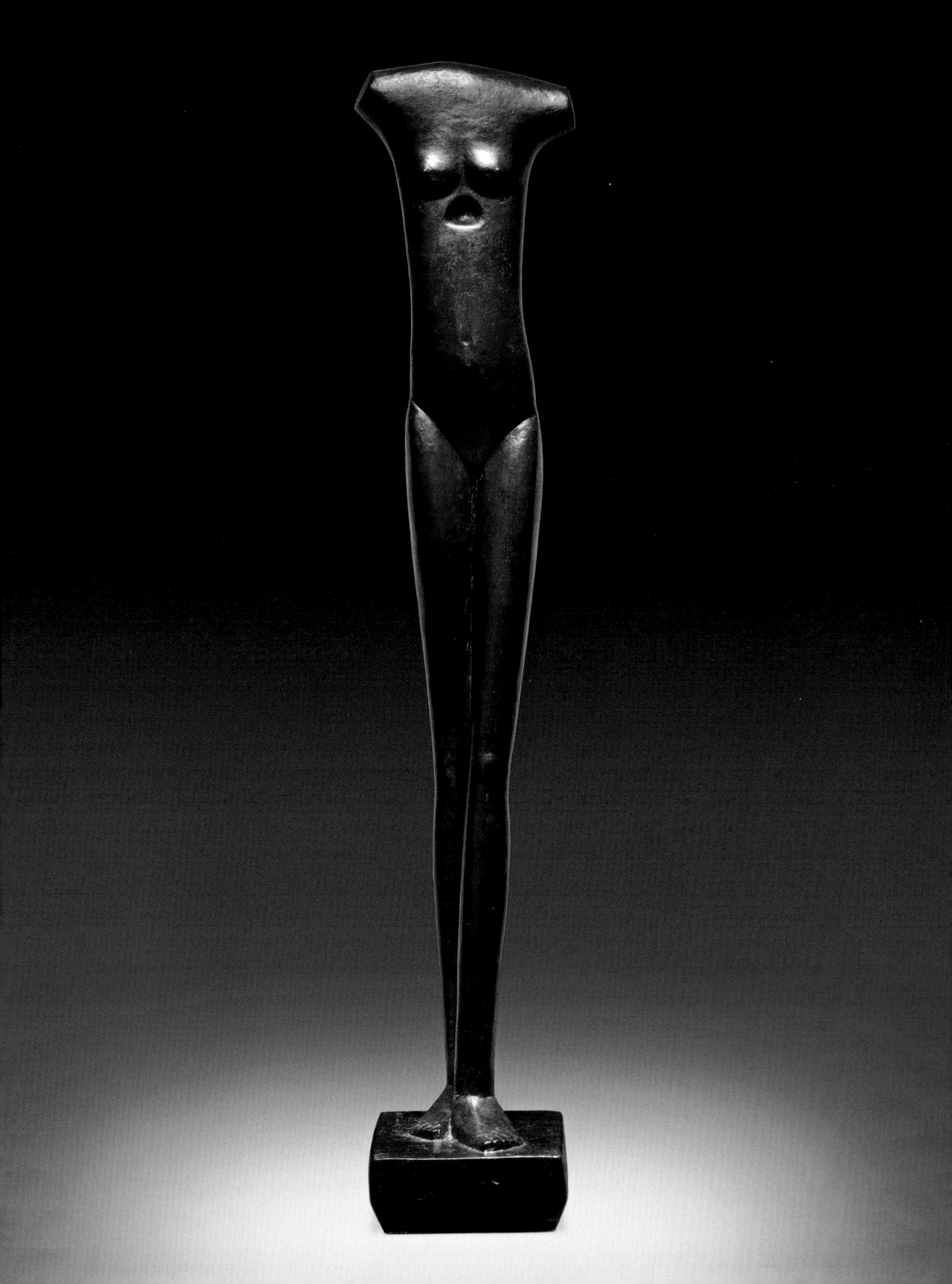

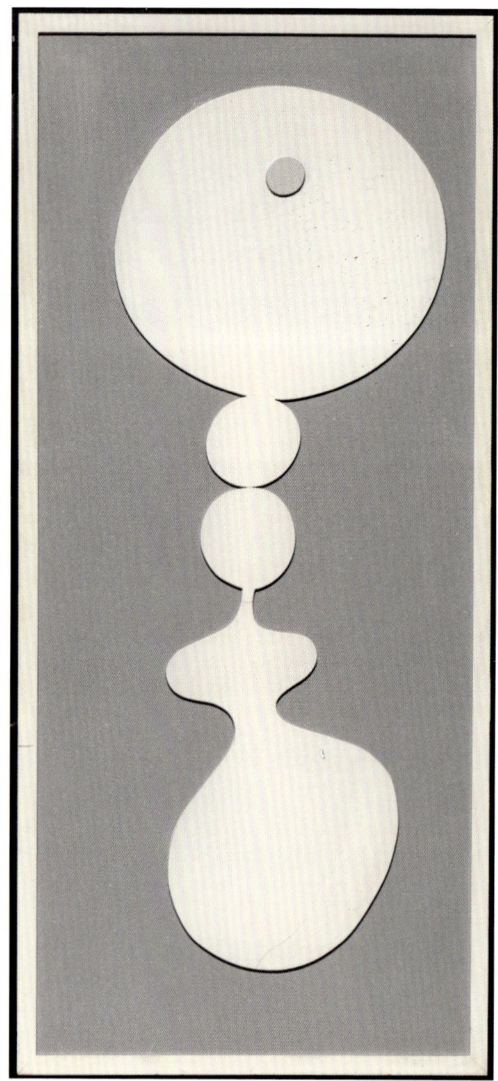

Jean (Hans) Arp

German, 1886–1966

Le fils du nombril (The Son of the Navel), 1957

This buoyant, lighthearted image is composed of white shapes that look as if they are floating against a gray background. The whole is punctuated by a small circle of gray on the uppermost and largest circular shape. Arp titled it *Le fils du nombril (The Son of the Navel)*. The ambiguity of the title suggests that Arp saw this as a figure of sorts, vaguely human yet clearly abstract, and with a strong, playful personality. The relief, typical of Arp's "constructed paintings," demonstrates his penchant for biomorphic forms. This composition began as a drawing in 1922 and was realized as a relief only in 1957, an example of Arp's characteristic reworking of many of the same themes and motifs across time in new ways. In reliefs of the 1950s, he employed contrasting colors and the suggestion of collage. The thickness of the cutout forms makes them seem to float above the surface by creating shadows that also reinforce the sharp lines. Arp was a pioneer of abstraction, a founder of the Dada movement, and also created Surrealist and Constructivist works. His most characteristic and appealing mode is the sort of biomorphic conception of subject and composition seen in this relief.

Relief and oil on board
141 x 62.2 cm (55½ x 24½ in.)
Gift of Richard and Sally Leahy, 2011.320

Joan Miró

Spanish, 1869–1954

Nuage et oiseaux (Cloud and Birds), 1927

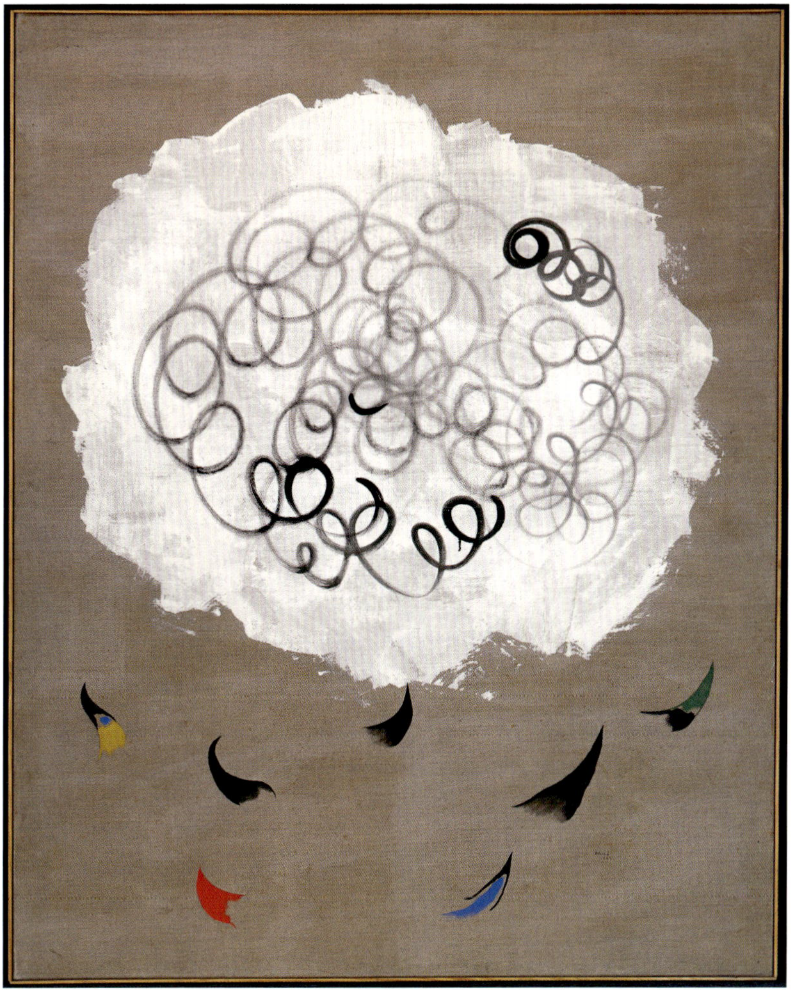

Painted on a raw, unprimed canvas, this picture looks like a monumental doodle. It belongs to a series of eighteen pictures that Miró made on this support, a rarity in 1927. A stark patch of white paint—filled in with looping, scribbled strokes of black—suggests a cloud, while half a dozen colored wisps and wedges below indicate birds in flight. But both cloud and birds sit stubbornly on the surface of thc fabric, refusing to recede into illusionistic depth. The Surrealist writer Louis Aragon described this effect three years later: Miró "makes paintings on colored canvas, painting there only a white patch, as though he had not painted in that spot, as though the canvas were the painting."

A Spanish native, Miró visited Paris in 1919 and settled there the following year. He gravitated to the Surrealist avant-garde, a group of artists and writers who shared an interest in exploring and representing the unconscious mind. Although he had received several years of Academic training in Barcelona, the young artist quickly de-skilled his approach, jettisoning his naturalist technique in favor of a willfully naïve, childlike manner suited to describe and elicit unconscious mental activity. Miró never formally joined the Surrealist movement, but André Breton, the poet and philosopher who served as its anchor, declared him "the most Surrealist of us all."

Oil on canvas

146 x 114 cm (57½ x 44⅞ in.)

Sophie M. Friedman Fund and Charles H. Bayley Picture and Painting Fund, 1980.273

Gerhard Marcks

German, 1889–1981

Pomona, 1932

Marcks carved this figure of the Roman goddess of fruit trees after a 1928 trip to Greece and Rome intensified his passion for early Greek sculpture. Drawn to Expressionism early in his career, he turned away from this movement, seeking instead a simplified image of nature. For him, the severity of Archaic Greek sculpture encouraged a kind of purity and solidity of form. The strong, robust figure of the nude Pomona is presented in a frontal seated position, with one foot resting on a block. Her features are generalized, and her slight smile recalls the famous smiles of Archaic Greek statues. Marcks relished the natural quality of his materials, here the hardness and warm color of the Austrian limestone. For many sculptors in the early twentieth century, carving directly into the block of stone, without relying on specialist marble carvers or on any kind of reproductive tools for executing sculpture, became a statement about truth and integrity, almost a moral imperative. Marcks purposefully left the signs of his tools in the finished sculpture, as in the carefully controlled, regular chisel marks evident on the flesh of the figure.

Made in 1932, this idyllic image was one of the last works Marcks created before he was swept up into the crisis of Nazi rule in Germany. Though not Jewish himself, his support for his Jewish friends and colleagues and his refusal to support the Nazi cause led to dismissal from his teaching position, the removal of his art from German museums, and the inclusion of his works in the 1937 exhibition of "degenerate art."

Austrian limestone

H. 95.3 cm (37½ in.)

Charles Amos Cummings Fund, 58.18

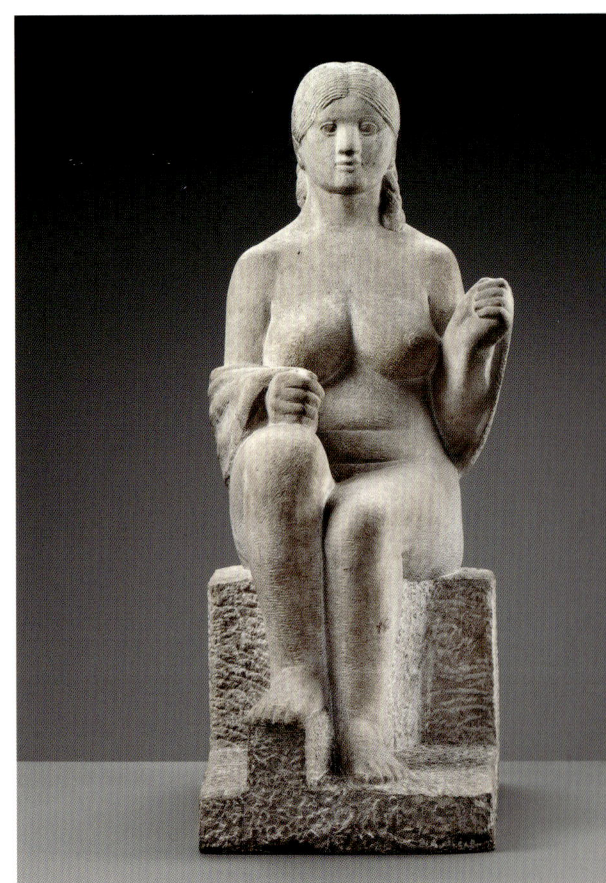

Max Beckmann
German, 1884–1950
Double Portrait, 1946

The theme of this portrait is friendship. It depicts two of the artist's most stalwart supporters through the upheavals of the Second World War and was painted as a present to one of them, Curt Valentin. Seated at right, Valentin was Beckmann's dealer; as a Jew, he was forced to flee Germany in 1937. In Berlin he had conducted a clandestine trade in the work of "degenerate" artists, like Beckmann, banned by the Nazi regime, and he continued to advocate for Beckmann across the Atlantic, selling in New York the few pictures that the artist could send from Amsterdam before the German invasion, and continuing to agitate on behalf of "degenerate" artists throughout the war. In Beckmann's portrait, Valentin holds a lighted candle, signaling his role as keeper of the flame for the condemned avant-garde through those dark years.

The portrait's other sitter, holding a full glass at left, is Hanns Swarzenski, a specialist in medieval art, much admired by Beckmann, who had likewise fled Germany for the United States in 1938. He secured a position at Princeton University, where he organized an exhibition of Beckmann's watercolors after the war. In the summer and fall of 1946, both Valentin and Swarzenski went to see Beckmann in Amsterdam. Although their visits did not overlap, he chose to paint them together as advocates and allies in his struggle. Eight years later, Valentin bequeathed the picture to Swarzenski, who shortly thereafter became a curator at the Museum of Fine Arts, Boston. Swarzenski, in turn, left it to the Museum on his death.

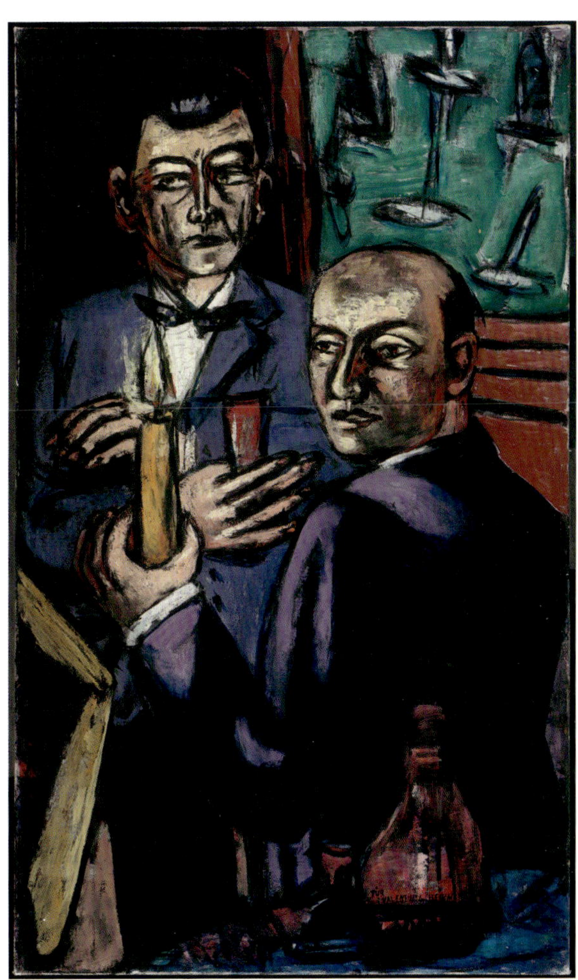

Oil on canvas
130.8 x 75.6 cm (51½ x 29¾ in.)
Gift of Dr. Hanns Swarzenski, 1989.348

Max Beckmann
German, 1884–1950
Still Life with Three Skulls, 1945

Beckmann's angular, aggressive style, nourished by his exposure to contemporary avant-garde developments in Paris and Berlin, placed the artist in personal danger after the rise to power of the Nazi Party. In 1937, after being designated a "degenerate" artist and stripped of his teaching post in Berlin, Beckmann fled to Amsterdam. There he remained for a difficult decade, painting this sardonic picture during the final weeks of the occupation.

The composition contains various props of a *vanitas* still life, a category of painting invented in the Netherlands during the seventeenth century that deploys ordinary objects as symbols of mortality. The playing cards scattered across the table, the empty bottle at right, and the snuffed candle at left all serve as reminders that life and its pleasures are quickly extinguished, hollow, a game of chance. In a traditional *vanitas*, the human skull is the ultimate marker of mortality, quite literally grave in its significance. But Beckmann's tumble of skulls, with their gaping mouths and hollow eyes, instead create a macabre impression of laughter—a bleak joke blurted out in a moment of hopelessness.

When he completed the picture, Beckmann wrote in his diary, "Quite a funny painting—just as everything else is totally funny and becomes more and more ghastly. . . . On the whole nothing will ever be as impossible as the present situation of poverty and dissolution."

Oil on canvas
55.2 x 89.5 cm (21¾ x 35¼ in.)
Gift of Mrs. Culver Orswell, 67.984

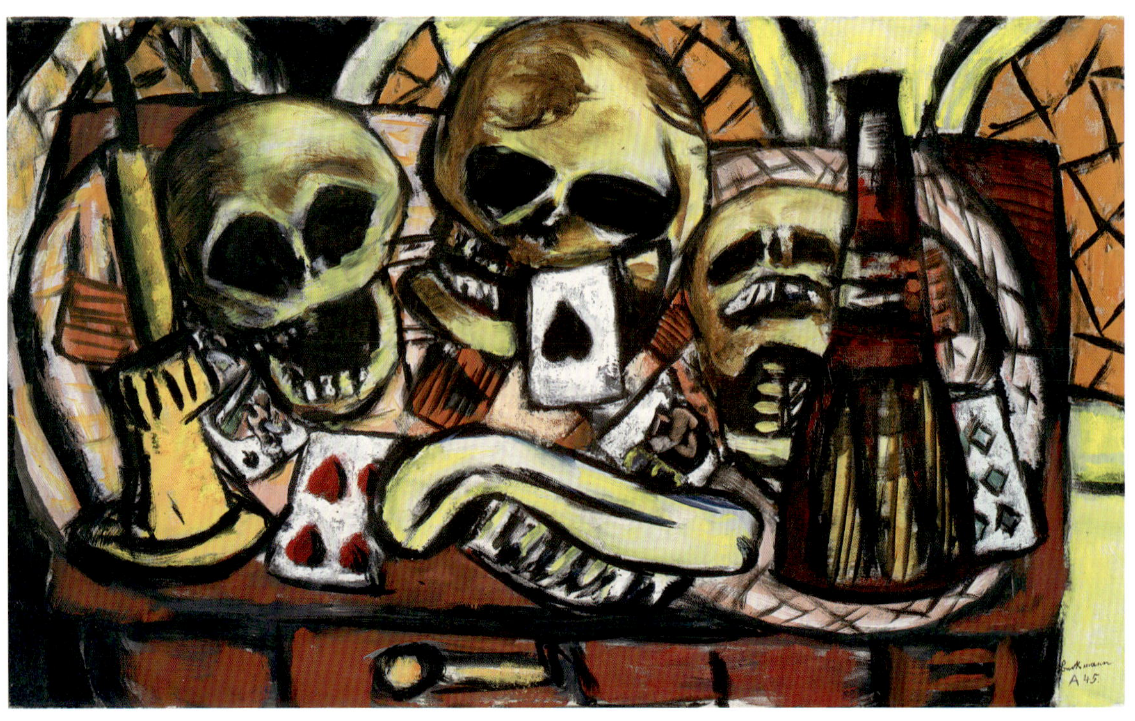

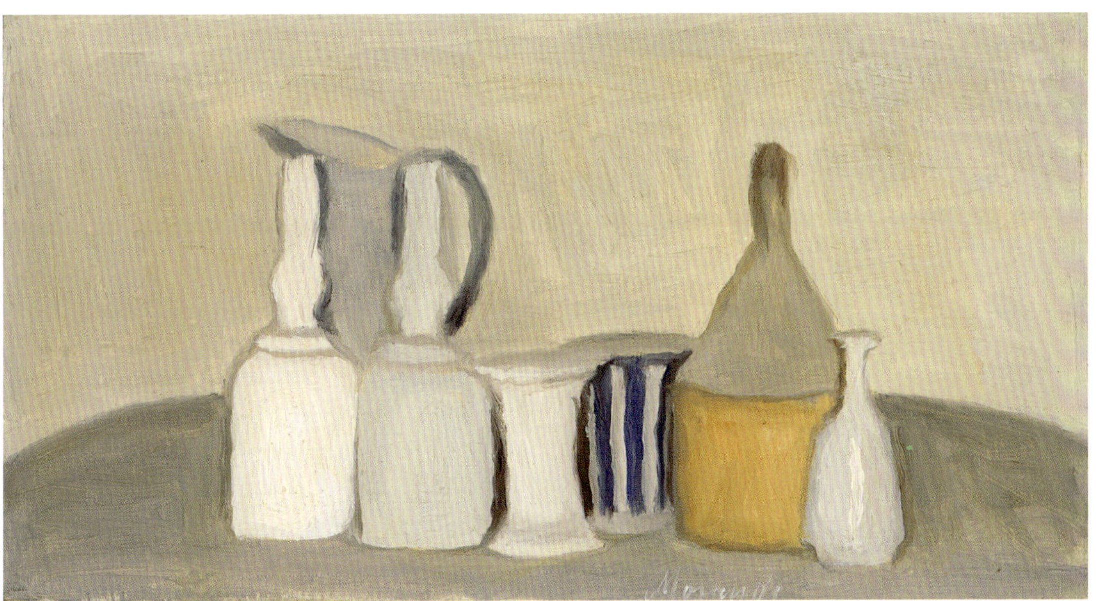

Giorgio Morandi
Italian, 1890–1964
Still Life of Bottles and Pitcher, 1946

Morandi's still lifes are essays in economy. Small vessels, thoughtfully arranged, appear to us at once as real objects, caressed by light and enveloped by space, as geometric forms in elegant proportion, and as strokes of paint, a veil of muted color.

Morandi spent his whole career in the university city of Bologna, where he was exposed as a student to various early twentieth-century avant-garde movements: Cubism, Futurism, La Pittura Metafisica (Metaphysical Painting). His style developed in conversation with these contemporary currents but remained deeply personal, more contemplative in tone than the Futurists' brash experiments, more committed to the solidity of forms than the Cubists' pursuit of fragmentation. His work is sometimes associated with the so-called *rappel à l'ordre*, a return to classical tradition that swept Europe in the wake of the First World War.

Like Picasso, Morandi admired Cézanne, but the lessons he learned from the nineteenth-century master were far removed from those qualities that interested Picasso. Morandi's watchfulness, his effort always to see familiar objects anew, reveals his debt to Cézanne. Like Cézanne's, Morandi's still lifes are populated with a familiar cast of characters: the same homely bottles, pitchers, and vases appear again and again in his work. He painted variations on this particular arrangement three times, in 1946, each one a triumph of simplicity.

Oil on canvas
25.1 x 45.1 cm (9⅞ x 17¾ in.)
Tompkins Collection—Arthur Gordon Tompkins Fund, 61.662

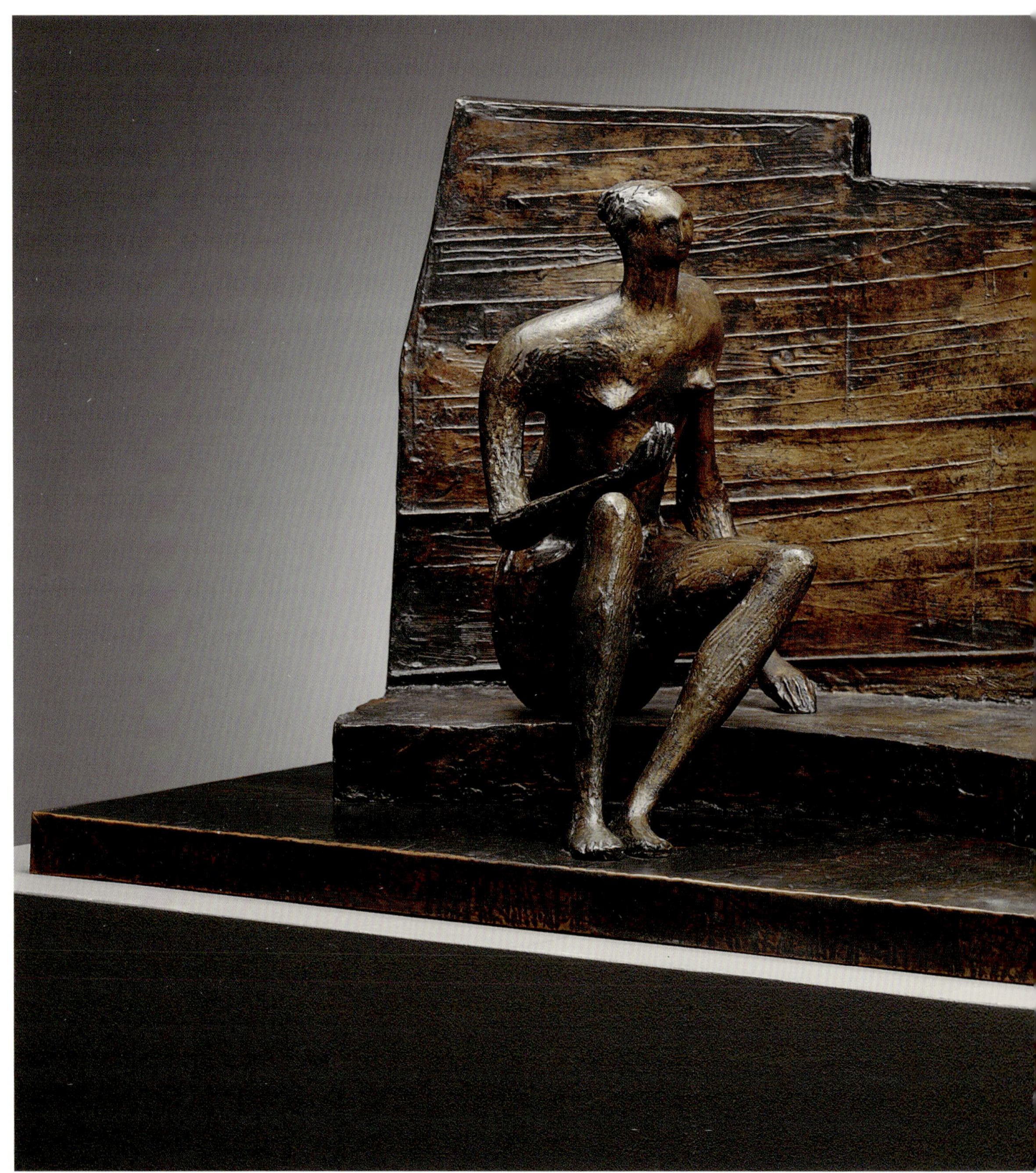

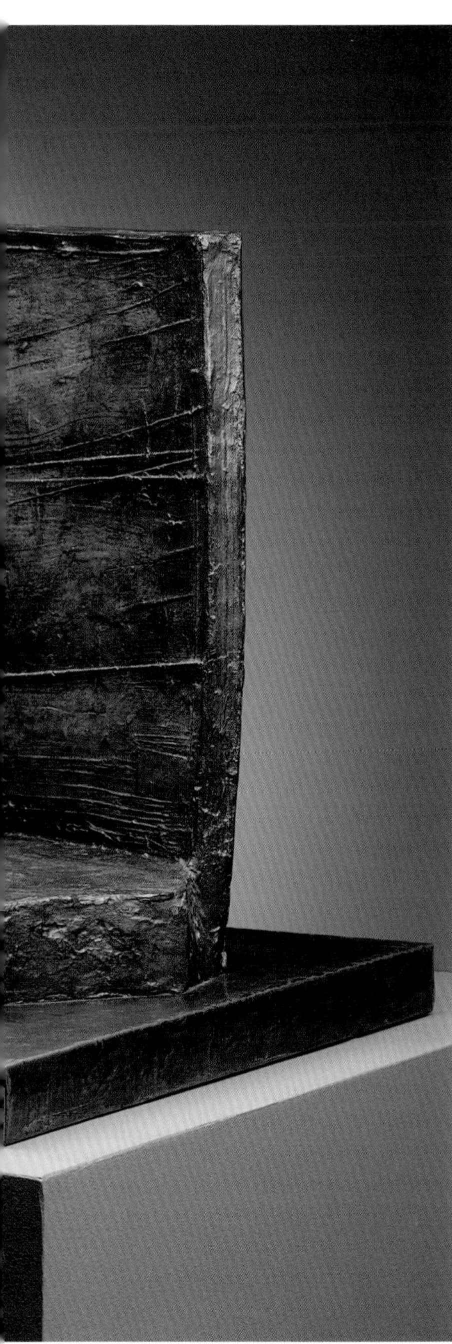

Henry Moore
English, 1898–1986
Seated Figure against Curved Wall, modeled 1956–57, cast 1959

"Sculpture, for me, must have life in it, vitality. It must have a feeling for organic form, a certain pathos and warmth." Thus Moore expressed the approach that guided him in the representation of his favored subject, the human figure. Moore, the most famous and influential British sculptor of the twentieth century, received major commissions for works in North America as well as in England. From the beginning, he developed a great interest in sculpture from all around the world, especially Africa, Oceania, and South America. He was dedicated to working directly in natural materials, and early in his career he worked primarily in stone. His bronzes retain the rough, direct touch of the model in clay or plaster, evident here in the varied surface textures.

Moore's large-scale works for outdoor settings are meant to interact with the landscape and space around them. In his smaller works he explored the way shapes and volumes relate organically with the surrounding space on a more intimate scale. Here, his female figure sits, holding her right hand as if supporting a book. The forms of the body are stretched and manipulated to create a play between small and large, slender and robust, attenuated and expanded, so that thin limbs and small head, for example, are grounded by the fuller, rounded pelvis. To set the form in space, Moore placed the figure against a simple curving wall, creating a foil for its shapes and volumes.

Bronze
69.2 x 91.4 x 53.7 cm (27¼ x 36 x 21⅛ in.)
Harriet Otis Cruft Fund, 59.477

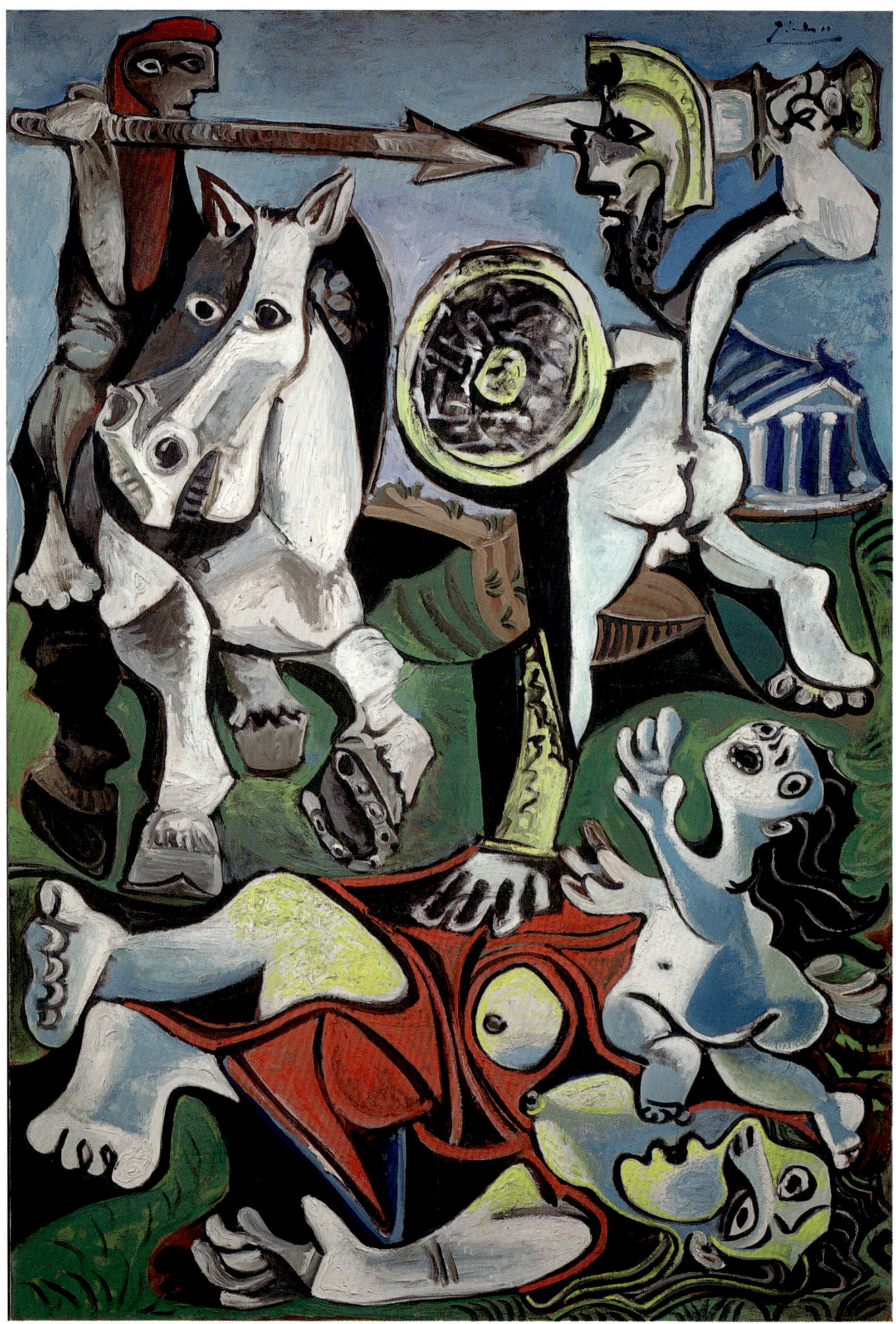

Pablo Picasso
Spanish (worked in France), 1881–1973
Rape of the Sabine Women, 1963

In a televised address on October 22, 1962, President John F. Kennedy announced the discovery of Soviet missiles armed with nuclear warheads in Cuba. Across the world, in a rambling eighteenth-century farmhouse overlooking the Mediterranean, Picasso followed the news with dismay: the United States and the Soviet Union sat on the brink of nuclear war. That very night, the artist embarked on a series of paintings in response to the crisis that culminated in this work, his last great history painting.

Inspired by contemporary events, the picture nonetheless depicts an episode from Roman history, recounted by the ancient authors Livy and Plutarch. Suffering from a shortage of marriageable women, early Romans carried off the wives and daughters of the neighboring Sabine tribe. The Sabine men launched a retaliatory attack, but the abducted women intervened to broker a truce between their Sabine kinsmen and their new Roman husbands. With his image of a Roman and a Sabine trampling a woman and child in their eagerness to join battle, Picasso transformed his classical subject—famously portrayed by Nicolas Poussin and Jacques-Louis David in paintings Picasso admired at the Louvre—into a protest against Cold War military escalation. The picture remains both a monument to the Cuban missile crisis and a timeless outcry against fratricidal warfare.

Oil on canvas
195.3 x 131.1 cm (76⅞ x 51⅝ in.)
Juliana Cheney Edwards Collection, Tompkins Collection—Arthur Gordon Tompkins Fund, and Fanny P. Mason Fund in memory of Alice Thevin, 64.709

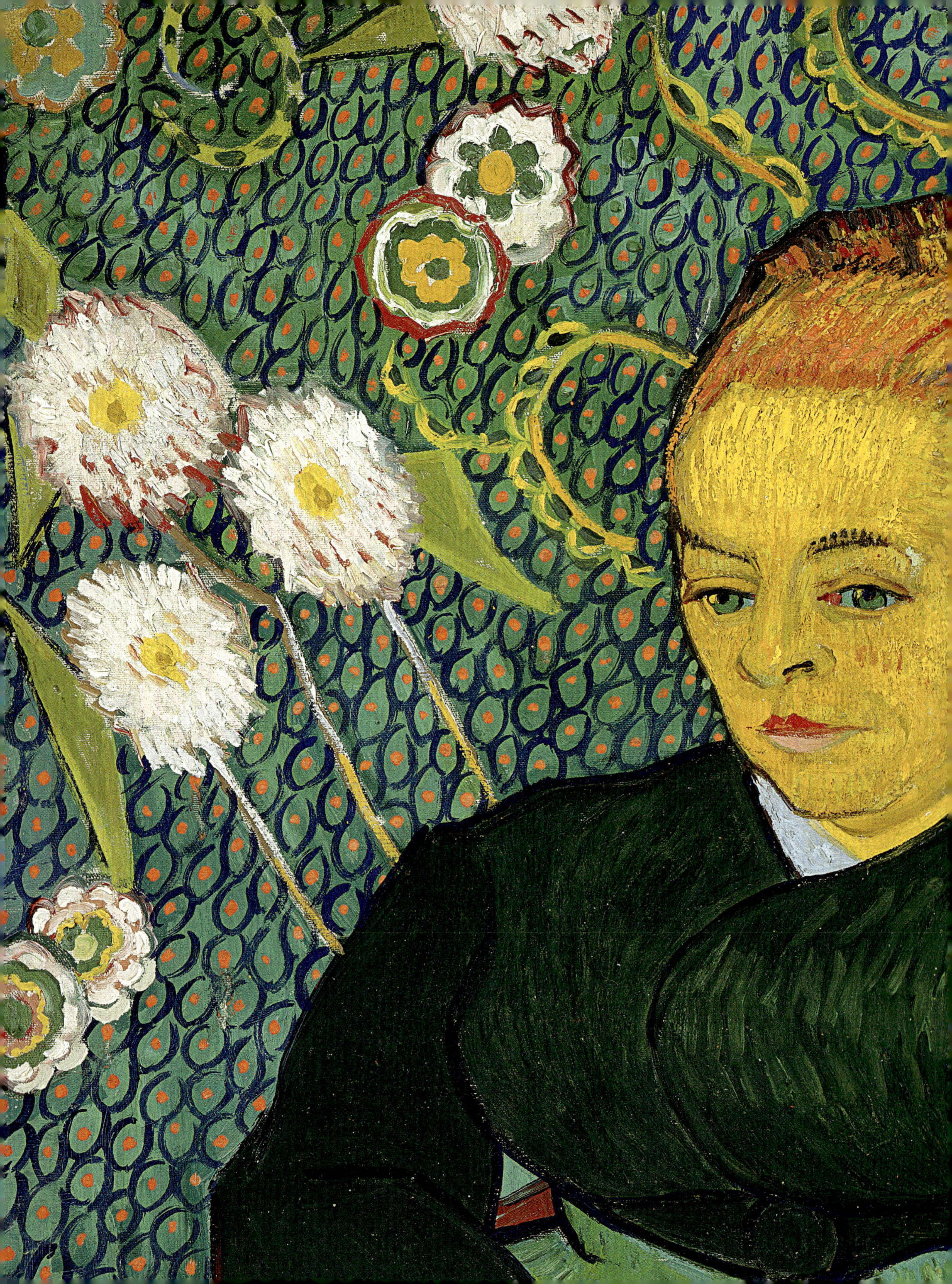

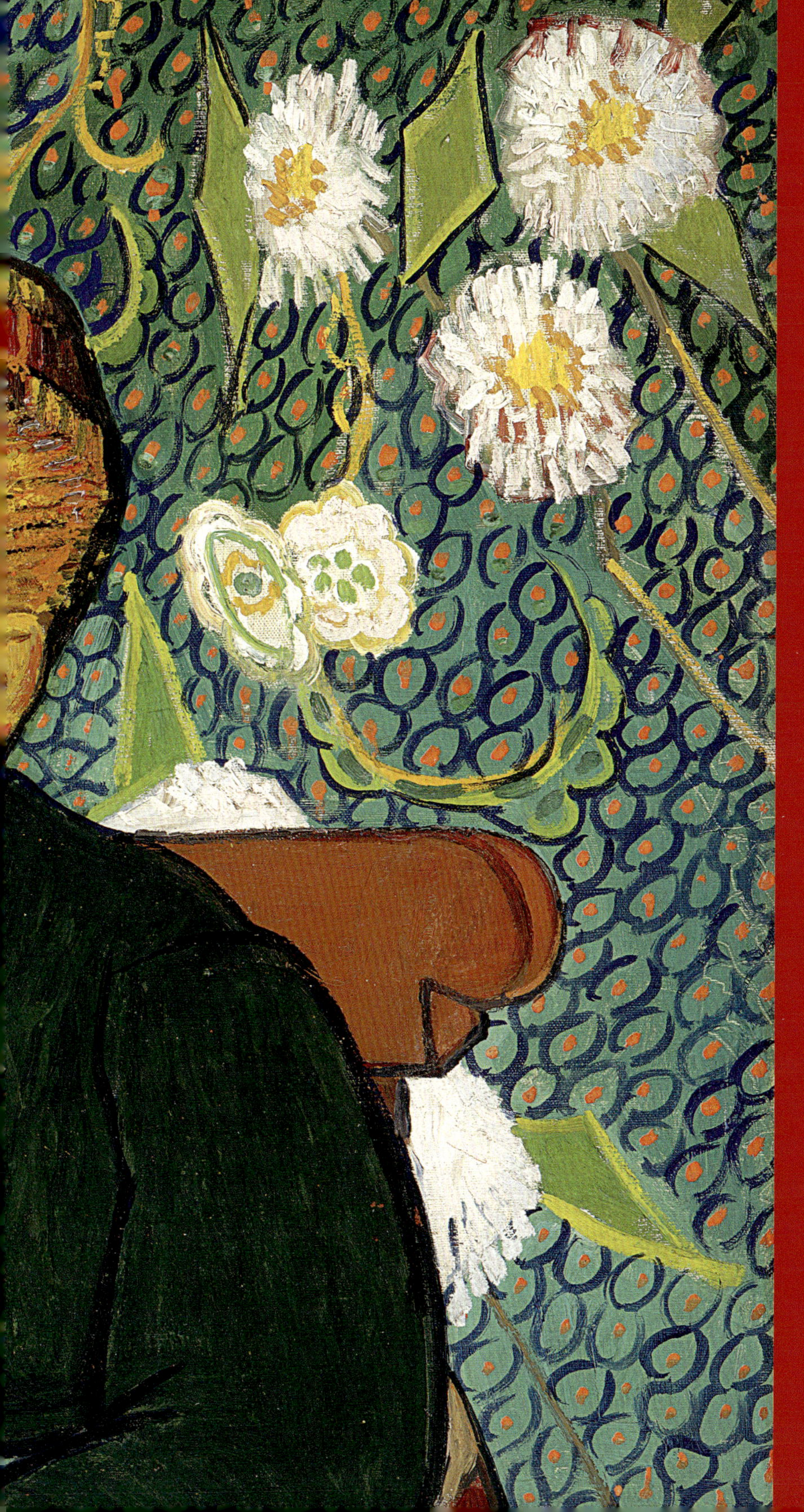

further reading, index, credits

Further Reading

The following general resources are suggested as potential starting points and can lead the reader to more detailed information about particular artists, movements, and themes.

The Lure of the Past

Baker, Malcolm. *Figured in Marble: The Making and Viewing of Eighteenth-Century Sculpture*. London: Victoria and Albert Publications, 2000.

Bann, Stephen. *Romanticism and the Rise of History*. New York: Twayne, 1995.

Barringer, Timothy, et al. *Pre-Raphaelites: Victorian Art and Design*. Exh. cat. London: Tate Publishing, 2012.

Bindman, David. *Warm Flesh, Cold Marble: Canova, Thorvaldsen, and Their Critics*. New Haven: Yale University Press, 2014.

Crow, Thomas E. *Emulation: Making Artists for Revolutionary France*. New Haven: Yale University Press, 1995.

Draper, James David, and Guilhem Scherf. *Playing with Fire: European Terracotta Models, 1740–1840*. Exh. cat. New York: The Metropolitan Museum of Art; New Haven: Yale University Press, 2003.

Hubert, Wellington, ed. *The Journal of Eugène Delacroix: A Painter of Passion*. London: Folio Society, 1995.

Naginski, Erika. *Sculpture and Enlightenment*. Los Angeles: Getty Research Institute, 2009.

Paul, Carole, ed. *The First Modern Museums of Art: The Birth of an Institution in 18th- and Early-19th-Century Europe*. Los Angeles: J. Paul Getty Museum, 2012.

Potts, Alex. *Flesh and the Ideal: Winckelmann and the Origins of Art History*. New Haven: Yale University Press, 1994.

Sérullaz, Arlette, et al. *Delacroix: The Late Work*. Exh. cat. New York: Thames & Hudson; Philadelphia: Philadelphia Museum of Art, 1998.

Vaughan, William. *Romanticism and Art*. New York: Thames & Hudson, 1994.

Representing Nature

Brown, David Blayney, et al. *J. M. W. Turner: Painting Set Free*. Exh. cat. Los Angeles: J. Paul Getty Museum, 2014.

Chu, Petra ten-Doesschate. *The Most Arrogant Man in France: Gustave Courbet and the Nineteenth-Century Media Culture*. Princeton: Princeton University Press, 2007.

Clark, T. J. *Image of the People: Gustave Courbet and the 1848 Revolution*. Princeton: Princeton University Press, 1982.

Costello, Leo. *J. M. W. Turner and the Subject of History*. Burlington: Ashgate, 2012.

Fusco, Peter, and H. W. Janson, eds. *The Romantics to Rodin: French Nineteenth-Century Sculpture from North American Collections*. Exh. cat. Los Angeles: Los Angeles County Museum of Art. New York: Braziller, 1980.

Galassi, Peter. *Corot in Italy: Open-Air Painting and the Classical Landscape Tradition*. New Haven: Yale University Press, 1991.

Jones, Kimberly A., et al. *In the Forest of Fontainebleau: Painters and Photographers from Corot to Monet*. Exh. cat. Washington, DC: National Gallery of Art; Houston: Museum of Fine Arts; New Haven: Yale University Press, 2008.

Lambert, Ray. *John Constable and the Theory of Landscape Painting*. New York: Cambridge University Press, 2005.

Murphy, Alexandra R. *Jean-François Millet*. Exh. cat. Boston: Museum of Fine Arts, 1984.

Murphy, Alexandra R., et al. *Jean-François Millet: Drawn into Light*. Exh. cat. Williamstown, MA: Clark Art Institute, 1999.

Reynolds, Graham. *The Early Paintings and Drawings of John Constable*. New Haven: Yale University Press, 1996.

Shackelford, George T. M., and Fronia E. Wissman. *Impressions of Light: The French Landscape from Corot to Monet*. Exh. cat. Boston: Museum of Fine Arts, 2002.

Tinterow, Gary, Michael Pantazzi, Vincent Pomarède, et al. *Corot, 1796–1875*. Exh. cat. New York: Metropolitan Museum of Art, 1996.

Zafran, Eric, ed. *Fantasy and Faith: The Arts of Gustave Doré*. Exh. cat. New York: Dahesh Museum; New Haven: Yale University Press, 2007.

Academies and Official Art

Boime, Albert. *The Academy and French Painting in the Nineteenth Century*. Oxford: Oxford University Press, 1971.

Brettell, Richard R. *French Salon Artists, 1800–1900*. Exh. cat. Chicago: Art Institute of Chicago, 1987.

Denis, Rafael Cardoso, and Colin Trodd, eds. *Art and the Academy in the Nineteenth Century*. New Brunswick, NJ: Rutgers University Press, 2000.

Des Cars, Laurence, et al. *The Spectacular Art of Jean-Léon Gérôme (1824–1904)*. Exh. cat. Milan: Skira; London: Thames & Hudson, 2010.

Hunisak, John M. *Carvings, Casts and Replicas: Nineteenth-Century Sculpture from Europe and America in New England Collections*. Exh. cat. Middlebury, VT: Middlebury College Museum of Art, 1994.

Lafont-Couturier, Hélène, et al. *Gérôme & Goupil: Art and Enterprise*. Exh. cat. Paris: Réunion des musées nationaux, 2000.

Ormond, Richard, et al. *Franz Xaver Winterhalter and the Courts of Europe, 1830–70*. Exh. cat. London: National Portrait Gallery, 1987.

Prettejohn, Elizabeth, and Tim Barringer, eds. *Frederic Leighton: Antiquity, Renaissance, Modernity*. New Haven: Yale Center for British Art, 1999.

The Second Empire, 1852–1870: Art in France under Napoleon III. Exh. cat. Philadelphia: Philadelphia Museum of Art, 1978.

Weinberg, H. Barbara. *The Lure of Paris: Nineteenth-Century American Painters and Their French Teachers*. New York: Abbeville, 1991.

Town and Country

Alsdorf, Bridget. *Fellow Men: Fantin-Latour and the Problem of the Group in Nineteenth-Century French Painting*. Princeton: Princeton University Press, 2013.

Bailey, Colin B. *Renoir, Impressionism, and Full-Length Painting*. Exh. cat. New York: The Frick Collection; New Haven: Yale University Press, 2012.

Bailey, Colin B., et al. *Renoir Landscapes, 1865–1883*. Exh. cat. London: National Gallery, 2007.

Boggs, Jean Sutherland, et al. *Degas*. Exh. cat. New York: Metropolitan Museum of Art; Ottawa: National Gallery of Canada, 1988.

Brettell, Richard R. *Impression: Painting Quickly in France, 1860–1890*. New Haven: Yale University Press, 2000.

Butler, Ruth. *Rodin: The Shape of Genius*. New Haven: Yale University Press, 1993.

Cachin, Françoise et al. *Manet, 1832–1883*. Exh. cat. New York: Metropolitan Museum of Art, 1983.

Clark, T. J. *The Painting of Modern Life: Paris in the Art of Manet and His Followers*. Princeton: Princeton University Press, 1984.

Elderfield, John, et al. *Manet and the Execution of Maximilian*. Exh. cat. New York: Museum of Modern Art, 2006.

Fried, Michael. *Manet's Modernism, or the Face of Painting in the 1860s*. Chicago: University of Chicago Press, 1996.

Groom, Gloria, et al. *Impressionism, Fashion, and Modernity*. Exh. cat. Paris: Musée d'Orsay; New York: Metropolitan Museum of Art; Chicago: Art Institute of Chicago.

Herbert, Robert. *Impressionism: Art Leisure and Parisian Society*. New Haven: Yale University Press, 1988.

House, John, et al. *Renoir*. Exh. cat. London: Hayward Gallery; Paris: Galeries nationales du Grand Palais; Boston: Museum of Fine Arts, 1985.

Kendall, Richard. *Degas and the Little Dancer*. Exh. cat. New Haven: Yale University Press; Omaha, NE: Joslyn Art Museum, 1998.

Kendall, Richard, and Jill Devonyar. *Degas and the Ballet: Picturing Movement*. Exh. cat. London: Royal Academy of Arts, 2011.

Lindsay, Suzanne Glover, Daphne Barbour, and Shelley Sturman. *Edgar Degas Sculpture*. Washington, DC: National Gallery of Art, 2010.

Loyrette, Henri, and Gary Tinterow. *Origins of Impressionism*. Exh. cat. New York: Metropolitan Museum of Art, 1994.

Moffett, Charles S., Ruth Berson, et al. *The New Painting: Impressionism, 1874–1886*. Exh. cat. San Francisco: Fine Arts Museums, 1986.

Morton, Mary, et al. *Gustave Caillebotte: The Painter's Eye*. Exh. cat. Washington, DC: National Gallery of Art; Chicago: University of Chicago Press, 2015.

Patry, Sylvie, ed. *Inventing Impressionism: Paul Durand-Ruel and the Modern Art Market*. Exh. cat. London: National Gallery, 2015.

Pissarro, Joachim, et al. *Pioneering Modern Painting: Cézanne and Pissarro, 1865–1885*. Exh. cat. New York: Museum of Modern Art, 2005.

Rathbone, Eliza E., and Shackelford, George T. M. *Impressionist Still Life*. Exh. cat. Washington, DC: The Phillips Collection, 2001.

Reff, Theodore. *Degas: The Artist's Mind*. Cambridge: Harvard University Press, 1987.

Shackelford, George T. M., et al. *Degas and the Nude*. Exh. cat. Boston: Museum of Fine Arts, 2011.

Thomson, Richard. *Art of the Actual: Naturalism and Style in Early Third Republic France, 1880–1900*. New Haven: Yale University Press, 2012.

Tucker, Paul. *Monet in the 90s: The Series Paintings*. Exh. cat. Boston: Museum of Fine Arts; New Haven: Yale University Press, 1989.

Wildenstein, Daniel. *Monet*, 4 vols. Cologne: Taschen, 1996.

Beyond the Impression

Barron, Stephanie. *German Expressionist Sculpture*. Exh. cat. Los Angeles: Los Angeles County Museum of Art; Chicago: University of Chicago Press, 1985.

Barron, Stephanie, and Wolf-Dieter Dube. *German Expressionism: Art and Society*. New York: Rizzoli, 1997.

Brettell, Richard R., et al. *The Art of Paul Gauguin*. Exh. cat. Washington, DC: National Gallery of Art, 1988.

Brettell, Richard R., et al. *Gauguin and the School of Pont-Aven*. Exh. cat. Paris and London, 1997.

Cachin, Françoise, Joseph J. Rishel, et al. *Cézanne*. Exh. cat. New York: H. A. Abrams in association with the Philadelphia Museum of Art, 1996.

Cernuschi, Claude. *Re/Casting Kokoschka: Ethics, Aesthetics, Epistemology, and Politics in Fin-de-*

Siècle Vienna. Madison, NJ: Fairleigh Dickinson University Press, 2002.

Cork, Richard. *Wild Thing: Epstein, Gaudier-Brzeska, Gill*. Exh. cat. London: Royal Academy of Arts, 2009.

Ehrhardt, Ingrid, and Simon Reynolds, eds. *Kingdom of the Soul: Symbolist Art in Germany, 1870–1920*. Exh. cat. Munich: Prestel, 2000.

Feilchenfeldt, Walter, et al. *The Paintings of Paul Cézanne: An Online Catalogue Raisonné*. www.cezannecatalogue.com.

Greene, Vivien. *Divisionism, Neo-Impressionism: Arcadia and Anarchy*. Exh. cat. New York: Guggenheim Museum Publications, 2007.

Kendall, Richard, et al. *Van Gogh and Nature*. Exh. cat. Williamstown, MA: Clark Art Institute, 2015.

Krämer, Felix, et al. *Dark Romanticism: From Goya to Max Ernst*. Exh. cat. Ostfildern, Germany: Hatje Cantz, 2012.

Lampe, Angela, and Clément Chéroux, eds. *Edvard Munch: The Modern Eye*. Exh. cat. London: Tate Publishing, 2012.

Lloyd, Jill. *German Expressionism: Primitivism and Modernity*. New Haven: Yale University Press, 1991.

Ockman, Carol, Kenneth E. Silver, et al., *Sarah Bernhardt: The Art of High Drama*. Exh. cat. New York: The Jewish Museum, 2005.

Peters, Olaf, ed. *Degenerate Art: The Attack on Modern Art in Nazi Germany, 1937*. Exh. cat. Munich: Prestel, 2014.

Rathbone, Eliza E., et al. *Van Gogh Repetitions*. Exh. cat. New Haven: Yale University Press, 2013.

Rewald, John. *The Paintings of Paul Cézanne: A Catalogue Raisonné*. New York: Harry N. Abrams, 1996.

Salm-Salm, Marie-Amélie zu. *Vienna 1900: Klimt, Schiele, Moser, Kokoschka*. Exh. cat.. Paris: Réunion des musées nationaux, 2005.

Shackelford, George T. M., et al. *Gauguin Tahiti*. Exh. cat. Boston: Museum of Fine Arts, 2004.

Thomson, Richard, et al. *Toulouse-Lautrec and Montmartre*. Exh. cat. Washington, DC: National Gallery of Art, 2005.

Van Gogh, Vincent. *Vincent van Gogh—The Letters: The Complete Illustrated and Annotated Edition*, ed. Leo Jansen, Hans Luijten, and Nienke Bakker. 6 vols. Amsterdam: Van Gogh Museum, 2009.

Woll, Gerd. *Edvard Munch: Complete Paintings*, 4 vols. London: Thames & Hudson, 2009.

Into the Twentieth Century

Angliviel de La Beaumelle, Agnès, ed. *Joan Miró 1917–1934*. Exh. cat. Paris: Centre Pompidou; London: Paul Holberton, 2004.

Bishop, Janet C., et al., eds. *The Steins Collect: Matisse, Picasso, and the Parisian Avant-Garde*. Exh. cat. San Francisco: Museum of Modern Art; New Haven: Yale University Press, 2011.

Bois, Yve-Alain, et al. *Piet Mondrian, 1872–1944*. Exh. cat. Boston: Little, Brown, 1994.

Büttner, Philippe, ed. *Surrealism in Paris*. Riehan: Fondation Beyeler, 2011.

Cowart, Jack, et al. *Henri Matisse: The Early Years in Nice, 1916–1930*. Exh. cat. Washington, DC: National Gallery of Art; New York: Abrams, 1986.

D'Allesandro, Stephanie, et al. *Matisse: Radical Invention, 1913–1917*. Exh. cat. Chicago: Art Institute of Chicago; New York: Museum of Modern Art; New Haven: Yale University Press, 2010.

Dickerman, Leah, et al. *Inventing Abstraction, 1910–1925: How a Radical Idea Changed Modern Art*. Exh. cat. New York: Museum of Modern Art, 2013.

Einecke, Claudia, Roger Benjamin, Guy Cogeval, Sylvie Patry, et al. *Renoir in the Twentieth Century*. Exh. cat. Ostfildern, Germany: Hatje Cantz, 2010.

Fergonzi, Flavio. *Morandi: Master of Modern Still Life*. Exh. cat. Washington, DC: Phillips Collection, 2009.

Foster, Hal, et al. *Art Since 1900: Modernism, Antimodernism, Postmodernism*, 2nd ed., 2 vols. New York: Thames & Hudson, 2011.

Klemm, Christian, et al. *Alberto Giacometti*. Exh. cat. New York: Museum of Modern Art; Zurich: Kunsthaus Zürich, 2001.

Kosinski, Dorothy M., Jay McKean Fisher, and Steven A. Nash. *Matisse: Painter as Sculptor*. Exh. cat. Baltimore: Baltimore Museum of Art; Dallas: Dallas Museum of Art, Nasher Sculpture Center; New Haven: Yale University Press, 2006.

Krauss, Rosalind. *The Originality of the Avant-Garde and Other Modernist Myths*. Cambridge, MA: MIT Press, 1985.

Mahler, Louise, et al. *Picasso Sculpture*. Exh. cat. New York: Museum of Modern Art, 2015.

McCully, Marilyn, ed. *Picasso—The Early Years, 1892–1906*. Exh. cat. Washington, DC: National Gallery of Art; New Haven: Yale University Press, 1996.

Rabinow, Rebecca, Douglas W. Druick, et al. *Cézanne to Picasso: Ambroise Vollard, Patron of the Avant-Garde*. Exh. cat. New York: Metropolitan Museum of Art, 2006.

Richardson, John. *A Life of Picasso*, 2 vols. New York: Random House, 1991.

Weiss, Jeffrey S., et al. *Picasso: The Cubist Portraits of Fernande Olivier*. Exh. cat. Washington, DC: National Gallery of Art; Princeton: Princeton University Press, 2003.

Index

Page numbers in italics refer to illustrations.

Credits

Grateful acknowledgment is made to the copyright holders for permission to reproduce the works as follows.

Figure 1, p. 20: © T. E. Marr photography, courtesy of Museum of Fine Arts, Boston

pp. 130 (fifth detail), 159, 160: © 2016 Fondation Oskar Kokoschka/Artists Rights Society (ARS), New York/ ProLitteris, Zürich

pp. 164–65 (detail), 166 (second detail), 189: © 2016 Artists Rights Society (ARS), New York/SIAE, Rome

pp. 166 (first and third details), 184, 187, 188: © 2016 Artists Rights Society (ARS), New York/VG Bild-Kunst, Bonn

pp. 166 (fourth detail), 186: © 2010, Gerhard-Marcks-Stiftung, Bremen

pp. 166 (fifth detail), 185: © 2016 Successió Miró/Artists Rights Society (ARS), New York/ADAGP, Paris

pp. 171, 178, 180: © 2016 Succession H. Matisse/Artists Rights Society (ARS), New York

pp. 172, 173, 174, 192: © 2016 Estate of Pablo Picasso/Artists Rights Society (ARS), New York

pp. 182, 183: © 2016 Alberto Giacometti Estate/Licensed by VAGA and Artists Rights Society (ARS), New York

pp. 190–92: Reproduced by permission of The Henry Moore Foundation